ALASKA

POLYCONIC PROJECTION

SCALE OF MILES

0   50   100   150   200   250

SCALE OF KILOMETRES

0   50   100   150   200   250

State Capital _____ ✪
Judicial Division
Headquarters _____ ◉

THIS
IS
ALASKA

By the Same Author

THIS
IS
ALASKA

Harry Kursh

PRENTICE-HALL, INC.   Englewood Cliffs, N. J.

F
910
K8

43351

To my brother Bill, and his family:

Lil, Rochelle, Laura, and Leo

> *"Every joy is gain*
> *And gain is gain, however small."*
>
> Robert Browning

ACKNOWLEDGEMENTS

ALTHOUGH ALMOST A CENTURY HAS ELAPSED SINCE AMERICA PURchased Alaska from Russia, it has been only in recent years that reliable and comprehensive facts about Alaska have been compiled by governmental and private agencies, within and without Alaska.

In preparing this book I frequently found it necessary to develop original information, or to search out comparatively obscure files by talking with hundreds of persons in Alaska, New York City, Seattle and Washington, D. C. In Alaska alone, I conducted more than 300 formal, intensive interviews with Federal and State officials and private citizens in all walks of life.

I wish to record here those agencies and individuals to whom I am particularly indebted for their cooperation. I want to make it clear, however, that if any errors have crept into the book, I am solely responsible for them, as well as for all opinions not specifically attributed to others.

For their help in reviewing this manuscript for factual accuracy, I am especially grateful to: Mr. Claire O. Banks, secretary, Greater Anchorage Chamber of Commerce; Mr. Maurice G. Gebhart, executive director, Alaska State Housing Authority; Dr. Robert B. Wilkins, secretary, Alaska State Medical Society; Mr. Robert A. Baker, president and founder, Matanuska Valley Bank, formerly executive vice president of Alaska's largest bank, the First National of Anchorage.

And to the following individuals in Washington and Alaska, I am especially indebted for their personal guidance and encouragement, and the time they gave me:

Lt.-Gen. Frank A. Armstrong, Commander-in-Chief, Joint Command, Alaskan Command; Maj.-Gen. C. F. Necrason, Commander, Alaskan Air Command; Brig.-Gen. M. O. Edwards, Chief of Staff, Alaskan Command; Col. J. B. Baker, Col. W. C. Gribble, Jr., Col. Dave Woods, Lt.-Col. Philip D. Wachtel, Jr., Lt.-Col. Gordon Gray, Lt.-Col. Lawrence T. Keohane, Maj. Philip Peacock, Maj. Roy Haynes, Maj. William S. Elmore, Maj. J. F. Sunderman, Chief, Air Force Book Program, Department of Defense; Capt. Edmond R.

McCarthy, Capt. John Monahan, Capt. Charles O. Weir, Mr. Albert R. Sears, Mr. Bob Knox, Senior M/Sgt. Robert E. Nance, T/Sgt. S. Z. "Gabby" Moran.

Mr. Dwight F. Rettie, Information Officer, Bureau of Land Management, Washington; Mr. Henry Scharer, Deputy Director, Office of Information, Department of Commerce; Mr. J. O. Kilmartin, Chief, Map Information Office; Mr. Carlos Whiting, Chief, Office of Information, Bureau of Reclamation; Mr. Richard Quintus, Mr. Robert L. Jenks, Mr. Frank M. Reed, Branch Manager, Alaska Small Business Administration; Mr. Joseph Hong, Administrative Assistant, Alaska State Housing Authority; Mr. Cliff Cernick, Editor, Fairbanks *News-Miner;* Mr. Bert Stimple, Miss Doris Dooley, Mr. Ross Miller, Miss Margaret Hornbeck, Mr. Harley D. Hurst, Mr. Clyde A. Rowen, Mr. Russell F. Eddy, Mr. Ken Sheppard, Mr. Tom Pavich, Mr. Robert Reeve, Mr. Charles Willis, Miss Sheila Tunney, Mr. and Mrs. Keath Heathely, Mr. and Mrs. Ben Calderon, Mr. and Mrs. Johnny Lane, Mr. and Mrs. Jack Rhodes, Mr. and Mrs. Dave Levine, Mr. and Mrs. Ray Slack, Mrs. Ruth Matson, Mrs. Jane C. Reed, Miss Sue Rydberg, Miss Carolyn E. Robinson, and Miss Charlotte Johnson.

I want to record here also my appreciation for the indefatigable typing and research services rendered by Mrs. Pearl Oremland, a friend and neighbor of Peekskill, New York.

Finally, to Miss Evelyn Singer and Mr. John Walsh for their indulgence and ever-present editorial guidance and wisdom I am always deeply grateful.

HARRY KURSH
Peekskill, New York
1961

Table of Contents

The most-wanted skills in Alaska . Wages and salaries . Working conditions and problems . The future

Contrasts in housing . Availability of housing . Pur-
chasing and financing homes . Building lots . The
Alaska State Housing Authority, ready to help you
. Problems and the future

The general picture . Doctors and their fees . Hospitals in Alaska . Public health: facts, myths, problems
. Disease and "frozen" lungs . The problem of biting
insects . The problem of sanitation . The future

High regard for education . The school system and
standards . Unincorporated schools . Incorporated
schools . Schools for natives . How teachers are employed . Salaries for teachers . Colleges and universi-
ties . The University of Alaska . The Alaska Methodist University . The future

The Federal public domain in Alaska . Uncle Sam's
landlord, the Bureau of Land Management . The
"language" of the Federal public domain . Classification of land . Vacant public domain . Land records .
Locating and identifying land . Homesteading: free
land for the asking! . Qualifications for homesteading . How to stake a homestead . How to get land for
homesites, business or recreation . "Gambling" in oil
and gas leases . Prospecting on public lands

APPENDIX A: *SCHOOLS IN ALASKA*   252

> A complete list of all elementary and high schools, public and private, including universities and community colleges.

APPENDIX B: *HOSPITALS IN ALASKA*   253

> A complete list of general hospitals by location, number of beds available, and sponsorship.

APPENDIX C: *CHAMBERS OF COMMERCE*   254

> A complete alphabetical list of all Chambers of Commerce in Alaska, together with addresses.

APPENDIX D: *PRESS AND BROADCASTING IN ALASKA*   255

> A complete list of all news, radio and television media in Alaska, listed according to cities and towns.

APPENDIX E: *ALASKA AIRCRAFT OPERATORS AVAILABLE FOR HIRE FOR HUNTING AND FISHING TRIPS*   256

> A complete list of aircraft operators, by cities and towns, available for hire and experts in hunting and fishing trips, coded according to their hunting and fishing specialties and addresses. Also a list of scheduled air carriers, to, from and within Alaska.

APPENDIX F: *AVERAGE HOURLY WAGES PAID TO WORKERS IN SIXTEEN OCCUPATIONS, IN ANCHORAGE AND FAIRBANKS*   259

> A tabulation of wages paid to skilled workers, according to sixteen different occupations, showing average hourly wages and range of wages from low to high.

SOURCES OF INFORMATION, ANNOTATED   260

> A complete list of sources of information in Alaska, according to subject matter about which information

CHAPTER 1

HOW TO UNDERSTAND ALASKA

> *"In a voluntary society, the only constant factor . . . is the factor of change."* Erwin D. Canham, Editor, *The Christian Science Monitor,* in an address at Fairbanks, Alaska.

ALASKA WAS DISCOVERED FOUR TIMES BY AMERICANS. FIRST IN 1867 when Secretary of State William H. Seward disclosed an agreement to buy a remote Russian territory that was to have a town, a peninsula, and a "Folly" named after him.

Second, at the turn of the century when the cry of "Klondike gold" stirred Americans everywhere; and like an army of ants lured by a huge mountain of sugar, they went streaming toward the West Coast, intent on boarding anything that floated, as long as it deposited them in Alaska, preferably near a convenient pile of gold from which each could carry away his own little fortune.

Then, after years of great disenchantment with the gold pickings, after years of supreme indifference to the existence of Alaska, there came the discovery that our polar backdoor was open. It had to be shut. It had to be guarded. Hence, prior to, during, and after World War II, we sent tens of thousands of soldiers, sailors and airmen and armies of civilian construction workers to Alaska; and many remained to become Alaskans.

Finally, there was that momentous occasion in the United States Senate, at exactly 8 o'clock in the evening, June 30, 1958. A long and sometimes bitter struggle abruptly ended with the pronouncement of five historic words, "So the bill has passed." Alaska, the 49th State, had joined the Union!

15

All Alaska erupted with joy. Bells were struck 49 times. Forty-nine huge bonfires, fed by 49 tons of wood, were set ablaze, and kept burning by 49 logs tossed on the fires. Alaskans had been accustomed to calling the United States *the Outside, the lower 48,* or simply *the States.* Now it was *the other 48.*

Then they came again to Alaska. Day after day, from every state, came reporters and feature writers and big-name columnists, radio and television journalists, and documentary film producers, laden with tape recorders and electronic magic—and with myths about Alaska, but with no particular desire to dispel the myths. Within weeks, Americans discovered Alaska again. Another Klondike was unleashed, a Klondike of curiosity, a Klondike of adventurous yearning, a Klondike of ambition for new careers, new jobs, new business opportunities.

Alaska became a magic word, a new enchantment. Traffic on the Alaska Highway, inbound, almost doubled overnight. Airline passenger traffic on flights to Alaska zoomed.

Countless thousands of Americans wrote letters to every government agency in Washington that was thought to have had anything at all to do with providing information about Alaska. They wrote to the Office of Territories, the White House, the Interior Department, the Air Force, the Secretary of State, the Forest Service, the Bureau of Mines, the Geological Survey, the Library of Congress, the Superintendent of Documents. They wrote to the Department of Labor, seeking information about jobs in Alaska, even though at the time there was fairly severe unemployment in Alaska. (In September, 1957, the Alaska Employment Security Commission had answered 356 such letters; shortly after statehood, a year later, there were 2,447 letters to be answered.)

The Director of the Bureau of Land Management in Washington received a long distance telephone call from a young man in New York. The caller wanted an immediate grant of a homestead in Alaska and instructions, please, for driving to his homestead. Like many others burdened by innumerable myths concerning Alaska, he had thought that Alaska was covered by a network of modern highways each conveniently leading to a beautiful homestead which could be had almost for the asking. He was disappointed when informed of the facts. Homesteads? Yes. But not that easy. You've got to work for it and, like the pioneers of old, you may have to carve your own road to reach it.

Unfortunately, when newcomers arrive in Alaska, as in the days of Klondike gold, there is considerable disillusionment because few come with knowledge of the *real* Alaska, the Alaska that is not all ice and snow and Eskimos and igloos, the Alaska that is indeed more than twice the size of Texas but considerably emptier, the Alaska that is not all Arctic in climate, not a gigantic, wall-to-wall honky-tonk colorfully decorated with Klondike Kates and assorted misfits, and the Alaska that is truly America's last frontier, but perhaps the most comfortable frontier in history.

The real Alaska is almost a paradox of geography, history, economics and social order. But when all the facts are in place, the real Alaska is no more a paradox than any other state because it is a story of people, of Americans.

The purpose of this book is two-fold: to correct the many misunderstandings and erroneous impressions regarding Alaska; and to discuss in a positive, objective manner the known facts of every conceivable phase of Alaskan life.

To understand the real Alaska, however, it is not enough to collect and evaluate historical and current statistics. It is equally important to view all Alaskan data in perspective. In this regard, one factor, at least, must be kept constantly in mind: because Alaska is a frontier society, *it is a dynamic, spirited, restless, imaginative, changing society.*

It is a society that thrives on hope and challenge, and in meeting challenge has sought a sense of fulfillment. It is a society that has no desire to boast of the fastest, the biggest, the mostest. It is a society that values a handshake as much as a contract. It prefers to forget yesterday and dream of tomorrow. Many have deliberately abandoned comforts in other states, but only (paradoxically!) to work toward creating similar comforts for themselves in Alaska.

But with or without comforts, Alaskans are there because they thrive on challenge and have rediscovered the dignity of dreams and labor.

Accordingly, I have chosen to take first things first in this book—the real Alaska in terms of its geography and climate; and the real Alaska in terms of the people: Who are they? Where do they live? How do they live? What do they think? What are their relationships with each other? With *cheechakos* (newcomers)? How do they get around?

It may surprise many to learn from these facts that the *concentra-*

tion of population in Alaska, in spite of the state's massiveness, makes for an existence that cannot be characterized as isolated. It may also prove surprising to learn that it is entirely possible for an Alaskan to live where he may never see snow.

Among the thousands of letters received by various Alaskan agencies from Outsiders, three questions are most frequently asked: (1) What is the cost of living in Alaska? (2) How do you get a job in Alaska? (3) What is the housing situation?

These questions are important and are answered here in separate chapters. But the answers are not based on a mere collection of official statistics. To be sure, such data are important. But having in mind the importance of understanding the real Alaska in perspective, I also gathered the bread-and-butter facts in order to report in everyday language exactly what it costs an Alaskan for a bottle of milk, a bottle of whiskey, a place to live, or to borrow money in order to build a place to live. In the chapter on employment we learn not only how many people are employed or unemployed in Alaska, but exactly where they are employed and how they got their jobs.

As we shall see, Alaskans have good reason to be proud of their educational standards and schools. However, not to be ignored in any society are its medical and health resources. In many American cities and towns there is a lack of adequate hospital and medical facilities, including doctors. In Alaska the problem is no different quantitatively, but the *nature* of the problem is different. To show the extent of this difference I took particular pains to gather the facts not only from medical authorities within Alaska, but from those outside. Many Alaskans themselves, for instance, do not know that several years ago a rather comprehensive study was made of medical and health problems in Alaska. The results of this study were published in a voluminous report by the University of Pittsburgh's Graduate School of Public Health. I utilized this report as a basis for my own search for facts, and to provide a three-dimensional view.

If there is one phase of life in Alaska that has perhaps never been distorted or exaggerated it is the great outdoors—hunting and fishing are, in a word, superb! Accordingly, my report on Alaskan wildlife is principally for the purpose of describing what Alaskans hunt and fish for, and where and how they go about it.

Apart from the opportunities for spiritual rediscovery, the tangible opportunities in Alaska lie mainly in the direction of business. To a great extent, however, business in Alaska may be geared to future developments in population and natural resources. Hence, the subject of Alaska's population is further evaluated in this connection, along with a discussion of Alaska's industries and resources. Here, too, it is important to note again that cold statistical data, while valuable, is insufficient. Thus, to provide perspective, I have obtained the sort of collateral information that does not show up in statistical data but should prove of value to the business-minded reader.

Closely linked to Alaska's industries and resources, indeed to Alaska's future as a whole, is the subject of the public lands. Many still do not understand that big as Alaska is, the new state does not own everything. In fact, only about one-third of the land in Alaska will eventually belong to the 49th State. The remainder will constitute the public domain, or Uncle Sam's land. From any point of view, personal or business, home or farming, recreation or prospecting, it is essential to understand how the public domain is organized, administered, and disposed of—in short, how to get land in Alaska. Having previously written a fairly comprehensive book on America's public domain, *How to Get Land from Uncle Sam,* I have been able to present this subject from a background of considerable advantage.

Part of the public domain story in Alaska, a part that has aroused great interest, is homesteading. Essentially, homesteading in Alaska, as elsewhere, means settling on the land for purposes of farming. Yet for an understanding of the real land story in Alaska we shall note, too, that homesteading can mean getting land for non-farm purposes. Still, agriculture may play a major role in Alaska's future, although it is not now significant. Therefore, I have added a discussion of agricultural life in Alaska.

The book closes with a report on the defense forces in Alaska and the politics and government of the new state. Although these subjects have been placed last, they should not be treated lightly. Most people are interested in knowing exactly where Alaska stands vis-à-vis Russia. Why not? Alaska is next door to Russia and lies across the most likely aerial invasion route of North America. But it is also important, in understanding the real Alaska, to appreciate the economic and social significance of a rather large defense force stationed there, and what may happen if the size or nature of this force is altered.

I have also endeavored to analyze and emphasize the significance of statehood. Some of us are apt to think that statehood simply meant adding a 49th star to the flag, amidst considerable hullabaloo for the aggrandizement of Alaska. But when Alaskans fought for statehood there was more than self-exaltation in mind. There were certain obvious and not-so-obvious advantages to statehood. These advantages are discussed toward the close of the book in order to help provide a basis for judging Alaska's political and economic future.

Unfortunately, no one book on Alaska could possibly provide all the answers. Some people, for example, may desire more specific information about weather in a particular town, or about how to get to Alaska by auto, or about business conditions in Homer, or jobs for teachers, nurses and electronics technicians in Anchorage, or housing in Seward, or hunting and fishing in the Panhandle. In a changing society like Alaska, the answers to specific questions may vary as much tomorrow as they do years from now. However, to help make this book a permanent reference, I have added various appendices and bibliographies containing comprehensive sources of information for just about any type of question that may be asked about Alaska today or tomorrow or in the next generation. These sources of information should prove indispensable.

Finally, I must say that my sole aim in visiting Alaska was not to become an Alaskan, but to see the state and the people as they perhaps have never seen themselves, and as outsiders would like to see them. In this respect, I went in search of facts that seldom see the light of publicity and also went behind the scenes that have received much publicity. In doing so, I was able to see and understand the real Alaska. I also had the *advantage* of being an Outsider. I could compile an objective report. If I have fulfilled this role, then I shall be pleased that this book has been a useful contribution to the literature on Alaska, and has been helpful to those who may themselves contribute to Alaska's future.

CHAPTER 2

THE TRUTH ABOUT ALASKA'S
CLIMATE AND GEOGRAPHY

> *"The emptiness of Alaska can be viewed in two ways. The optimist will note there is plenty of room for more people. The pessimist will see it as proof that it is hardly habitable."* Anchorage Daily Times, August 20, 1959

A CURRENT JOKE IN ALASKA CONCERNS THE STORY OF A BOMbastic Texas mayor who telephoned the Governor of Alaska to congratulate him on the achievement of statehood. Said the Texan: "You may be the largest state in the Union now, but just you wait a bit. It won't be long before we Texans get to building a pipeline to Alaska. Then we'll blow some hot air through it, and by the time you're melted down you won't have a state but half the size of Delaware!"

Alaskans can afford to join in the laughter. The joke reflects one of the most prevalent misconceptions concerning Alaska's climate and geography. To begin with, the name Alaska, said to originate from the Indian word, *aliashka,* meaning "great land," is quite apt.

Alaska's combined area exceeds 586,000 square miles. Four more states the size of Alaska would almost equal the entire United States. A map of Alaska superimposed over a map of the United States would show the top of Alaska at the Canadian border above Minnesota, the southeastern leg of Alaska running through Georgia, and southwestern Alaska passing in an arc through Oklahoma, Texas,

Mexico, and California. The east-west borders of Alaska would cover the distance between Indiana and Colorado.

Because of its size, Alaska is a land of striking contrasts. There are fjords, glaciers, volcanoes, dense forests, great treeless plateaus, fertile valleys, windswept plains, innumerable bays, and five great river systems. The Yukon River cuts through the entire width of Alaska and pours 180,000 cubic feet of water *per second* into the Bering Sea.

There are four time zones in Alaska and three vast primary mountain systems: the Pacific, the Alaska, and the Brooks systems. The Pacific mountain system runs parallel to the south and southeast coastlines; the Alaska system encompasses famed Mt. McKinley in the interior and runs southwest to the Aleutians; the Brooks, with many formidable peaks, ranges east-west across Alaska above the Arctic Circle.

Less than one-fourth of Alaska is in the North Frigid, or Arctic zone. Southwest and southeast Alaska are in the same latitude as Scotland. There are some places in Alaska where it snows far less than it does in some areas of New England, or the north central states, like Wyoming or Montana; and there are certain times of the year when the only ice and snow to be seen *in all Alaska* is on the mountain peaks, as in the Rockies during the summer.

In short, there is no such thing as a "typical" Alaskan scene or climate. Physiographically and climatically, there are no features common to all Alaska. The Texan who boasted of "melting down" Alaska was misled by Hollywood's traditional license to adjust the facts.

Actually, because the contrasts within Alaska are so sharp, the best way to understand the real Alaska's geography and climate is to consider the state region by region.

SOUTHEASTERN ALASKA—THE "PANHANDLE"

The "leg" of Alaska that borders the Canadian province of British Columbia is generally known as southeastern Alaska, or the "Panhandle." It stretches like an unassembled jigsaw puzzle along the coast for some 700 miles.

In reality, the Panhandle is an enormous archipelago—barely attached to the mainland. It is virtually cut off from Canada by massive glaciers and mountain ranges that rise sharply to heights of more than 9,000 feet. Almost every town of any consequence in the Panhandle—Petersburg, Sitka, Wrangell, Ketchikan, and Juneau, the state capital—is practically an island, accessible only by air or sea. The only exceptions are Haines and Skagway, neighboring towns in the northern portion of the Panhandle. Haines is linked to Canada via the Alaska Highway at Haines Junction. From Skagway, it is possible to go to Whitehorse, British Columbia, over the White Pass & Yukon Railroad, a picturesque ride on some 110 miles of narrow-gauge rails.

As an attraction for tourists, the Panhandle is one of Alaska's greatest assets. It is a region of incomparable beauty, with snow-capped mountains and countless fjords, America's "Scandinavia." Fleets of fishing vessels roll gently in the harbors of colorful villages, many of which—like Sitka, the old Russian capital—still show the influence of Old World architecture. Great forest stands of spruce, cedar and hemlock, making up in density what they lack in height, are among Alaska's most important natural resources.

The mildest climate to be found in Alaska is in the Panhandle. A booklet prepared by the Defense Department for servicemen to be stationed in Alaska states that "it is no colder in the Panhandle than in Maryland." Influenced by the Japanese current, temperatures in the Panhandle rarely fall below zero. Often, when it is snowing in Oregon and blizzards are tormenting New York City, there is no snow in the Panhandle. The winters are exceptionally mild and the summers delightfully cool, although occasionally some Panhandle towns will experience a few days of summer temperatures in the 80's.

The average January temperatures in the Panhandle range from a low of 21° F. in Skagway to 32° F. in Sitka and Ketchikan. In July, the average temperature for most towns is well above 50° F. However, more indicative of the relatively mild climate in the Panhandle is the number of days in the growing season—the period between the last killing frost in the spring and the first frost in the fall. The growing season ranges from 111 days in Skagway (May 27 to September 15) to 172 days in Juneau (April 28 to October 17).

But climate in the Panhandle has been so unpredictably mild that there are often wide variations in growing season. There have been times, for instance, when the Ketchikan area has been free of frost for as many as 268 days, whereas the *average* is 156 days.

On the other hand, the same physical features—sea, current and mountains—which influence the Panhandle's climate also contribute to its most distinguishing characteristic: rain. In the words of the U.S. Weather Bureau, the Panhandle is in "the zone of dominant maritime influence," which means a raincoat is always kept handy at the office. It has been said that more rain falls in southeastern Alaska than in any other place in the United States, and the official Weather Bureau data lend substantial support to the statement. In at least one Pandhandle town there has been 14 inches of rainfall during a 24-hour period. The Weather Bureau's records (sometimes despised by tour promoters) show that "maximum *monthly* amounts of precipitation of around 30 inches or more have been realized at about 25 per cent of the reporting stations in southeastern Alaska." The greatest amounts of rain in the Panhandle usually occur in September, October, and November.

Another feature of climate in this region is fog. It comes frequently and is persistent. Many Alaskans cite it as a strong argument in favor of moving the state capital from Juneau to Anchorage, a suggestion that has been both bitterly resisted and unsuccessfully promoted.

SOUTHWESTERN ALASKA

This region of Alaska consists largely of the leg that starts as the Alaska Peninsula and thins out across the Pacific in a series of stepping-stone islands, the Aleutian Chain, pointing ominously at the Kamchatka Peninsula of Russian Siberia. It also includes the comparatively large islands of Kodiak and Unalaska.

As a whole, southwestern Alaska is unattractive. It is dotted with volcanoes and glaciers and almost unbroken horizons of low-lying bush and moss, although active volcanoes seen from the air in the "valley of 10,000 smokes" are an intriguing sight.

In this region, a tree is a rare sight, and wildlife sanctuaries have been established on a number of islands, where animals could scarcely be safer from the incursions of man. Some grassy and gently sloping portions, particularly on the islands of Kodiak, Unalaska, Chirikof, and Umnak, have made it possible to graze such livestock as cattle and sheep, and government reports indicate that at least seven ranches have been established on Kodiak.

One of the most spectacular events, sometimes called "the greatest wildlife show on earth," takes place annually in this region. It is the round-up of fur seals in the Pribilof group of islands, some 700 air miles west of Anchorage. Every Thursday morning at eight o'clock, during the months of July and August, the Reeve-Aleutian Airways office in Anchorage is filled with people waiting to be flown to the Pribilofs to watch nimble natives cut small groups of seals out from vast herds, surround them, kill them with clubs, and skin the animals with uncanny efficiency.

The climate in southwestern Alaska is almost identical to the Panhandle, having similar temperatures, growing seasons, rainfall, and fog. But the winters are *not* mild. During the winter this region is afflicted by a seemingly interminable series of wind storms which frequently make it dangerous, if not impossible, to remain outdoors.

Oldtimers say that they expect wind storms on an average of once every four or five days during the winter. In the words of the U.S. Weather Bureau: "These storms frequently cover a large area, and a single storm may produce strong winds all along the chain from Attu to the tip of the Alaska Peninsula. The islands experience strong winds from practically all directions, depending upon the position and course of the intense storms. Wind speeds of 70 to 90 mph occur almost monthly during the winter season at some of the [weather] stations along the islands. Occasionally these storms retain considerable intensity as their centers move eastward across the Alaska Peninsula."

As a matter of fact, had it not been for the venturesome flying in the early days of Alaskan aviation by such intrepid bush pilots as Bob Reeve, president of Reeve-Aleutian Airways, many of the areas in this region would have remained inaccessible. Reeve is credited with developing the techniques that have made Aleutian flying routine and safe.

SOUTH CENTRAL ALASKA

The generally accepted boundaries for south central Alaska are: on the east, the Canadian border; on the west, a line about perpendicular to the middle of the Alaska Peninsula; on the south, the Gulf of Alaska; on the north, an arc of mountains consisting of the Wrangell and Alaska ranges, encompassing the cities of Cordova, Valdez, Seward, Anchorage, Dillingham. This is a mixed region of mountains, flat lands, and valleys. It includes the great Mt. McKinley, highest mountain in North America, about midway between Anchorage and Fairbanks, and the lush Matanuska Valley, about 50 miles above Anchorage, principal agricultural center of Alaska.

South central Alaska is perhaps the most settled region of all; nearly half the population of Alaska may be found in the highly modernized Anchorage circle, within a radius of ten miles.

Climatically, this region of Alaska has been compared with Nebraska, Colorado and Iowa. Although winter brings longer periods of darkness than in southern Alaska, sub-zero temperatures are not as frequent as schoolboy geographies might indicate. The climate is marked by a gradual transition from maritime to mountain influences. With the exception of the area around Cordova, where precipitation is almost as heavy as in parts of the Panhandle, the average annual rainfall drops abruptly. It averages around 14 inches a year in the Anchorage area.

At the peak of the winter, for a period of about 30 to 40 days, this region will experience sub-zero temperatures ranging from an occasional low of -46° F. to -19° F. But these sub-zero temperatures are not as uncomfortable as they may seem because there are mountainous shelters. Anchorage, for example, is surrounded on a 270-degree arc by the picturesque Chugach Mountains, which usually reduce wind forces in Anchorage. Average January temperatures range from a low of about 9° F. to 28° F.; and July temperatures average well above 50° F. throughout the region. The frost-free growing season varies from 93 to 149 days.

INTERIOR ALASKA

The "heartland" of Alaska, sometimes called "central" Alaska, comes geographically closer to representing what most Outsiders would visualize as being "typically Alaskan."

It is bounded on the north by the Brooks Range and on the south by the Alaska Range and stretches from the Canadian border to the Bering Sea. It has been described, in a booklet issued by the Alaska National Bank of Fairbanks, the principal interior city, as "an intermontane region of great valleys, rolling hills and uplands, of spruce and birch forests and large rivers, including the Yukon, Kuskokwim, Tanana, and Kobuk, which are the principal navigable streams of Alaska."

In addition to Fairbanks, interior Alaska includes the towns of Nome, Kotzebue, and Nenana.

It is in this region that Alaska's temperature extremes occur. The temperature in Fairbanks, for example, has been known to exceed 100° F. in summer, dropping to -60° F. and -70° F. in winter.

Winter in Fairbanks, the most populous city of the interior, second largest city in Alaska, brings prolonged periods of darkness and such extreme cold that even the hardiest soul cannot remain outdoors very long. On December 21, dawn begins at about 10 o'clock in the morning, and sundown starts shortly after 1:30 in the afternoon.

During the winter, people who work indoors are not apt to see daylight for months. Keeping the engine and oil and water from freezing in an automobile is a constant problem. An automobile left outdoors overnight usually starts rolling again on "square" tires, the rubber having frozen flat to the ground. Conversely, summer brings long days of sunshine. One of the annual events in Fairbanks is a midnight outdoor baseball game played without benefit of lights.

The average January temperature in Fairbanks is -11° F.; July average is 60° F. The growing season is about 90 days.

The region, as a whole, is perhaps the driest in Alaska, with average annual rainfall ranging from a low of less than 7 inches in the Fort Yukon area to a high of 20 inches around the town of Holy Cross. Fairbanks itself seldom experiences more than 12 inches of rain annually; and when the snow falls there is usually such a complete absence of wind that the flakes come down gently, almost as artificially as white cornflakes in a vintage stage setting.

THE ARCTIC SLOPE

The Arctic slope is the most rugged region in Alaska. It ranges northward from the foothills of the Brooks Range, and extends across the state. It is truly the romanticized, storied region of Alaska.

In the winter the region is bare, windswept, desolate. It is the only place in Alaska where the typical, if not only, inhabitants are Eskimos, although most live not in igloos but in white frame houses, and the typical "skin" boat is apt to be powered by an outboard motor which almost any Eskimo can strip and rebuild in the dark.

The principal settlements (they could hardly be called towns) are the Eskimo villages of Wainwright and Barrow, and some would also include Kotzebue, which is practically on the border between the "interior" and the Arctic Circle. In Barrow, the ice breaks up for only a few weeks during the summer, perhaps just long enough to allow vessels to bring fresh supplies for another year.

The average January temperature in Barrow is -17°, but a better indication of the short summer season, when July averages 40° F., is the extremely limited period between killing frosts: 17 days. According to those who have lived or worked in the Arctic slope region, "you can't be sure about the weather from one day to the next, except that it will be cold." While nearly all the snow may be melted before June, giving way to exquisite displays of flowers and berries in the sheltered valleys, by mid-October you could expect to walk across any river in the area.

A NOTE OF CAUTION ABOUT ALASKAN CLIMATE

There is a vast difference between a general discussion of climate and specific weather. This is especially true of Alaska, where there is still much to be learned about climate. According to a U.S. Weather Bureau study it seems "well to emphasize that the climate of Alaska is an extremely marginal factor for many fields of human endeavor, and demands careful consideration. To ignore the implications of local climatic conditions may be to invite disaster, but taking advantage of known facts may provide the necessary margin to assure success and avoid years of effort which may result in eventual failure."

In other words, the Weather Bureau statement is a warning. Do not take climate in Alaska for granted. If you are at all concerned about weather in any particular town or area, for personal, recreational or business purposes, obtain reliable and direct information from sources in that area, the U.S. Weather Bureau or the local Chamber of Commerce (*see appendix section*).

PERMAFROST: BY-PRODUCT OF ALASKAN CLIMATE

Permafrost—permanently frozen ground—is a condition that may be found in about 60 per cent of Alaska. In the far northern reaches, permafrost has been explored to a depth of 1,200 feet, whereas in the south it occurs only rarely and to a depth of two to three feet.

Permafrost may create a host of problems, particularly in building construction, sanitation, digging for a source of water, and farming. Once, at a military construction project in the north, it was found that the structure had shifted dangerously because the heat generated by the foundation materials had melted the permafrost zone around it. Ironically, the problem was solved by the installation of a permanent electronically controlled refrigeration system to keep the foundation frozen in the permafrost!

Permafrost is one of the great challenges of northern Alaska. It has been only in recent years that engineers and scientists have undertaken to study its characteristics. If and when permafrost problems are overcome, the results will be as vital and as electrifying as turning a desert into a flowering valley of truck gardens. Permafrost does *not* make an area uninhabitable. It merely discourages settlement and adds to the burden of living. But there is great confidence in Alaska, thanks to the work of U.S. Army engineers and Defense Department research agencies, that in the forseeable future the permafrost problem will be licked.

Dr. C. Earl Albrecht, a former Commissioner of Health in Alaska, struck an encouraging note. Writing in the *American Journal of Public Health,* he said:

"We know that the Russians have over 15,000,000 people living on permafrost, with cities of a quarter of a million population (more than the entire population of Alaska!). The realization that Russia and Siberia have some of this know-how and we do not is annoying. The need for American engineers to solve these problems is obvious and fortunately several groups are at work."

CHAPTER 3

MEET THE REAL ALASKANS:
WHO THEY ARE, WHERE THEY LIVE,
HOW THEY LIVE

> *"Alaska is a friendly country, a trusting country. People believe in Alaska and each other."* Albert R. Sears, Director, Civilian Personnel, Alaskan Air Command

THE COMBINATION OF BEING THE LARGEST STATE IN THE UNION and having the smallest population gives Alaska a statistical portrait of extreme isolation, "bush" living. The population density is less than one person per square mile, compared with an average U.S. density of more than 50 per square mile. In some areas of Alaska, a "village" may consist of a handful of Indians or Eskimos or a cluster of hunters' shacks in a permanent camp. Nearly half the 287 inhabited areas of Alaska contain less than 100 persons. In some 30 per cent of the remaining inhabited areas, the population is between 100 and 200. From these figures it is possible to "prove"— and many have done just that—the isolated existence of Alaskans.

However, expect to find most Alaskans living a dull, insular life and you may expect to be disappointed. Actually, nearly three-quarters of all Alaskans live in and around the four largest cities: Anchorage (60,000); Fairbanks (38,000); Ketchikan (10,500); and Juneau (9,500).

The great majority of Alaskans live comfortably in modern urban and suburban communities. There are, to be sure, rugged individualists who prefer to live in comparatively primitive shacks or log cabins, miles from town, but even these dwellings are usually equipped with modern conveniences—electricity, running water, telephones, and sometimes automatic oil or LP-gas heat. A visitor to Spenard or City View, suburbs of Anchorage, might well believe he had never left Hempstead, Long Island, the outskirts of Los Angeles, or the suburbs of Denver. Many parts of Juneau, in fact, resemble the quiet, picturesque, hilly streets of San Francisco.

The most distinctive feature of life in Alaska is that it represents a melting pot of Americans from every state in the Union. Consequently, *most* Alaskans tend to live, work and build in the American tradition. Progress is apt to be characterized by bigger and better split-level homes and well-kept lawns, a car in every garage, supermarket shopping, PTA meetings, weekly Rotary luncheons, Lion lectures, and a Chamber of Commerce in every town with two or more merchants.

The most rapid period of population growth for Alaska occurred after World War II. In October, 1867, when a sixteen-year-old boy raised the first Stars and Stripes over Alaska, there were only about 500 white persons in the territory and approximately 33,000 aborigines (Eskimos, Indians and Aleuts). Since then the native population has remained almost static, but the total population has increased from 128,000 in 1950 to more than 220,000, including about 47,000 military personnel and their dependents, most of whom are stationed at Elmendorf Air Force Base and Ft. Richardson, outside Anchorage, and at Ladd and Eielson Air Force Bases near Fairbanks. However, the military and their dependents have been in Alaska in such great numbers and for so many years that Alaskans tend to consider them part of the total resident population.

For the most part, newcomers from other states should have no difficulty in adjusting to life in Alaska. There is little in Alaskan social and cultural life that may seem foreign or unique to Americans.

A CLOSER LOOK AT ALASKANS

When an Alaskan says "native," he generally refers to an Eskimo, Indian, or Aleut, of whom there are approximately 35,000.

Most Eskimos live in the far north, the Indians in the southeastern areas, and the Aleuts, a relatively small number, in the southwestern areas, chiefly the Aleutian Islands and the Alaska Peninsula. Many of the natives have retained their cultural and tribal traditions, but nearly all speak English and in almost every respect are "Americanized."

There are also about 5,000 other non-whites in Alaska, mostly American Negroes and Filipinos. The latter came long ago to work in the fishing industries.

Among non-native Alaskans there are basically two categories of Americans: those who came to Alaska for a specific job or under military assignment and chose to remain; and those who came to find a new way of life. According to an Alaskan market study published by Benton and Bowles of New York, the "average Alaskan is a newcomer. He and his family have lived in the 49th State for only eight or ten years."

YOUTHFUL AND YOUNG AT HEART

Essentially, Alaska is a youthful state. There are proportionately more younger people in Alaska than in any other state. The number of children under five years of age is twice the national average; and the number of Alaskans over 65 is half the national average. Some 42,000 are between five and seventeen years of age; 52,000 are between 18 and 44; and 24,000 are between 45 and 64.

This youthful composition of Alaska is one of its principal assets and clearly a basis for rapid growth.

But in recent years Alaska has been attracting an increasing number of newcomers who are young more at heart than in age. Many arrive having successfully raised a family elsewhere and then grown restive with a sedate, almost routine way of life.

Typical was the story of Mr. and Mrs. Ed Perkins, formerly of Seattle, both around 60 years of age. He had been a carpenter, she a teacher. To explain why they came to Alaska and why they enjoy their new life in the 49th State, Mr. and Mrs. Perkins like to tell the story of a friend who came to visit them at the cabin they had built themselves, overlooking an exquisite view of sea and mountains near Cook Inlet, not far from Anchorage. Plainly puzzled and constantly looking about the cabin, the friend would remark, "I don't know why you left the comforts of your Seattle home where all you had to do was push a button; here you don't even have electricity. You even have to carry water to flush that 'modern' toilet you brag about!"

"He kept that up all the time he was here," Mrs. Perkins said, "and he couldn't even see the inlet below us, or the mountains across, or the woods behind us. And while he was here we talked about a camping trip we were going to take. He said, 'Camping trip! Great Scot, you're camping all the time!' "

Most people, young and old, have chosen to remain in Alaska because they are lured by the state's great outdoors or the sense of adventure that comes with working and living in a land that still throbs with pioneer spirit. A 42-year-old New Yorker I met near Anchorage, where he was building his own home in a heavily wooded area, told how he had abandoned an active partnership in a prospering business in New York and decided to settle in Alaska after having made a vacation trip to the new state. "It's the spirit of the place that gets you," he said. "Everybody's busy building something. It's exciting."

The great spirit of Alaska is infectious. It is the common denominator of Alaskans everywhere and derives from a sense of sharing in the challenge of building something new. It is mass togetherness.

I shall never forget my conversation with a young former Brooklynite, an intelligent, well informed man who had not completed high school. Of his eight years in Alaska, he said:

"The most wonderful thing about Alaska is that everybody works together and helps each other. You don't feel as if you are alone in the world. When I lived in Brooklyn, I think I was the most selfish man alive. I wouldn't go around the corner or lift a finger to help anyone, unless I knew it would also help me.

"I've changed up here and love it. One night I got a phone call from a new neighbor, moved in only a few months before, and I had hardly known him. His car had broken down, and he wanted to know if I could come out to help him. I put my coat on, hopped in my car and took off. It was an 800-mile round trip!"

The former Brooklynite's sentiments are echoed by the Rev. Richard T. Lambert, of Fairbanks, who has said: "This is really not a get-rich-quick area, nor is it a place where one could drift easily alone, living to oneself. One must come expecting to depend upon others and helping other people in turn."

A unique example of the "Alaska spirit" was the time the canneries of Cordova were caught short-handed by an unexpected bonanza in the salmon run. It turned out to be the largest catch in nearly a generation, but help was urgently needed to pack the catch. Almost everyone in town—men, housewives, children, shopkeepers, teachers, even the local banker—turned to in force, donning oilskins and aprons to help the canneries.

Just as horsethieving in the old West was an odious sort of crime, stealing property in Alaska is considered an abominable act of anti-neighborliness. A stroller down a main street in any town is apt to pass auto after auto filled with an assortment of supplies and personal valuables, but not one door locked. A wealthy Alaskan, who leaves his home for an annual business trip to Los Angeles, and has been doing so for 18 years, has never locked his front door. Many Alaskans have no front-door locks.

THE ALASKAN PERSONALITY

Alaskan youthfulness and spirit are without doubt the most important "natural" resources in Alaska, motivating Alaskans to work hard. The same spirit also generates a friendliness, a warmth, a charm and informality that may be seen anywhere: crossing the street, at the corner drugstore, or at a PTA meeting. It may be seen at almost any swank cocktail lounge where men in slacks and sweaters mingle freely with women in evening clothes. In fact, a type of dress usually consisting of an "Eisenhower" jacket and slacks or whipcord trousers is called the "Alaska tuxedo" because so many men show up dressed that way at social events.

But it is not an affectation, a calculated attempt to be different. It is a way of life in Alaska. The message is obvious, Alaska's way of saying, "I am a non-comformist, a rugged individualist at heart. I like being with people but I don't like people telling me what I should or shouldn't like for myself."

I saw a rather vivid demonstration of this couldn't-care-less attitude on several occasions in Anchorage. Involved was a husky young man who sported a thick, red beard, an immense handle bar mustache, begrimed coveralls, and an old felt hat cut to fit atop his head like a precarious fez. At the end of a day's labor on his homestead, not having a car, nor time to change into something more formal, he would drive into Anchorage aboard his open tractor, roll casually along the modern shopping section (Fourth Avenue) and maneuver into a parking-meter space just as if he were coming to town in a chauffered limousine. He'd jump from his tractor, pause to chat with friends, or go window shopping, or stop in at a cocktail lounge, and at no time did anybody stare at him as though he were an odd-ball.

WHERE AND HOW ALASKANS LIVE

The great majority of Alaskans live comfortably in conventional homes within city or town limits. As a matter of fact, there has been an increasing demand for apartment dwellings in Alaska's larger cities. In the urbanized centers there are modern supermarkets, ranch homes, split level homes, and Cape Cods, with and without attached garages. There are movie houses, cocktail lounges, bowling alleys, the usual shortage of parking space, and the ubiquitous pneumatic drill, symbol of a changing society.

In contrast, almost every urban area has its share of Alaskans who live in comparatively crude shacks or log cabins, erected by do-it-yourselfers making use of backyard timber. Some "shacks" are authentic leftovers of the Klondike age, but usually with all the comforts of modern living. Some Alaskans even *prefer* the Klondike look. In one log cabin, the type seen in travelogues on Alaska, I saw a roomful of the most luxurious Hollywood-fashion, white leather furniture money could buy. The owner, an Alaskan businesswoman who preferred the "esthetic appeal" of a log cabin, was also partial to modern furnishings. But she would never trade her log cabin for a mansion.

As a rule, Alaskans are fairly gregarious. But this does not mean they gather in throngs. Most simply enjoy informal get-togethers with friends and just talking around coffee at the kitchen table. (According to the American Telephone and Telegraph files, Alaskans do more talking on the telephone than people in any other state. Alaskans average 630 calls per person annually, compared with 426 for the U.S. average.)

Making conversation in Alaska is easy. When strangers meet, the usual ice-breaker is, "And where are you from?"

Alaskans go to movies, listen to radio, watch television, read a great deal—and drink! They do far more drinking than any other group in the United States, a fact that is immediately obvious to visitors. In most towns, there are cocktail lounges and package liquor stores everywhere. Comedian Joe E. Brown once quipped that Fourth Ave. in Anchorage is the "longest bar in the world," a rather pungent description for nearly half a mile of an almost unbroken line of cafés on both sides of the street. Some cafés strive to attract tourist trade by perpetuating the atmosphere of a honky-tonk, with swinging doors and bleached blondes playing decrepit pianos amidst swirling clouds of smoke. But most cafés are of the cocktail-lounge variety, and others are rapidly converting to a more sedate ambiance for the home trade. At any rate, drunkenness on the streets is rare.

All told, there are about a dozen radio stations and five television stations in Alaska, within the range of perhaps 90 per cent of the population. Except for local shows, which feature such popular programs as illustrated talks on hunting and fishing, nearly everything on Alaskan television is on film. Most events of any significance may be at least a week old before appearing on Alaskan TV screens, and sometimes the impact and thrills are gone because the details will have been obtained from radio or newspapers. For example, I once asked a 38-year-old family man who had accumulated considerable wealth through a successful business (restaurant) after 13 years in Anchorage, "Since you have made so much money, what is there that you would most like to do now? Return to your hometown, live it up?"

"No," he said unhesitatingly, "but I'd sure give a thousand bucks to see a big league ball game."

"Don't you see baseball on TV?"

"Yes. But it's stale. The thrill's gone. I always know the score."

Of six daily newspapers in Alaska, perhaps only the two in Anchorage and the one in Fairbanks resemble modern journalism. But even these do not place great stress on national or international affairs, unless there are Alaska angles to the story. Alaskans who desire to keep up with world affairs usually subscribe to the weekly news magazines or the air editions of the *New York Times.* Quite a few pay 30 cents for same-day Seattle newspapers delivered by air, but an impartial observer would have to say that the 30 cents is wasted, for the Anchorage *Daily News,* and *Times,* and the Fairbanks *News-Miner,* widely and efficiently distributed at 10 cents each, are equal if not superior to the Seattle newspapers.

Most Alaskans do not seem to be particularly sports-minded. Except for high school teams and service teams, there is little in the way of organized sport. But Alaskans are certainly fun-minded and will participate actively in community festivities and fairs.

Perhaps the most colorful event in Alaska—if not in the entire North country—is the annual Fur Rendezvous, held in February in Anchorage. The Fur Rendezvous converts Anchorage for several days into a carnival city, and attracts Alaskans from everywhere. It is part of a tradition that goes back to early 19th-century Alaska, when fur buyers met with Indians to trade, and after trading would celebrate their deals with fire water. During the modern Fur Rendezvous, Eskimos come from the north to display their crafts, perform dramas, dances, and sports; and there are dog-sled races in the streets of Anchorage, sometimes for stakes running into thousands of dollars. Men and trucks sometimes work through the night, carting snow from the outskirts to spread about the streets of Anchorage in order to assure good dog-sled racing! The event even draws one contestant from as far away as Massachusetts.

There are more culturally advanced forms of entertainment in the major cities, such as concerts and theatrical productions which usually play to standing-room-only audiences. Sometimes the performances are by local talent and are quite ambitious. Anchorage, for instance, has a large symphony orchestra of its own, as well as a choral group numbering 100 to 120 voices, which participate in an annual June music festival. But local community groups have been increasingly sponsoring concerts by well known musicians and artists invited from the great halls of New York, Chicago and Los Angeles.

Alaskans are avid readers, and support their libraries. A recently constructed library in Anchorage is one of the best-equipped and most modern I have seen anywhere in the world, and there was hardly an afternoon or evening that I did not see the library crowded with school children and adult readers. Typically, the library subscribes to scores of Outside publications in order to satisfy the Alaskans' hunger for news and knowledge. Several magazines are published in Alaska. One of these, the *Alaskan Sportsman,* is of exceptional quality in its fiction and non-fiction and tends to reflect the true spirit of Alaskans.

SOCIAL INTERRELATIONS

Nowhere in Alaska is there any evidence of resentment toward *cheechakos,* newcomers. A possible exception is Juneau, where many of Alaska's oldest families have been established and the few newcomers may feel a certain social "chill" in the air.

But as a rule *cheechako* is a friendly term and newcomers are made to feel welcome. Yet Alaskans can be piqued readily by any sudden intrusion of new ideas—or talent—particularly if such intrusion tends to make some Alaskan enterprise, or institution, or personality, seem mediocre by comparison.

To a great extent this may be due to fear, or insecurity. Many Alaskans have been successful in business, society, or politics as a result of individual tenacity and hard work and sometimes sheer courage, rather than superior talents. As a frontier society, Alaska has attracted many whose abilities are somewhat lukewarm, because it has been relatively easy for them to reach the top and remain there in a frontier setting, as compared with a highly competitive society. Mediocrity is frequently apparent, particularly in business. Accordingly a smart *cheechako,* no matter how skilled, ingenious or experienced, does not impose new ideas drastically or suddenly. He learns to take his time.

WOMEN IN ALASKA

For the most part, women in Alaska lead a typically American family life, tending to home, children, and garden, and they read about Dan McGrew and the "lady known as Lou" with as much curiosity as women who have never been to Alaska. What is perhaps most characteristic of women in the 49th State is that many work, either part-time or full-time; many join their husbands in outdoor fun; many are quite handy with paint brushes and tools around the house.

Doris Dooley grew so handy with tools soon after her arrival in Fairbanks, about 10 years ago, that she was able to start her own business, leasing, installing, and maintaining soda dispensing machines and popcorn vendors. It is not unusual to see Doris, a handsome blondish woman in her forties, hop off her truck in Fairbanks, with a kit of plumbing tools on her way to a repair or installation job. In some other state she'd probably be a candidate for town eccentric. But in Fairbanks she's just another Alaskan making a go of things.

Women in Alaska enjoy an unparalleled social and economic equality with men. There are women in trades, politics, business and law enforcement. In Anchorage, a familiar sight is the attractive *motorcycle* policewoman, assigned to traffic enforcement.

Before statehood, there were many laws passed protecting the rights and interests of Alaskan women in such matters as minimum pay ($1.50 per hour), equal pay for equal work, and protection of property rights in marriage and divorce. These laws remain in force.

One aspect of life, however, that affects women in particular, especially housewives with children, is what Alaskans call "cabin fever," supposedly a syndrome of boredom and monotony arising from long periods of darkness and cold during the winter. Cabin fever is said to be epidemic in the interior.

Many ministers and physicians (there are no private psychiatrists in Alaska) told me that "cabin fever" is the principal social "disease" in Alaska and that it accounts for a higher-than-average rate of alcoholism and suicide. Another result of cabin fever, according to many Alaskans, is the standard joke known as "the spring break-up," indicated by a high rate of separations and divorces after the winter.

Statistical data support the view that incidences of alcoholism and suicide in Alaska are above average. But if the rate of divorce in Alaska is any indication of cabin fever, the disease is not nearly as bad as many make it out to be. The latest divorce rate in Alaska was about 2.6 per 1,000 population, but there was almost an identical divorce rate for the entire U. S.

However, more significant is the fact that the divorce rate in Alaska in 1945 was much higher—3.9 per 1,000—and has been declining steadily ever since, whereas the divorce rate in the U. S. has remained practically unchanged.

These statistics, of course, are subject to varying interpretations. It is entirely possible, for example, that when a marriage breaks up in Alaska one of the partners is apt to leave the state and obtain a divorce elsewhere. But the *steadily declining* rate of divorce in Alaska cannot be ignored in view of Alaska's increasing population during the same period. My own feeling is that Alaskan marriages tend to be more firmly cemented because husband and wife share a common goal and affection for their way of life and the new state of Alaska. One minister put it nicely: "If a man and wife stick it out together in Alaska for one full year, not even the Lord can tear them apart."

A rather common misconception about women in Alaska is the oft-heard remark, even among Alaskans, that women go to Alaska to get a man because men outnumber women seven to one.

Single women arrive in Alaska constantly, but not many. Most come to take jobs as teachers or as government workers in Federal Civil Service. There is no basis, however, for accepting the seven-to-one ratio. A liberal estimate would bring it down to more manageable proportions, three to one. Nonetheless, Alaska is no huge man-trap for single women. Most young men in Alaska are already married. There is, however, a definite ratio of three *unmarried* males to one *unmarried* female in Anchorage and Fairbanks—thanks to the unusual preponderance of military personnel in those areas.

But do not conclude that life for unmarried females in Alaska is dull. It is anything but that, particularly in Anchorage and Fairbanks. For one thing, both these cities supply adequate recreational and social resources where young couples can have fun. In both cities, there are many socials at community and religious centers, and there are a great variety of clubs, social, fraternal, professional, and recreational. In Anchorage alone, there are more than 150 active social and professional societies. In addition, the social resources in both cities are substantially augmented by large and well-run functions at the various military bases.

Dating and social life is extremely informal, and there is little chance for monotony because Alaska's young folk represent not the monolithic cultural pattern of a single community, but backgrounds as diverse as America itself.

One evening, as I sat in the living room of a modern home shared by three young unmarried female teachers, discussing with them the subject of their social lives in Alaska, one of them, from a small upstate New York town, said: "I love the informality here and the variety of young men Alaska has. They all seem to come from different cities and different backgrounds, and if a young man feels like seeing you, he doesn't seem compelled to conform to a pattern of social intercourse; he doesn't make a ceremony of it over the telephone, for instance. He just comes knocking at your door."

At that very moment, there was a knock at the door. Four strikingly handsome airmen from Elmendorf were there. "Just passing by," said one. "Thought we'd come in and say hello."

"Come on in," the girls called out in unison, laughing, and soon the room was filled with a babble of happy small talk and blithesome spirits. My visit ended abruptly when all went out for pizza and Cokes.

RELIGION IN ALASKA

The density of churches in Alaska is high. One community of 1,500 supports nine churches! There are almost 100 churches between Anchorage and Fairbanks. Every conceivable denomination is represented. Increasingly, the churches are playing a vital role in the social lives of Alaskans, providing a variety of welfare and counselling services, including a Hospitality House in Fairbanks for job-seeking girls in need. Recently, a $5,000,000 college was started by the Methodist Church in Anchorage, and plans have been made for an almost year-by-year expansion of the college.

But Alaskans apparently are not fervent about their religion. A well known religious leader in Alaska said, smilingly, "Alaska is still a missionary country as far as religious life is concerned. People who come here are essentially escapists, non-conformists.

"This is a weekend country. Anyone who has any kind of camping gear and a car takes off with his family on weekends. I don't blame them. I'd join them if I could, and sometimes I do."

Cooperation between religious groups is excellent, although there seems to be an undercurrent of animosity between the major denominations and those of what some call the "fringe" religions, of which there are many in Alaska, operating from store-front churches. But discrimination of any sort, religious, racial, or social, is almost non-existent. It is definitely anti-social to be a bigot in Alaska.

TRAVEL IN ALASKA

Many arriving in Alaska for the first time are surprised to find that Alaskans travel about with ease, even in winter. Of the many strange notions held by Outsiders regarding travel in Alaska, none was more ludicrous than that revealed by a *cheechako* who thought that during the winter, if he had to call for a taxi in Alaska, he'd find himself hopping into a dog sled operated by an Eskimo crying, "Mush!"

In some northern portions of Alaska—and in the isolated bush—the dog sled or snow shoes are still the only means of travel in winter. But even these are rapidly giving way to the airplane.

Alaska is the flyingest place in the world. Everybody, it would seem, has a pilot's license—housewives, ministers, doctors, nurses, lawyers, Indians, Eskimos, Aleuts, salesmen, politicians, hunting and fishing enthusiasts. In fact, many sportsmen who had utilized airplanes avocationally for hunting and fishing have become professional bush pilots.

A few days before my visit to the University of Alaska at Fairbanks, an 18-year-old Indian girl landed on the campus in her own airplane to register as a freshman for the coming semester. She had flown, I was told, some 600 miles over extremely rough country.

According to Alaska Airlines, "78.7 per cent of the population use air transportation regularly. The average Alaskan flies 28 times as much and as frequently as the citizen in the continental United States." Indeed, it is the airplane that is really responsible for the "opening" of Alaska's interior. In this regard, the U.S. Air Force played a significant role shortly after World War II, proving that it was feasible to fly heavy equipment into the heartland of Alaska.

There are about 130 fields and terminals for scheduled air transport in Alaska. Added to these are almost 300 landing strips scattered about the state. An Alaskan, if he does not fly his own airplane, will hop aboard anything from a bush pilot's Piper Cub to a DC-7C or jet as casually as a banker takes a taxi to lunch on Wall Street.

HIGHWAY TRAVEL

The only highway link between Alaska and the continental U. S. is the famous "Alcan" or Alaska Highway, which goes through the Yukon Territory, Alberta and British Columbia. It is perhaps the most publicized highway in the world because it is an adventure in scenic grandeur. Unfortunately, it is also a gruelling trip and has perhaps been over-glamorized to the point where many making the trip are totally unprepared for its hazards. Because most of the highway is gravel-surfaced, except in Alaska, among the more common accidents are broken windshields and headlamps and fuel tanks, shattered by flying rock. An Air Force captain related a hair-raising experience which, he said, "took 20 years off my life."

He had been traveling on the Alaska Highway with his family. His wife was beside him in the car, his children were in a trailer. He happened to look in his rear-view mirror just in time to see flames licking out of the trailer. A flying rock had split his fuel tank, and a spark apparently touched off a fire. He brought his car to a screeching halt, raced out and rescued his children. "Another minute," he said, quivering, "and I would have been without a family."

While such dramatically dangerous incidents are infrequent, a trip to Alaska via the Alaska Highway is more enjoyable—and safer!— when it is properly planned and all official advisories are heeded.

The Alaska Highway was built as an emergency measure during World War II. Its location was hurriedly chosen. Its 1,523 miles from Dawson Creek in British Columbia to Fairbanks were constructed by 14,000 men in less than ten months. For hardy truck drivers transporting urgently needed war materiel, the highway was adequate. But for passenger vehicles, the highway trip was an adventure in every respect.

But there has been considerable improvement since the end of World War II, and further improvements are being made continually. The entire portion of the highway in Alaska, some 300 miles, has been paved. But nearly all of the highway that goes through Canada is gravel. Many prefer to make the trip in winter because hard-packed snow actually makes the trip smoother, cleaner, and safer—provided speed limits are strictly observed. In the spring, however, motorists have to battle mud; and in the summer they contend with flying gravel and massive clouds of dust.

Proper preparation for a trip on the Alaska Highway entails careful, advance planning. It means, for instance, you must allow at least five or six days to cover the entire distance, never driving in excess of about 40 mph. It means finding out in advance what spare equipment should be carried and what protective measures should be taken against flying gravel.

Veteran travellers of the Alaska Highway recommend that at least two good spare tires be carried at all times. They also recommend a good insect repellent during summer travel; tire chains, a shovel, and a bucket of sand in winter. They also advise motorists to place wire screens around headlamps and windshields, and that a bar of soap, or some effective hole-filling device, be kept handy to plug a gas-tank leak.

All along the Alaska Highway there are a number of service stations, adequately spaced, to take care of most highway needs: oil, gas, spare parts, repairs, lodging, food. However, the services vary considerably. Some garages make only minor repairs and have no spare parts. Some lodges offer rooms without bath and no running water. Perhaps the best source of information for planning a trip via the Alaska Highway is "Travel in Alaska," a five-cent booklet sold by the Superintendent of Documents, U.S. Government Printing Office, Washington, D. C. (For other sources of information for Alaska Highway travel, see the appendix.)

ROADS IN ALASKA

Before World War II, the only significant road in Alaska was the Richardson Highway, which links the gulf port of Valdez to Fairbanks, a distance of 365 miles. Today, not including the Alaska Highway, there are some 2,000 miles of good paved roads in Alaska, constituting a well-travelled network of primary and secondary systems, connecting the two most populated areas in the state—Anchorage and Fairbanks—and the towns between and around these areas.

The primary system connects the Alaska Highway, Fairbanks, Anchorage, Valdez and Seward. These roads are kept open the year round. On most other roads, the snow is not removed after November, and some roads are closed until May or June. However, thanks to years of the most advanced highway engineering service in the world—the U.S. Bureau of Public Roads, when Alaska was a territory—nearly all of Alaska's cities and towns employ the best-known snow-removal techniques; there are nearly 3,200 miles of streets and roads in and around Alaska's towns, and these are rarely closed on account of snow. The 70,000 motor vehicles in Alaska have no trouble getting around.

The Alaska Railroad

The only railroad of any consequence in Alaska is the Alaska Railroad, owned and operated by the U. S. Government, under the supervision of the Department of the Interior. It covers a distance of about 500 miles, from Seward to Fairbanks, via Anchorage. It has branch lines to serve the Army's port of Whittier, the Air Force Base in Fairbanks, and the agricultural center of Palmer, near Anchorage.

Completed in 1923, the Alaska Railroad has played an important part in encouraging settlement in Alaska. More than half the people in Alaska live in what is known as the "railbelt," cities and towns near tracks and terminals, such as Anchorage and Fairbanks. Alaskans make good use of the railroad for personal travel and freight. There have been few occasions when the railroad has not earned a profit, although its rates are not out of line with comparable costs in Alaska.

The railroad's employees are Civil Service workers whose wages average about 40 to 45 per cent above similar occupational groups in the Pacific Northwest.

Alaskan trainmen are known as the friendliest people in the state. Often, during the hunting and fishing seasons, an outdoorsman will choose a likely hunting and fishing camp-site while seated at the train window, and the train will come to a halt, allowing the outdoorsman time to get off. In a day or two, the train will stop again at the same spot to pick him up. The trainmen also have a system for communicating with prospectors and homesteaders living in isolated areas, the bush. They will pick up messages from stakes along the tracks, deliver mail, even take shopping lists to drop off groceries on the return trip. According to unofficial reports, trainmen have shopped for and delivered: wedding rings, women's underclothes, false teeth, bird seed, pet dogs, and an artificial leg.

The only other common-carrier railroad in Alaska is the Canadian-British owned White Pass & Yukon, which connects Skagway with White Horse in Canada's Yukon Territory. Only some 20 miles of its 111 miles of trackage are in Alaska. The ride along this railroad's narrow-gauge tracks is popular with tourists and vacationing Alaskans. It takes about six hours to cover the entire route, but daily schedules are maintained only between May and September.

TRAVEL BY WATER

Since 1954 there has been no passenger service to and from Alaska on American ships. During the summer months only—from about late May through September—several Canadian cruise ships carry passengers along the picturesque Inland Passage from Vancouver, British Columbia, to Panhandle ports (Ketchikan, Wrangell, Petersburg, Juneau), ending their excursions at Skagway. The vessels are operated by Canadian Pacific (1320 Fourth Avenue, Seattle); Canadian National (Vancouver, Canada); and Alaska Cruise Lines (Joseph Vance Building, Seattle).

As a rule, however, there is very little space aboard the cruise vessels for one-way passengers, since most space is reserved for those who have signed for round-trip "package" tours, which are becoming increasingly popular. A cruise along the Inland Passage, with its endless vistas of fjords and glaciers and densely timbered islands, has been compared many times with an ocean voyage to Norway, except that the waters of the Inland Passage are as smooth as a lake on a windless day.

Throughout Alaska, especially in the Panhandle, many own boats for transportation as well as pleasure. But there is within Alaska no local port-to-port scheduled passenger service on ships, except for a state-operated passenger-car ferry, which runs on a regular schedule between June and November at Juneau, Haines and Skagway. Once a month, a large, modern mailboat, the M.V. EXPANSION, operated by Capt. Niels P. Thomsen (Box 537, Seward, Alaska) makes a run to 35 ports in the Aleutian Islands. The mailboat offers accommodations for 12 passengers. Alaskans consider it an unusual and colorful voyage, for which the cost averages $258 for the entire trip.

Waterborne cargo service to and from Alaska is provided largely by Coastwise Lines and the Alaska Steamship Company, operating from Seattle. In the Panhandle, a substantial amount of cargo is carried between ports on locally operated barges.

For many years, the Alaska Steamship Company has been the principal over-water freight carrier for Alaska and has played an important, albeit sometimes controversial, part in the development of Alaska. More than 60 steamship companies have come and gone in the Alaska trade, but the Alaska Steamship Company has been in business since 1895, when it started with one ship. Today, it operates 15 vessels and carries an average of 400,000 to 600,000 tons of freight to and from Alaska. In a typical year, its ships (as large and as modern as any in ocean-going freight anywhere) will average more than 800 calls at 65 different ports, ranging from Ketchikan to Kotzebue. In recent years, the Alaska Steamship Company has spent several million dollars to modernize its cargo-handling facilities. This has resulted in recently announced lower freight rates and, perhaps most important for Alaskans who like to do mail-order buying in the continental U.S., it has also resulted in considerably less spoilage and damage of in-transit cargo.

THE FUTURE

Since statehood, many Alaskans have been hopeful that facilities for travel and transport within Alaska will greatly increase. No doubt they will.

For several years a little known Congressional group, the Alaska International Rail and Highway Commission, under the chairmanship of Senator Warren C. Magnuson, has been studying the travel and transport problems and needs of Alaska. The Commission has recently expedited its work by holding a series of hearings in Alaska and by hiring the noted Battelle Research Institute of Ohio to make a scientific study of Alaska's rail, highway and waterway needs. As soon as the Commission offers its recommendations, perhaps sometime in late 1961 or early 1962, there will undoubtedly be a great increase in Federal assistance toward expanding Alaska's travel facilities.

It is almost certain, for example, that the Commission will recommend a direct rail link between the continental U.S. and Alaska. This will undoubtedly require some form of Federal participation, either through subsidies and loans to a private railroad or an expansion of the government-owned Alaska Railroad. Another and perhaps more immediate possibility is improvement and expansion of the Alaska Highway through the joint cooperation of the U.S. and Canadian governments.

Meanwhile, within Alaska many new highways are already under construction or in the planning stage. Alaskans are most hopeful that within the next decade there will be at least one highway crossing the entire east-west width of Alaska, particularly Fairbanks-to-Nome. A small part of this highway leading out of Nome has already been built. When such a trans-state highway is completed, it should touch off a new Klondike of travel to and settlement within Alaska. It should also provide fresh challenge and opportunities for business and homesteading.

Every improvement in transportation to, from and within Alaska has altered life in the 49th State, diluting its frontier characteristics, hastening settlement, creating new business opportunities, opening new frontiers for exploration of natural resources. In this regard, Alaskans are watching the jet age with keen interest. Already, trans-Polar passenger jets are making regular stops in Anchorage on flights between Europe and Asia. Anchorage and Fairbanks have already established plans for airport improvements to accommodate increasing jet air traffic.

As fast as jet aviation enters Alaska, the frontier will disappear. Some oldtimers in Alaska don't think this is progress. But it is inevitable. Jet aviation will perhaps do for Alaska in a decade what the Conestoga wagon did for the old West in a couple of generations.

CHAPTER 4

THE ECONOMIC FACTS OF LIFE IN ALASKA: COSTS AND STANDARDS OF LIVING

> *"A Congressional Committee was told that Alaskans would be willing to 'live on beans' to make a go of statehood. This is the spirit that may have to be applied. . . ."*
> B. Frank Heintzleman, former Governor of Alaska

A FLORIDA NEWSPAPER, PERHAPS NOT ENTIRELY IMPARTIAL, recently published a feature article about the high cost of living in Alaska. It gave the impression that Alaskans are either millionaires or starving fools. The article told how a visitor from Florida had paid $2.50 for a haircut in Alaska, 50 cents for a shoeshine, 90 cents for a thin hamburger, and 75 cents for a peanut butter sandwich—without jelly! As a final thrust at scaring visitors away from Alaska, it reported that a car wash had cost $5. At that, it was a bargain because the price had been marked down from the usual $6. The story neglected to mention that the auto in question had just come off the Alaska Highway with an impossible accumulation of grime, for the removal of which $5 was perhaps a bargain, indeed.

In the light of cold statistics, it cannot be denied by even the most ardent Alaskan partisan that prices in Alaska are high and the cost of living is in fact higher than in any other state. But as mentioned in the introductory chapter, it is important to view all statistical data regarding Alaska in perspective. If this is done, we should note that most reports on Alaska's cost of living are not entirely accurate because they neglect to mention certain compensating factors, which we shall examine here.

First, the background, or the causes for Alaska's high cost of living.

Alaska produces very little. Nearly everything is imported from the continental U.S. via Seattle. Consequently, the high cost of transportation is a principal reason for Alaska's high cost of living. The problem of transport is compounded by the fact that most ships, planes, and trucks making deliveries to Alaska frequently return almost empty. The cost of "back haul" is, therefore, added to the cost of inbound freight. Hence, the cost of living in a particular town in Alaska will tend to vary directly with its distance from Seattle. That is why, for instance, an Alaskan living in Nome or Fairbanks may consider a glass of orange juice a luxury, whereas an Alaskan in Juneau or Anchorage may have orange juice for breakfast every morning.

Two other important factors in Alaska's high cost of living are: (1) the high cost of doing business in Alaska; (2) the general inability—or neglect—of Alaska's few local producers and businessmen to reduce prices by employing more efficient methods of production.

In computing the selling prices of their products or services, Alaskan businessmen must take into account the higher wages they pay, the need to maintain large inventories (sometimes as a hedge against shipping strikes), the high cost of heating, and the high cost of rents, as well as substantially higher interest rates on borrowed capital.

On the other hand, efficiency is not always feasible for Alaskan businessmen because efficiency often implies greater volume of business and in most cases the Alaskan market is too small to absorb increased volume. An efficient concrete block plant in Anchorage, for instance, invested rather heavily in modernizing its plant, but it usually operates at about one-fourth capacity. On occasion, Alaskan farmers have had to pour gasoline over mounds of potatoes in order to prevent a glut on the market.

Milk, potatoes, and eggs account for more than 75 per cent of Alaska's farm production. The present Alaskan market could absorb perhaps a five-fold increase in these products. But Alaskan farmers are faced with their own high costs of doing business, such as the high cost of purchasing machinery, gasoline, heating fuel, feed, fertilizer, and processing materials. As a result, Alaska's farmers do not increase volume and must frequently compete with agricultural products—including fresh milk, potatoes, and eggs—shipped by air from Canadian and U.S. farms, whose far greater production is efficient enough to absorb the cost of air-freighting to Alaska. Conversely, if an Alaskan farmer "over-produces," he cannot ship his products to markets in other states because he cannot compete in other states.

Finally, lack of competition must be considered as a factor in Alaska's high cost of living. Because Alaskans have long been accustomed to paying high prices, some merchants continue the "custom" of charging high prices even though circumstances, from time to time, may enable them to reduce prices. As we shall see, keen competition among clothiers and package liquor stores in Alaska does account for the fact that clothing and liquor prices in Alaska are only slightly above average U.S. prices.

THE COMPENSATING FACTORS

Perhaps most neglected in reports on Alaska's high cost of living is the fact that Alaskans receive higher wages than other Americans. Federal Civil Service employees, for instance, constitute the largest single group of workers in Alaska, and they receive a 25 per cent cost-of-living bonus, although the bonus was originally applied under the rule that Alaska was an "overseas territory."

In order to meet the high cost of living, Alaskans also tend to adjust their *standards* of living. A haircut may cost $2.50 and a shoeshine 50 cents, but Alaskans "stretch" the time between haircuts and shine their own shoes. They will live in smaller homes, dine out infrequently, take lunch to the office, shop with extreme care, search for bargains at sale time, and waste little.

Nothing varies in Alaska as much as the standard of living. Within one street in one town it is possible to see families and individuals living in anything from a shack reminiscent of Hoovervilles to exquisitely modern split-levels. These conditions reflect not only rather liberal zoning regulations but the need for some people in Alaska to "adjust" their standards of living. In some cases, those living in comparative shacks may be earning as much as those living in the split-levels, except that a shack dweller may be compensating for the fact that he also owns an airplane and a homestead, and frequently goes hunting and fishing. In some other community, Outside, under pressure to keep up with and look like the Joneses, he'd be unable to "compensate." In the same light, family income is frequently augmented by working wives, who feel no social pressure simply because they have to work. This, too, helps families compensate for the high cost of living. Single persons usually compensate by sharing rent and cars, and cooking for themselves.

But while on the subject of income, covered in detail in the next chapter, it should be noted here that a higher weekly or per-hour wage in Alaska does not necessarily add proportionately to a higher net income. A higher income may place the wage earner in a higher tax bracket, in which case a certain percentage of the higher wage that is supposed to compensate for the high cost of living comes off the top for taxes. Uncle Sam's Internal Revenue Service is not authorized to make allowances for the higher costs of food, clothing and housing in Alaska.

STANDARDS OF LIVING IN ALASKA

A newcomer who is prepared to "adjust" his standard of living, as oldtime Alaskans do, should have no trouble meeting the high cost of living, assuming he obtains employment comparable to what he might have had before coming to Alaska. If a newcomer, for example, wants to feed his children as much milk as he might have provided for them back home, he might have to get them accustomed to less *fresh* milk and more of the reconstituted and recombined (but equally nourishing) varieties of milk that abound in Alaska. A study made by the armed forces once showed that the per capita consumption of *fresh* milk among servicemen in Alaska was about 33 ounces daily; but the civilian consumption was less than 7 ounces daily. Among Alaskans, therefore, the difference in milk consumption is made up with "powder." In fact, some Alaskan farmers believe that even if they could reduce their fresh milk prices they might not sell more, because Alaskans have become conditioned to non-fresh milk and have learned to prefer it over fresh milk. Such a preference is not difficult to acquire in Alaska. The technology of reconstituted and recombined milk has advanced considerably. It is sometimes difficult to discern any difference between the taste of non-fresh and fresh milk.

The term "standard of living" is nebulous. It cannot be measured precisely or comparatively. Who can say what is a "high" or "low" standard of living? Who can say that a standard of living has "improved" or "deteriorated"? Can a hermit who wants to be a hermit, nothing more, nothing less, "improve" his standard of living if given free access to all the gold in Ft. Knox? Who enjoys a "higher" standard of living: a man in Scarsdale, New York, with a $50,000 house, a car for every member of the family, TV sets in every room and an irksome, ulcer-breeding job on Madison Avenue; or the Alaskan who has abandoned Madison Avenue, lives in a simple Cape Cod, is never irritated by an erratic commuter's schedule, and goes fishing and hunting to his heart's content?

Standard of living is a highly personal business. Those who have chosen to settle in Alaska are the first to admit that back home there were more "conveniences" and flashy status symbols. But they are quite satisfied to settle for "less" in Alaska. An Alaskan considers his standard of living tremendously "improved" if he has had some good luck in hunting or fishing and has been able to stock his freezer with the rewards thereof. It is no coincidence that 37 per cent of Alaskan households in the Anchorage-Fairbanks area own freezers, compared with a U.S. average of 20 per cent. But even this figure can be misleading because many Alaskans also rent lockers at a monthly cost of about 50 cents per cubic foot for the purpose of storing the frozen prizes of their hunting and fishing trips and from their backyard or homestead gardens.

I recall rather vividly the evening I went to visit with a young couple, in Alaska eight years, originally from New York City. When the husband went to the pantry for some matches, out tumbled a veritable avalanche of 1-pound tins of king salmon. Embarrassed by his mishap, he explained that he had had some remarkable luck on his last fishing trip and had perhaps overstocked his pantry with the salmon, which he had canned himself, at a cost of approximately 27 cents per tin. Incidentally, dinner that night was moose steak, taken from the freezer, thanks to the husband's last hunting trip.

"How would you appraise your present standard of living in Alaska?" I put this question to more than 300 persons from all walks of life in Alaska. The replies were remarkably uniform, in two distinct categories. All the oldtimers, those who had been living in Alaska 10 years or more, said that they were enjoying a "higher" standard of living in Alaska. Those who were comparative newcomers said that they had to put up with a "lower" standard of living. The oldtimers no longer compared their standards in Alaska with what they had left behind in other states. The newcomers, on the other hand, continually compared their mode of living in Alaska with their "back home" standards. In short, an oldtimer tends to remember when "things were much worse."

A male high school teacher, for instance, told me that when he first settled in Alaska, in 1949, the street on which he had bought a home was not paved. There were no sewers and water had to be purchased from a tank truck. He appraised his standard of living in Alaska as being "quite high now" because he lives in an improved house on the same street, which is paved, landscaped, and has sewers. Yet, according to his own description of the town and home he had left in Minnesota, if he were to return to his hometown he'd enjoy a considerably "higher" standard of living.

Newcomers, conscious of having a "lower" standard of living, express little or no regret for having settled in Alaska. They are not concerned about standards of living. This, as we have discussed earlier, is a reflection of the "spirit" of Alaska. Their rewards in life come from being a part of America's last frontier and in helping to build the frontier. For them, every gain is joy "and gain is gain, however small." They derive gratification by participating in the "spirit" that moves Alaskans to seek constant improvement. Sometimes, when improvements come, the gain is not so small. One Alaskan oldtimer, now rather wealthy, proudly told me how back in 1952 he had purchased a lot for $850 on what was then the outskirts of Anchorage because he had anticipated rapid expansion of Anchorage in that area and subsequent improvements, such as the installation of paved roads and sidewalks. He said he had made the purchase against the advice of his best friends. But seven years later, the lot on the "outskirts" became one of Anchorage's leading streets and he sold the lot for $32,500!

COST OF LIVING: OFFICIAL FACTS

Since World War II, numerous official studies have been made in Alaska to obtain reliable economic data regarding the cost of living. Consequently, that notable American rule of thumb—the cost of living index—may be applied to Alaska as an accurate yardstick.

With respect to essential living costs—food, housing, clothing, and personal services (*e.g.,* barbershop service, dry-cleaning, beauty parlor)—here is the cost of living "rule" for Alaska: Taking 1958 prices in Seattle as a base 100, the comparative cost of living in five key Alaskan cities ranges from 121 to 154. Specifically, it is 121 in Sitka; 122 in Ketchikan; 124 in Juneau; 140, Anchorage; 154, Fairbanks.

In other words, an Alaskan living in Fairbanks can expect to pay 54 per cent more than the same goods and services might cost in Seattle; in Sitka it would be 21 per cent higher.

However, just as there are variations in the cost of living indexes between cities in Alaska, there are also important differences between certain items that are included in the "shopping basket" from which the cost of living index is computed. Fresh fruits and vegetables in Fairbanks, for example, may be almost double the Seattle index, which accounts for the relatively low consumption of citrus fruits in Fairbanks.

THE COST OF FOOD IN ALASKA

According to the Alaska Extension Service (U.S. Department of Agriculture), the average Alaskan family spends approximately one-third of its income for food. This is about 10 per cent higher than the average family expenditure for food in the continental United States.

Food prices in Alaska have been under continuous study since 1949, when the marketing economics staff of the Alaska Extension Service published its first *Quarterly Report on Alaska's Food Prices*.

Data for the *Quarterly Report* are carefully compiled from prices turned in by volunteer shoppers who visit three to six retail establishments in key Alaskan cities each month. The shoppers note various prices according to brand and size of volume-selling items. The prices are then averaged for publication in the *Quarterly Report,* a technique similar to the famous 40-item "market basket" utilized by the U.S. Bureau of Labor Statistics as a standard for determining changes in food prices.

In Alaska, the total price for the 40-item "market basket" (including flour, meats, dairy products, fruits, vegetables, and canned goods) will range from approximately $20 in Ketchikan to $27 in Nome. The average for all Alaskan cities will be about $23. According to the Extension Service, a "typical family of four in Alaska will spend from $1,900 to $2,600 yearly" for food, depending on locality.

Following is a table of what average *per capita* expenditures may be for Alaskans in ten different cities.

City	Average Annual Per Capita Expenditures for Food
Anchorage	$538
Fairbanks	605
Juneau	513
Ketchikan	498
Kodiak	525
Nome	661
Palmer	605
Petersburg	490
Seward	541
Sitka	494

Those interested in comparing specific food prices between Alaskan cities may do so by writing to: Marketing Economist, Alaska Extension Service, Box E, Palmer, Alaska. Copies of the *Quarterly Report* are free.

THE COST OF HOUSING

The subject of housing is discussed in detail in Chapter 6. It should be noted here, however, that Alaskans generally allocate about 25 to 35 per cent of their incomes toward housing—apartment rentals, house rentals, or mortgage and maintenance payments. However, unlike a pound of butter, it is difficult to equate housing costs between cities in Alaska because, as elsewhere, the quality of housing varies, except that in Alaska the variations are considerable. As an illustration: the three young, unmarried teachers I talked with in Anchorage had been living in a fairly modern frame house almost in the center of town. They had rented the house furnished and their total cost for rent, fuel, and utilities came to less than $160 per month, which they shared. The house was neatly and tastefully furnished, had two bedrooms, a fair-sized living room, a modern kitchen, and an attached garage. In Fairbanks, the cost of renting a similar house in a comparable location would be substantially more. But if the teachers were to limit themselves to the same budget allocation for housing in Fairbanks, they'd perhaps have to live in a less spacious house on the outskirts of town, and the furnishings would be nothing to write home about.

The Cost of Clothing

Prices of wearing apparel throughout most of Alaska are comparatively low; that is, when compared with other cost of living items. In many instances, clothing may be purchased in Alaska, particularly in Anchorage, at prices equal to those found in any large city Outside for comparable quality. Astute shoppers in Alaska frequently make substantial savings on clothing costs simply by waiting for clearance sales, which are held periodically in Alaska as elsewhere. The official cost of living index shows apparel prices in Alaska ranging from a low, in Ketchikan, of about 10 per cent over Seattle prices, to a high (Juneau) of about 20 per cent above Seattle.

However, the official cost of living index may be slightly misleading because the quality of clothing sold in Alaska is unquestionably superior, perhaps equal to apparel sold in some of New York's Fifth Avenue shops. While this may seem strange, there is good reason for it. Alaskan clothing merchants, more than others, have long since adopted the attitude that the cost of shipping a quality item is no more than the cost of shipping an inferior one. Also, since returning rejected merchandise is an unwelcome expense and a high one, it is, in the long run, simply good business to sell quality merchandise.

Some comparisons are interesting. A woolen woman's coat bearing a Forstmann label and Milium lining sold in an Anchorage department store for $48 at the same time an identical coat was selling for $42.95 in a New York shop off Fifth Avenue. A man's dress suit in Anchorage was $49.95, compared with a similar suit selling in New York at $44.50. In children's wear, boys' flannel shirts selling at 99 cents to $1.49 were identically priced in New York stores.

Services and Taxes

With the exception of medical-care costs (see Chapter 7), the cost of most personal, home and auto maintenance services is substantially higher in Alaska than similar services in other parts of the United States.

For example, while the cost of laundering a man's shirt in almost any American city was approximately 25 cents, the same service in Anchorage was almost double. In most cases, the price of a three-course dinner for two with a good meat entree, in a rather unpretentious Alaskan restaurant, would range from about $7 to $8, not including tip; whereas a comparable dinner for two in Chicago or

New York might range from $3.70 to $4.50. Perhaps the only "service" cost in Alaska that is comparable with prices elsewhere in the United States is the cost of admission to a movie. At two modern motion picture theatres in Anchorage, adults usually pay $1 or $1.25.

As a general rule, it may be said that Alaskans will pay substantially more than other Americans for services involving food and hand labor, and comparatively less for services that may be dispensed on a mass basis, such as telephones, light and water utilities, garbage collection, and insurance.

Like Americans everywhere, Alaskans gripe about taxes. Almost every Alaskan city has a sales tax, averaging three per cent. The state tax on income is computed on the basis of 14 per cent of the Federal tax. An Alaskan paying a Federal income tax of $1,000, for example, will also pay a tax of $140 to the state.

COST OF LIVING: UNOFFICIAL

To provide what I believe may be a more down-to-earth perspective of living costs in Alaska, I did two things while traveling from town to town. (1) As any budget-conscious householder might do, I shopped around. I checked prices in stores and newspaper advertisements and compiled my own "unofficial" shopping list of prices on the basis of what I would have had to pay if I had gone shopping at the time the prices were posted, paying particular attention, as most Alaskans do, to "specials" and sales. (2) I also kept a "notebook census," carefully recording references to living costs whenever I visited with an Alaskan family, and I made it my business to visit all sorts of people, from millionaires to laborers, truck drivers and craftsmen, Federal Civil Service employees and members of the armed forces living off base.

What follows, then, is my own shopping list and revealing information about typical family living, costs and standards, in Alaska.

My personal shopping list:

Foods and Beverages

Item	Price
Sirloin tip roast (choice)	$ 1.49 lb.
Spare ribs	.69 lb.
Top round steak (choice)	1.29 lb.
Bacon, sliced	.69 lb.

Item	Price
Chicken, fryers	.39 lb.
Frankfurters	.59 lb.
Beef liver	.59 lb.
Eggs, small to large, grade A	.59 to .79 doz.
Milk, fresh	.42 qt.
Cheese, Swiss processed, 5-lb. carton	2.39
Butter, unsalted	.89 lb.
Coffee (unbranded)	.69 lb.
Coffee, instant (large jar)	1.09
Ice cream, half-gallon	1.15
Flour, 25-lb. bag	3.49
Baking chocolate, ½-lb. bar	.55
Chocolate syrup, 1-lb. can	.34
Shortening, 3-lb. tin	.75
Beef stew, 15-oz. tin	.45
Chicken, canned, 3¾-lb.	1.98
Corn on the cob, canned (medium)	.51
Chili with beans, canned, 40-oz. can	.79
Nuts, mixed, 3¾-oz. can	.69
Baby foods, strained (small jars)	.12
Tomato juice, canned, 46-oz. can	.34
Orange juice, frozen, 6-oz. can	.30
Potatoes, local, 10-lb. bag	.73
Tomatoes, Calif. beef steak	.25 lb.
Lemons (about 10-oz. size)	.29 ea.
Grapes, seedless	.25 lb.
Cereals, dry, 8-oz. box	.33
Seagram's "Seven Crown"	4.99 fifth
Johnny Walker Scotch	6.89 fifth
Calvert's Gin	4.89 fifth
Canadian Club	6.99 fifth
Walker's Imperial	4.89 fifth
Black & White Scotch	7.19 fifth

Household

Paint, DuPont (Flowkote)	6.69 gal.
Paint, outside white (Rudd)	5.89 gal.
Step ladder, wooden, 6-ft.	7.95
Ceiling fixture, kitchen, 8-in.	4.98
Percolator, electric "Mirro," 9-cup	9.88

Automotive

Inner tubes, 6:70-15	1.98
Anti-freeze (Prestone)	2.95 gal.
Muffler, installed, 1949-58 models	9.98
Headlamps, sealed-beam, 6 or 12 volt	2.60
Gasoline, regular and "extra"	.45 to .49 gal

Toys and School Supplies

Item	Price
Doll, stuffed, 30 in. high	1.79
Briefcase, children's	1.19
Ball point pen	.39
Coloring book and crayons	.21
Loose leaf paper (200 package)	.59
Lunch kit, including 10-oz. vacuum bottle	2.88

Women's Clothes

Coat, Forstmann label, wool, Milium lined	48.00
Stockings, 51 gauge, 15 denier	.88
Cotton dresses	4.98 to 7.98
Better print dresses	7.00 to 12.95
Summer suits	16.95 to 22.95
Dress suits	49.88 to 59.95

Men's Clothes

Suits, dress	49.95 to 79.95
Jackets, zippered	9.88 to 12.95
Shoes, average to good	11.95 to 23.95
Pajamas, flannel	2.88 to 4.98

Children's Clothes

Girl's nylon slips	2.44 to 3.44
Girl's corduroy jumpers	10.88 to 12.88
Boy's flannel shirts	.99 to 1.49
Toddler's cardigans	1.66 to 2.79
Girl's dresses	2.22 to 3.95
Boy's sport coats	9.88 to 19.95

Services and Miscellaneous

Television service call	5.00
Movies (adults)	1.00 to 1.25
Shoeshine	.50
Haircut	2.50
Dry cleaning, 2 suits, men's	2.50
Dry cleaning, 2 skirts	1.35
Laundry, 2 shirts	1.00
Alcoholic drink, highball	.75 to .90
Residential telephone, private (according to one of three zones)	8.00—8.75—13.50 per month

REVELATIONS FROM A NOTEBOOK

To learn about life and living in a "foreign" land, there is, in my opinion, no substitute for person-to-person talks on the scene, especially in the relaxed and confidential atmosphere of the living room. Accordingly, as the next best thing, I present below the unadulterated facts and impressions from my notebook, as transcribed from actual tape recordings made during scores of visits to Alaskan homes. I have chosen the four notebook histories that follow because they are quite typical and offer a cross-sectional view of Alaska and Alaskans. In my view, such notebook revelations make it possible to obtain a bread-and-butter appreciation of what otherwise might come out as lifeless statistics.

Mr. and Mrs. "A.": Both are in their early thirties. Have one child. Mr. A., from Indiana originally, was discharged from the Army in Alaska about 9 years ago, remained and married in Alaska and is employed as a laborer, working for the city of Anchorage. Mrs. A. does not work. Total income, approximately $7,000 a year. Possess a 1959 Volvo auto, purchased in Anchorage for $800 cash, plus trade of 1958 Volvo. Auto covered by $5-10-5,000 insurance, $100 deductible collision, and non-deductible comprehensive, at cost of $126 a year. They own their home: 2 bedrooms, each about 8 x 10; living room, 9 x 17; kitchen, 9 x 10; bathroom of simulated tile, old-fashioned bathtub on legs; all floors hardwood; interior walls, Cellotex; outside, siding of cedar; no basement; house heated by oil-fueled space heater, automatic; fuel kept in 55-gallon drums outside rear of house.

House purchased in 1955 for $4,000; paid $2,300 cash; seller took balance on mortgage, interest-free, although bank rate on mortgage would have been 8 per cent. House is on small lot, about ¼-acre; when originally purchased the house was not as large as at present. A 16 x 16 addition and improvements were made at a cost of about $3,000 for lumber, insulation, cabinets, lighting fixtures, new 220-v. wiring system, new hot water heater, new plumbing. Most parts were ordered from mail-order catalog. Mr. and Mrs. A. did all the work, hence no labor costs.

Average annual fuel bill for heat and hot water, $240; gas, for cooking, one large tank approximately every six months, cost $18.50. Average monthly electric bill, $23; garbage collection, $3 per month. Taxes: school district, $42.43; public utility district, $11.63; personal property tax, $25; insurance on home at rate of $11.20 per thousand.

Mr. and Mrs. "B.": Ages 36, 28, respectively. Both from Michigan; arrived Alaska 1956. Mrs. B. has Civil Service job as secretary at Elmendorf Air Force Base. Earns about $4,300 per annum, plus 25 per cent bonus; Mr. B. is liquor salesman, earns about $192 gross, per week; two infant children. Live in trailer, purchased for $2,000, financed through Federal credit union at interest rate of ½ of one per cent of unpaid balance; trailer has 2 bedrooms, living room, kitchen, bath, radio, TV, 2 small refrigerators. Rent in trailer camp, $45 per month, includes water and garbage collection; additional for electricity averages $7.50 per month. Mrs. B. pays $15 per week for full-time baby sitter, 8:30 to 4:30. Has no trouble getting baby sitter. Baby-sitting rates are low because of ample supply among dependents of military personnel. As Civil Service employee on base, Mrs. B. has option of sending children to all-day nursery run by base at cost of $15 per week per child, including hot lunch each day. Social life consists largely of visiting with friends on base and in Anchorage. During summer, frequent camping, fishing trips, with children, but not in trailer. Rarely go to movies. Prefer social visiting, especially when friends have invited *cheechakos* to the gathering.

Mr. and Mrs. "C.": Age, in late forties. Both from New York City. Arrived Fairbanks, Alaska early 1959; two teen-age children. Mrs. C. does not work but expects to do so after the family has had a chance to settle down, following excitement of arrival in Alaska. Mr. C. has $158 per week take-home pay as sheet metal worker; but he does not work every day. As soon as his union credentials are transferred to Alaska he will work full-time and overtime and will earn between $254-$300 per week, gross. Now live in rented house, at average cost of $200 per month, varying with use of utilities. House is comfortable but old, rooms small, kitchen exceptionally small, furnishings old-fashioned and worn. On hunting trip with son, Mr. C. accidentally shot son in leg. Son in hospital 5 days for X-rays, surgery. Was in private room, received 20 injections of penicillin, blood transfusions; total bill for hospitalization, $255. Private doctor's fee was $7.50 for first visit, $5 thereafter. Mrs. C. has had dental work in Alaska: two fillings, full-mouth X-ray series, cleaning. Total dental bill, $50. Children attend high school. Both content but complain of "too much homework."

Mr. and Mrs. "D.": In Alaska about 25 years; have lived in Fairbanks, Seward, Bethel, Anchorage. Like Anchorage best. Two children attending University of Alaska at Fairbanks, tuition free. Mr. D. is successful businessman with $500,000 line of credit at two Alaskan banks. Live in 5-bedroom house on about one-third acre. Each bedroom about 10 x 12; living room very large, panelled with costly woods; no basement; house heated by 2 circulating space oil heaters; oil kept in 500-gallon tank in open yard; fuel bill at 22 cents per gallon, averages $660 to $700 per year. House originally rented 17 years ago at cost of about $64 per month. Purchased for $8,000 from original owner. Subsequent improvements and additions (3 bedrooms upstairs) totalled $13,000, including cost of materials and labor. Improvements made between 1949-51. Total taxes on house about $400 per year. Mr. and Mrs. D. active in local politics, community affairs, fraternal organizations, business and social clubs. Principal recreation, meeting with friends at downtown hotel cocktail lounge or informal get-togethers at friends' homes. Dine out infrequently. Three TV sets in home, but family seldom watches TV. In Alaska prior to World War II, "life was a constant struggle, to earn a living." Improvements came rapidly after Korean war, when Mr. D. made most of his money in real estate and retailing. Until Mr. D. prospered, Mrs. D. frequently held part-time jobs as bookkeeper and secretary.

THE FUTURE

The relatively high cost of living in Alaska will perhaps remain a permanent feature of life in Alaska. But it is almost certain that the gap between the cost of living in Alaska and in the continental U.S. will steadily narrow. The rate of narrowing will depend almost directly on the rate at which business expands as a result of population growth in Alaska. A larger population will make it possible for Alaskan businessmen and farmers to capitalize on the advantage of volume selling and production. It will also stimulate new manufacturing industries, thereby reducing the need for Alaskans to purchase high-cost "imports."

More significant: a greater population increase will attract new businesses operated by competitive-minded retailers, including chain stores. Through more progressive and aggressive merchandising techniques, there will come further reduction in prices. The more entrenched Alaskan merchants who are unable or unwilling to meet price-cutting competition will get out of business. The successful establishment of several discount stores in Anchorage, for example, has already had a downward influence on the prices of auto parts, home appliances, radio and TV sets. The recent establishment of Alaska's first chain stores—Safeway and Woolworth—will have a revolutionary impact on prices within a few years. If these chain operations prove to be as successful as expected, more chain stores will be attracted immediately to the opening of outlets in Alaska.

The prospects for a somewhat lower cost of living in Alaska are excellent.

CHAPTER 5

HOW TO GET A JOB IN ALASKA

> *"People willing to work hard, with a sense of humor and a real dedication would be more successful in Alaska than almost anywhere else in the United States."* Charles F. Willis, President, Alaska Airlines

W HEN A STATE OFFICIAL IN ALASKA LEARNED THAT I WAS going to write a book about the 49th State, he made a special point of asking me to see him. As I stepped into his office, and before I could even offer my hand, he jumped from his chair, shook a finger violently at me and said, "For God's sake! Don't tell people to come up here for jobs!"

I was well aware of the reasons for his bitterness.

During World War II, the great need for manpower in Alaska received considerable publicity. Many stories were told about the extremely high wages and incentive bonuses paid to civilian workers, especially in construction. By and large the stories were quite true and were true again, although on a somewhat lesser scale, shortly after the Korean war—thanks to Uncle Sam's generosity with cost-plus contracts. But the impression that Alaska still suffers from a skilled labor shortage has lingered. Much worse has been the added distortion that almost anyone, even an unskilled laborer, can arrive in Alaska anytime, have his pick of jobs, and by putting in a lot of overtime return to the "lower 48" with a sizable bankroll.

Alaskans have seen increasing evidence of these lingering myths as month after month brings fresh numbers of new settlers—almost penniless, expecting to obtain jobs immediately. Such was the situation with a much-heralded group called the "Detroit 59ers," who had quit their jobs, sold their homes or given up comfortable low-rent apartments, to participate in a "wagon-train" exodus to Alaska. Within months after their arrival, many of them had to be "rescued" by Alaskan sympathizers and welfare agencies. Some, indeed, had to be rescued literally by the U.S. Air Force and Army Engineers after they had been trapped by flood waters in the bush, where they had been attempting to put up their own log-cabin homes.

So widespread is the notion of a labor shortage in Alaska that "Alaska job" promoters, advertising in popular magazines and newspapers, have done a thriving business "selling" jobs in Alaska, selling information about jobs, or both, but offering little in the way of truth, still less in the way of jobs, if any. Law enforcement agencies and Better Business Bureaus everywhere have had their hands full putting the "Alaska job" promoters out of business, much to the relief of the 49th State.

With a few occupational exceptions, *there is no labor shortage in Alaska*. There has been none for years; and barring another war or defense emergency, there may never be a critical labor shortage again in Alaska.

Knowing this, should anyone refrain from going to Alaska to carve a career, a new future? Not at all. There are jobs to be had and, as we shall see, ways of getting them. But it does mean that job-hunting in Alaska should be approached with intelligence or at least an understanding of the fundamental employment—and unemployment—picture. It is important first to understand the sources of employment, then to consider the facts about wages, problems, and the future.

SOURCES OF EMPLOYMENT

One of the most prevalent misconceptions about employment in Alaska is that the construction industry creates the greatest number of jobs. Not true! The largest employer in Alaska is Uncle Sam. Sometimes even Alaskans find this hard to believe. But the facts are incontrovertible.

The total civilian labor force in Alaska is about 64,000. Of these, about 15,000 to 18,000, may in any one year consist of Federal employees. Said a U.S. Department of Labor report: "The United States Government dominates the employment situation in Alaska to an unusual degree. Federal employees [in Alaska] constitute somewhat less than one-quarter of the total working force." *

According to a report by two analysts of the Alaska Employment Security Commission, "Civilian government workers, predominantly on Federal payrolls, made up about one-third of the non-agricultural total [of employment in Alaska]."

The average annual rate of employment in Alaska's private industry is about 30,000. The following table shows the industries and the average number they employ during the year.

Industry	Average Employment
Manufacturing, mostly fish-canning	4,700
Wholesale-retail	7,000
Construction	5,900
Trannsportation, communication, utilities	5,000
Services	4,000
Mining	1,300
Finance, insurance, real estate	1,000

In government, three Federal departments account for most of the civilian employment in Alaska: the Department of Defense, the Department of Commerce, and the Department of the Interior. These departments employ about 90 per cent of all Federal employees in Alaska.

Another important source of Federal jobs, although somewhat more restricted in occupational variety, is the Department of Health, Education and Welfare, which administers a number of medical and health facilities for Alaskan natives.

Finally, there is the U.S. Department of Agriculture, which employs clerical and professional personnel for its research and extension service activities in the 49th State.

Among agencies of the Department of Defense, the Air Force—with some 3,000 civilians on its payroll—is the largest employer and is known as the Alaskan Air Command with headquarters at Elmendorf Air Force Base, Anchorage. But its civilian employees are also at Ladd and Eielson Air Force Bases near Fairbanks. Ladd Air Force Base actually starts where the Fairbanks city line ends. Eielson is about 25 miles from Fairbanks.

The Army is the second most important employer of civilians within the Department of Defense. And within the Army, the Corps

* U.S. Department of Labor, Bulletin No. 1191.

of Engineers, with headquarters in a large, modern building in Anchorage, is the principal civilian employer.

For students in college, the Corps of Engineers in Alaska offers one of the most unique vacation-type civilian jobs. Each year, since 1949, the Corps of Engineers has offered numerous *temporary* appointments to undergraduates from accredited engineering schools who want to earn and learn between semesters. The jobs are "student aide appointments," and thus far have attracted candidates from every state, Europe, the Middle East and the Far East. The pay varies according to the college class of the appointee, usually being about $152 or $164 for a two-week period of 40 hours per week.

Student aides receive free round-trip transportation from Seattle. They may be assigned anywhere in Alaska, under professional engineers tackling a variety of projects. Many of the student aides live in low-cost barracks near the Corps of Engineers' headquarters, or in a contractor's camp. To be eligible student aide applicants must major in civil, structural, electrical, mechanical or architectural engineering, or allied fields of geology, mining, and chemistry. Inquiries and applications for these appointments are handled through: U.S. Army Engineer District, Alaska, Corps of Engineers, P.O. Box 1288, Anchorage.

Within the remaining Federal departments, the agencies providing employment are:

Department of Commerce: Federal Aviation Agency; Weather Bureau; Bureau of Public Roads.

Department of the Interior: Alaska Railroad; Bureau of Land Management; Fish and Wildlife Service; Bureau of Indian Affairs; National Park Service; Geological Survey; Bureau of Mines; Bureau of Reclamation.

Department of Health, Education and Welfare: Public Health Service.

Department of Agriculture: Soil Conservation Service; Forest Service; Extension Service; Agricultural Marketing Service; Research Service; Farmer's Home Administration.

State and local government agencies, of course, employ many Alaskans but usually only the teaching jobs go to Outsiders.

Who Gets the Jobs?

Except for certain skills not usually found in Alaska, nearly all jobs go to the available labor market—those who apply for the jobs directly at the plants and offices in Alaska. In spite of the "job promoters" in places like New York, Washington, Chicago, and West Coast cities, *extremely little* recruiting is done outside Alaska. For example, although the Alaskan Air Command employs more than 3,000 in jobs ranging from janitorial to professional, only about 17 per cent are what is known as "on transportation agreement," meaning those recruited from the Outside. About 15 per cent of those employed by the Alaskan Air Command are dependents of military personnel stationed in Alaska. The remainder are Alaskan residents.

There was a time, perhaps as recent as the frenetic post-Koreanwar period, when many construction workers had to be recruited from the Outside. That was due to an unusual spurt in defense construction—radar networks, airfields and the like. However, so many construction workers in the once urgently needed crafts—carpentry, bricklaying, electrical and metal trades—have remained in Alaska that to a great extent Alaska can today provide its own skilled labor force. In fact, because construction in Alaska is extremely seasonal, there is considerable unemployment in many crafts during the winter.

An interesting indication of Alaska's domestic "labor supply" was reported in the Fairbanks *News-Miner,* which showed the number of craftsmen employed and unemployed during a typical winter season in Fairbanks:

> Carpenters employed, 105; unemployed, 250
> Electricians employed, 71; unemployed, 58
> Iron workers employed, 2; unemployed, 28
> Painters employed, 50; unemployed, 42
> Plumbers employed, 70; unemployed, 255

The figures for other occupations were equally drastic, if not depressing. However, as we shall see, the term "unemployment" needs to be qualified in order to give perspective to the facts.

How You Get a Job in Alaska

About 9 out of 10 people working for the Government in Alaska are on Civil Service status. Residents in Alaska obtain these jobs simply by applying to the nearest Civil Service office or by visiting the respective government agencies to find out whether vacancies exist, or may come up. For Outsiders interested in getting advance information about Federal jobs in Alaska, the principal source of information is the Alaska Branch, Eleventh Civil Service District,

U.S. Civil Service Commission, Seattle. If you obtain a Civil Service job in Alaska, you may be asked to sign an agreement to remain in Alaska for two years. If you fulfill the contract, your round-trip transportation is paid by the Government. In some cases, the Government will also pay transportation costs for your entire family, household furnishings, and car.

However, you may seek and obtain highly valuable information about Federal job prospects by communicating directly with the Washington, D. C. headquarters of any of the various government departments in Alaska. For example, if you were an electronics technician, knowing that electronics occupations are common to the Federal Aviation Agency, the Weather Bureau, and the Air Force, you'd address an inquiry to each of these agencies in Washington, where your letters would be transmitted to a personnnel director who may send you a printed reply containing general information, or you may get a letter directing you to report to a particular office to be hired and started on your way to Alaska.

For a job in private industry, you should not go to Alaska without some advance assurance of a job waiting for you, or without sufficient funds to support yourself while job hunting. The best time of year for job hunting in Alaska is during the summer, when employment is at its peak. The worst time of year is during the winter, which for interior Alaska would range between October to March or April.

The most important source of information for jobs in Alaska is the Alaska Employment Security Commission, P.O. Box 2661, Juneau.

But not to be overlooked in the continental U.S. are the local state employment offices. There are more than 1,800 such offices throughout the nation, affiliated with the U.S. Employment Service. These state offices form a little-known network called the "public employment service system." A valuable special service of this system to the public is the "clearance program", which makes it possible for job hunters in one state to find employment in another state and conversely for employers in one state to find needed skills elsewhere. Alaska is part of this network. If you want to know whether there is a need for your particular type of occupation in Alaska, or even whether there are any job openings for your occupation, your local state employment office may come up with the fastest answer for you through the "clearance program."

For Outsiders seeking employment in Alaska's construction industry, an equally rewarding technique is to communicate with the various companies which have construction contracts in Alaska. Many of the larger construction companies have their main offices in the continental U.S. From time to time it is possible to obtain a list of such companies from the Department of Defense, in Washington, D. C. A major source of information regarding private contractors in Alaska is the U.S. Army Corps of Engineers, Washington, D. C.

There is also a magazine published in Anchorage, *Alaska Construction News,* which in almost every issue carries the names and addresses of almost all firms holding construction contracts in Alaska, together with such information as the dollar value of the contracts held, the type of work to be performed, and where the work is to be done. The magazine may be available to you through your local library and may be obtained directly from Alaska by subscription.

In New York City, there is a little-known but highly regarded publication covering the general subject of "overseas jobs," but it frequently carries news and information of interest to those seeking employment in Alaska. Called *Jobs Overseas,* it is a mimeographed periodical published by M. G. Enterprises of 101 West 42nd Street. The "enterprises" is a genial, energetic father-in-law of an Ivy-League university professor who began *Jobs Overseas* as a hobby. In effect, he has developed to a fine art the technique of gathering news about job opportunities abroad. He sells the information only through his publication and often corresponds personally with a network of "fans" throughout the world.

Periodically, the Superintendent of Documents, Washington 25, D. C., will have available for sale at nominal prices a variety of publications dealing with employment in America's overseas installations. Alaska is often mentioned in these publications. The technique for obtaining a publication that may be of value for job hunting in Alaska is to ask the Superintendent of Documents for a "list of publications" pertaining to Alaska and employment overseas. These lists are free and contain descriptions of the various publications available. From the list, you choose the publications that interest you, submit an order (for which a convenient form is attached to the list), enclose the amount required in cash (no stamps) and within two to three days after your order is received in Washington, the publications will be on their way in the mails to you.

Occasionally, however, publications pertaining to Alaska—and perhaps information of importance to job hunting in the 49th State —are not shown in the "list of publications" because the latter are not too frequently revised. Nonetheless, it is possible to keep in touch with all the latest government publications that may be issued regarding Alaska simply by asking the Superintendent of Documents to place your name on the mailing list for free copies of "Selected United States Government Publications." These are issued bi-weekly and are similar to the "list of publications," except that they are more current and are not necessarily confined to any particular subject.

For professionals, sub-professionals and technicians who may be interested in self-employment practices or job opportunities, there are also numerous professional societies and various state boards in Alaska. The societies and boards are reliable sources of information regarding their respective specialties, such as medicine, law, chiropractic. (See Appendix, "Sources of Information.")

THE MOST-WANTED SKILLS IN ALASKA

A question frequently asked of those who tell the truth about jobs in Alaska: "If there is really no labor shortage in Alaska, how on earth do Outsiders get jobs there?" The answer: in the same way that people anywhere obtain employment, by filling vacancies in existing jobs, or seeking newly created jobs in new or expanding businesses.

In Alaska, vacancies occur as a result of a fairly high turnover. Dependents of military personnel, who hold many jobs in Alaska, are frequently returning to the continental U.S. The turnover rates are highest in Anchorage and Fairbanks. Another factor in turnover, in government as well as private employment, is the weather. Some who arrive during the sunny, pleasant months suddenly find that they can't take the Alaskan winter, mostly the short days and long nights. The Federal Civil Service turnover rate is about four times greater than the similar rate for the continental U.S. Snow in Alaska is sometimes called "rotation dust."

The jobs that go begging most often in Alaska are those requiring professional education or technical training, although the latter should not be confused with skilled crafts, such as carpentry, masonry, plumbing. "Technical training" normally includes such skills as electronics, medical laboratory, engineering and meteorological aid.

There is also a consistent and growing demand for highly trained administrative and clerical office workers. A Civil Service official told me that any competent stenographer or stenotypist can arrive in Alaska anytime and "go to work for the Government in ten days."

When I asked a civilian personnel director in Alaska what occupations in Government or private industry have been among the most wanted skills in Alaska, he said: "Conditions as a rule tend to vary. But in general you can get an idea by examining the lists of the number and types of jobs that have to be filled through Stateside recruiting." I examined the lists and made the following tabulation:

Occupations Needed	Estimated No. of Jobs to Be Filled	Percentage of Jobs Filled by Outsiders
Airways operating specialists	400	98%
Electrical maintenance technicians	225	95
Teachers, all grades	225	95
Engineers	415	95
Nurses	210	85
Draftsmen technicians	150	85
Engineering aides	500	95
Meteorologists and aides	125	80
Construction inspectors	125	80
Forestry aides	100	75
Fishery management biologists	130	100
Accounts, auditors, budget officers, administrators	100	95
Administrative officers	50	90
Correctional officers	45	100

Professional positions, including *social workers, psychologists, welfare and recreational workers, biologists, physicists, geologists,* and *physical therapist,* almost always require 100 per cent recruitment from the Outside.

WAGES AND SALARIES

Generally, Federal jobs offer lower salaries and per-hour wages than comparable jobs in Alaska's private industry. But in this regard an important fact worth repeating is that the Civil Service worker receives a 25 per cent cost of living allowance in Alaska. The allowance is *not* subject to income tax.

Once it appeared as though the allowance might have lost its tax-free status when Alaska was admitted to statehood. Finally it had to be protected by administrative rulings because the allowance was originally designed to benefit Civil Service workers in overseas territories, not overseas *states*.

Skilled craftsmen who work for the Federal government are generally paid on an hourly basis, which does *not* include the 25 per cent cost of living allowance. But such workers are sometimes known as "wage board" employees because their hourly wage rates are based on rates established by official wage boards who attempt to establish a Federal hourly wage that is comparable with hourly wages for similar occupations in private industry.

But there is a significant difference. The government's hourly wage rates are fixed maximums; whereas the private craftsman's hourly rates are usually union-fixed minimums, which are often topped by "premiums" when employers are urgently in need of craftsmen, or when a project requires a craftsman to live in the bush, away from his home and family. Consequently, sometimes wage board employees of the Government receive lower wages than their counterparts on "premium" rates in private industry. However, officials point out that Government workers enjoy stable, year-round employment, which is not always true of craftsmen in private industry.

On the whole, average weekly earnings in Alaska exceed $100 per week for employees in most industries. A relatively recent study showed the average weekly wage for all "covered" (Social Security) employment in Alaska to be in excess of $120 per week, compared with a similar average of $83 per week for the continental U. S. The highest weekly pay averages occur in the construction industry, ranging from $180 to $190 per week. The lowest weekly averages are in manufacturing (largely canning) and in the service industries, *e.g.,* barbershops, restaurants, retail and wholesale.

However, averages in Alaska can be misleading if not properly interpreted. The average weekly wage, for example, does not reflect the total income of the wage earner. Many jobs, especially in manufacturing and construction, are seasonal. It is not unusual, however, for a construction worker in Alaska to earn a "year's" pay in six or seven months, since many construction workers are employed under conditions requiring premium rates and overtime pay at time-and-a-half and double time (after 35 to 40 hours). Among construction workers during the peak of the employment season, pay checks in excess of $250 to $300 per week are not unusual.

In fact, this "seasonality" of employment tends to appeal to many craftsmen in Alaska and is a source of acrimony between them and the communities in which they live. Many construction workers will live frugally while in Alaska during the peak of the employment season and then depart with large amounts of cash for sunnier climes during the winter. Resident Alaskans resent the idea of money which could stimulate business in Alaska leaving the state to be spent elsewhere. On the other hand, many craftsmen have chosen to remain in Alaska and do not really consider themselves "unemployed" during the winter because the time off simply enables them to pursue hobbies or just take things easy after months of having worked 70 to 90 hours, seven days, a week. A surprising number of them are amateur artists and spend their winters painting. Officially, however, they are "unemployed" and collect unemployment compensation checks.

The state's ceiling on unemployment compensation is $45 per week, to which may be added an additional $5 for each dependent, to a maximum of five dependents. To say the least, unemployment compensation officials face a rather complicated and sometimes delicate situation in Alaska. In the *Monthly Labor Review*, published by the U.S. Department of Labor, an expert once wrote: "Over the years, the unemployment compensation law [in Alaska] has operated to the advantage of [seasonal] industries by providing the workers with unemployment benefits that are, in a way, 'offseason' wages."

In interpreting averages, you must also keep in mind that the lows and highs tend to disappear. Many in the retail and service industries and in manufacturing receive less than $100 per week, which is low for living in Alaska. But quite a few of them are part-time employees or working wives with no particular interest in working a 40-hour week, or a 52-week year.

Because seasonality of employment is such an important factor in Alaska, employment figures are often reported in terms of "average annual employment." It is not unusual for some 25 per cent of the total labor force to be "unemployed" during the months of January, February, and March. A corresponding rate of unemployment in the continental United States—at any time of year—would obviously be catastrophic.

WORKING CONDITIONS AND PROBLEMS

When under Territorial status, Alaska's labor force was protected by a number of laws, some of which were among the most liberal of their kind in the U.S. Alaska was among the first lands under the American flag to have laws against child labor. A 1949 law gave women the right to sue employers for damages if denied equal pay for work equal to that done by men. Alaska was among the first to get a Fair Employment Practices Act, in 1953, prohibiting discrimination in employment on account of race, religion, color, or national origin. Minimum wages and overtime pay in excess of eight hours in one day, or 40 hours in one week, were also provided by law before statehood. However, as one of the conditions for obtaining statehood, Alaska had to agree to retain these laws, unless or until they were changed by the State Legislature. Accordingly, the laws remain in force because they have not been changed and perhaps never will be, unless they are further liberalized. The most powerful voice in the electorate is organized labor.

Generally, those who prefer a casual and relaxed working environment will find Alaska the ideal state. Indeed, some employers told me that their biggest personnel problem was "too much sense of humor." Typically, a large warehouse manager said, "The average man who works for me thinks life in Alaska is just one big lark. Sure, we all have fun and get along nicely together and go hunting and fishing together, and sometimes when the king salmon are running good we just close up shop and take off with our fishing poles. Mark Twain would have had a ball writing about working life in Alaska. But there have been times when I would have given my right arm for a good, serious-minded foreman."

A "serious-minded" worker in Alaska is apt to find opportunities and rapid promotion. In Fairbanks I talked with a 30-year-old man who had arrived in Alaska at the age of 26 to work as a clerk for the Air Force. But while working for the Air Force, he did some part-time work for a food-processing firm in Fairbanks. Now he is no longer with the Air Force, but has been made a partner in the food-processing company, without cash investment on his part, because he had given the company some fresh ideas on advertising and aggressive merchandising which proved profitable.

Government workers are perhaps endowed with the most pleasant and salubrious working conditions in Alaska, particularly those who are stationed at the larger bases where they frequently are entitled to "fringe" benefits in low-cost housing, food, medical care and recreational facilities. Ladd and Elmendorf Air Force bases are virtually cities within cities, boasting restaurants and cafés, large movie houses, gymnasiums, libraries, hobby shops, special staffs of experts for guidance and instruction on hunting and fishing, a complete array of personal service shops, banks, post offices, intra-base transportation and scheduled bus service to town, as well as religious and educational facilities, and perhaps the finest medical-dental care in all Alaska. At Ladd AFB, where the winters are sometimes severe, it is entirely possible for an employee to reach his office from his on-base apartment, take his meals, visit friends on the base, or spend after-work hours at one of several recreational centers without ever putting on a hat and coat, or without ever knowing that it is winter. This is made possible at Ladd AFB by a unique "utilidor" system of huge underground passageways which connect virtually all important on-base buildings, a recognized marvel of engineering.

Or consider, for example, one of the seemingly isolated Government installations, the Mt. Edgecumbe medical-educational agency run by the U.S. Public Health Service for Alaska's natives on some 253 acres of island near Sitka, the old Russian capital in the Panhandle. Apart from the fact that Mt. Edgecumbe is located in the heart of some of the greatest hunting and fishing country to be found —deer, bear, king salmon, Dolly Varden trout, steelheads, halibut, cod, red snappers, mallards, blue bills, and a variety of saltwater ducks—the social and recreational facilities are almost equal to anything that might be found in any large U.S. town, including bowling alleys! Mt. Edgecumbe employees are also eligible for furnished and unfurnished housekeeping and non-housekeeping apartments at relatively low prices, and cafeteria meals at costs ranging from 80 cents per dinner meal to about $12 per week for three meals a day.

Perhaps the main working-condition problems in Alaska are isolation from the mainland and lack of opportunity to reach the ethereal heights of executive success with big-corporate glimmer—and pay.

Actually, isolation is mainly a problem for those in the professions. The isolation is sometimes a matter of geography within Alaska, but more often than not it is a question of economics, not being able to afford the cost of flying to professional society meetings and conventions Outside. A number of professionals in the physical and medical sciences have left Alaska on account of this isolation.

"It is not a problem to be taken lightly," an Air Force electronics engineer in Alaska told me. "If you have any interest at all in progressing with the scientific advancements in your field, you must make a special effort in Alaska to get your hands on and read all the technical literature possible. Still there is no substitute for being able to meet constantly with others in your field."

Typically, an Alaskan physician said, "I'd give a month's income if I could attend some university lectures on the latest developments in certain surgical procedures, and I wish I could afford the cost of a trip to AMA conventions."

There are, of course, professional societies within the State of Alaska and statewide conferences are held, making it possible for colleagues to exchange views and ideas. But sometimes it is difficult for a professional society to get a majority of its members together at the same time. Not long ago, there was a meeting of Alaska's Public Health Service nurses in Anchorage. It was the first such conference in eight years! When the White House Conference on Education was called in 1955, it was essential for Alaska's representatives to the Conference to first meet with their colleagues within Alaska. But it wasn't easy. "The general difficulty of getting people together for meetings presented definite problems," said Lew Hanks, chairman of the Alaska Committee for the White House Conference.

Often, it is the state's capital that professional groups meet in and turn to for administrative assistance and sources of inspiration, especially in the drive to improve professional standards of practice, encourage research, and stimulate progress. But in this regard Juneau is perhaps the most implausible state capitol in the nation. It is geographically, economically and climatically isolated from the rest of the state and from the majority of people in the state. It is especially isolated from the state's most dynamic and most populated center, Anchorage.

In terms of up-the-ladder opportunities for would-be executives, there are few such opportunities in Alaska because there are few large companies in the state. Most large business organizations with dealings in Alaska maintain only branch offices. The main office may be in Seattle, Chicago, or New York, and considerably beyond the reach of those who'd like to be able to impress the chairman of the board or the vice president in charge of sales. Once a number of Alaskans who had left the state were sent questionnaires in an effort to find out why they had left. Quite a few replied that in Alaska they could "be only a minor clerk" and opportunities for promotion to big-money jobs were lacking. One respondent said almost bitterly, "Many enterprises exploit Alaska's natural resources, but their headquarters are in Seattle or Tacoma."

THE FUTURE

Population growth in Alaska will stimulate new business and provide expansion opportunities for established businesses. There will, therefore, be more job openings in Alaska and perhaps increased opportunities for career promotions. But unless population growth brings with it new industries, especially those based on developing Alaska's untapped natural resources, jobs and careers in Alaska will be quite vulnerable to the economic ups and downs. A slight cut-back in defense spending, for example, could make Alaska what the economists politely call an "area of labor surplus."

New settlers in Alaska would be wise not to burn their bridges behind them unless and until they are firmly established in the jobs or careers of their choice. But if those in Alaska should note that new industries are successfully developing, especially industries based on exploiting Alaska's natural resources, such as oil and gas, they could expect to share profitably in a historic economic boom.

CHAPTER **6**

CONTRASTS, UNLIMITED: HOUSING IN ALASKA

> *"Housing will be one of Alaska's major industries . . . with a growing young population, demand eats up supply as fast as new homes are built."* Fairbanks Daily News-Miner

NOT LONG AGO THE ALASKA STATE HOUSING AUTHORITY WAS confronted with a unique problem in human relations—how to make a woman accept a substantial sum of money that was rightfully hers, but which she insisted was not. The dilemma arose shortly after the Housing Authority had launched an urban renewal program in Fairbanks. Like similar programs authorized by Federal housing laws, the Fairbanks project was aimed at razing slums and replacing them with decent homes financed by private capital. Usually, the slums are condemned and the property owners compensated. It may be a time-consuming process, but not a particularly complicated one—unless it suddenly becomes difficult to locate property owners.

In this particular Fairbanks project, there were some difficulties in tracing titles. Many of the properties to be condemned were log cabins and shacks—genuine Klondike leftovers—which had been abandoned or "sold" to Klondike Kates and then converted into brothels. Over the years, clusters of these remnants became notorious red-light districts. One such district, in fact, had been quite active in Fairbanks until the early Fifties. But many of the original Klondike

79

Kates had long since retired from the profession, usually through marriage. They had integrated well, becoming exemplary and sometimes socially prominent mothers and grandmothers in cities and towns throughout Alaska. Meanwhile, they had carefully discarded their former addresses and all possible evidence of association therewith, because the red-light districts had become too well known throughout Alaska.

Accordingly, when a Housing Authority official confronted a woman with the news that she was entitled to a large sum of money for a condemned property in Fairbanks, he was not surprised to see the woman respond with a horrified stare. Feigning ignorance and innocence, however, she denied being the rightful owner. She was polite enough, insisting that there must have been a mistake, and as a perfectly honest woman she couldn't possibly accept someone else's money. The official, nonetheless, explained (rather discreetly) that the Authority's title tracers were quite expert at these matters and had been able to locate her, in spite of several aliases along the way. But the woman was adamant. It was not her property!

The official departed, a bit puzzled. Were the title searchers wrong? They weren't. A few days later, the woman telephoned and asked the official for a pledge of confidence and a midnight rendezvous at a remote location. When they met, the woman admitted she was the owner. All the aliases were hers, and she arranged to have the money due her transferred to a private bank account.

While this story, the last of its kind in the Housing Authority's files, is still good for chuckles, it did not signal the end of strange "human" problems for housing officials, who think it is equally puzzling (but not quite as funny) to find family after family coming to settle in Alaska without having made the slightest advance preparation for housing. After statehood, a housing official was appalled to discover a man and wife and five young children literally living in a station wagon. For more than a week, the family had been taking turns at sleeping lying down or sitting. They had been unable to find suitable housing within their means. The housing official worked around the clock to find shelter for the family.

Ever since the end of World War II, the demand for housing in Alaska has almost always exceeded the supply. The sudden influx of newcomers after statehood further aggravated the situation. Unless there are drastic changes, there may be a tight housing situation in Alaska for years.

Anchorage is typical of the housing story. At the last count, there were approximately 19,500 dwelling units in the city, but of these only about 7,500 were available for rentals. But each rental unit was occupied, and usually subject to a waiting list. The number of dwelling units in other towns is smaller, of course, but the ratio of rental units is about the same, as is that of the waiting lists.

There has always been a large demand for rental units on account of the fairly mobile nature of the population. But the tight housing situation also reflects Alaska's changing society. Many of the newcomers are not quite as content—as were many of the oldtimers—to settle in "substandard" cabins and shacks. Also, the oldtimers are changing. Many had been content, for years, to live in crude log cabins and "temporary" homesteads, which for them had been part of the lure of Alaska, the novelty or adventure of living like a pioneer. But as their families grew in size and income increased, and maturing years somewhat diluted their pioneering passions, some have been yearning for more of the "normal" comforts of life. Sometimes the change is evident in the colorful names some Alaskans give to their newly purchased modern homes, as for example a roadside lodge near Fairbanks called "Atlastahouse"!

Two other causes for Alaska's housing shortage have been high construction costs and builders' difficulties in obtaining loans for large-scale housing developments.

But you don't need to live in a station wagon, nor in housing beyond your means if you know the facts about housing and know what to do about it. First, however, let's consider the "quality" of housing in Alaska.

CONTRASTS, UNLIMITED

The striking contrasts of housing qualities in Alaska are immediately obvious to visitors. In fact, the contrasts form a part of the "color" of Alaska which appeals to tourists with cameras. They like to pause to photograph the rather odd appearance of an authentic Klondike log cabin sandwiched between modern homes (or shops!) in the heart of main street. But behind the "color" lie some interesting revelations, as shown, for example, in a survey of 132 dwellings that were located virtually in the heart of Fairbanks, prior to a slum-razing operation. Of the 132 homes, nearly 40 per cent were without flush toilets and baths; 115 were officially declared "substandard";

26 had no piped-in water; many were, in official words, "dilapidated firetraps."

Yet in Fairbanks (and Anchorage) there are residential areas which resemble the swank suburban communities of Philadelphia, New York, or Detroit, with large split-level or ranch-type homes and meticulous landscaping. Moreover, there are several thousand modern rental units in large apartment houses and housing developments. In Anchorage there is also modernity in the picturesque mosaic of the old and new.

In Anchorage, the Alaska Housing Corporation, a private company, owns about 1,260 furnished and unfurnished apartments at three different locations, all newly constructed. At one location, there is a 14-story apartment house with the simple, straight lines and glass-cornered apartments of up-to-date architecture. Rentals in these apartments range from $100 per month for an efficiency-type (one room and bath) apartment to $150 for a two-bedroom apartment, unfurnished. Furnished rentals are generally $15 per room additional. Utilities included in the rent are water and heat. Tenants pay their own electric bills, which during the winter may average $15 to $20 per month. Yet rent for less modern, less spacious units elsewhere in or near town may be equal to these. The conclusion is obvious: In Alaska, *rental price tags are no indication of housing quality.*

AVAILABILITY OF HOUSING

Just as job openings frequently occur as a result of "rotation," housing also becomes available in this manner. But the rate of availability is tied almost directly to the rate at which military personnel and their dependents leave Alaska. The same applies to the rate of turnover of Federal employees and to the seasonal departure of construction workers and disenchanted *cheechakos*. In most instances it is rental housing that becomes available, mostly furnished and unfurnished apartments.

In some instances, the turnover of rental units has been fairly high. In one Anchorage housing project, between 1953 and 1959, about 150 rental units were occupied by 1,200 families. In other words, during this period the average apartment had changed hands seven or eight times.

During the same period in Fairbanks, there were 900 families in 75 units; and in Ketchikan 150 families had occupied 50 units. Hence, the housing turnover rate in Ketchikan clearly shows a less mobile population—less military personnel, less Federal employees.

However, certain types of rental units are more available than others. Alaska is a youthful state. The most wanted apartments, therefore, are those with two or more bedrooms, to accommodate families with young children. As a result, two- and three-bedroom housing is more difficult to obtain than "efficiency" apartments.

Below is data obtained from the files of the Alaska State Housing Authority. It represents an indication of the availability—and rents—of various types of units in Fairbanks. It is also fairly indicative of housing in or near any large town in Alaska, including Anchorage, except that in the less populous areas the rents might be slightly lower. All the apartments in the table below include kitchens. The one-room apartments are usually of the "efficiency" type, having a small bathroom and a small area or corner of the studio-living room as a "kitchen," with a small refrigerator, stove and sink.

Type of Rental Unit	*Rating of Availability*	*Rent and Description*
Efficiency apartment	Good	$100-160 per month. Furnished, including water and heat.
1-bedroom apartment	Fair	120-175 per month. Furnished, including water and heat.
2-bedroom apartment	Poor	150-190 per month. Furnished, including water and heat.
1-bedroom house	Fair	125-135 per month. Unfurnished, utilities not included.
2-bedroom house	Poor	145-155 per month. Unfurnished, utilities not included.
3-bedroom house	Scarce	155 and up. Unfurnished, utilities not included.
Trailer camp sites	Good	45 per month. Average monthly costs for electricity, $15; about $20 per 100-lb. tank of propane gas for hot water, cooking, heating.

PURCHASING AND FINANCING HOMES

In a woeful report on housing, the Fairbanks *News-Miner* once observed: "Moderate priced housing is still unheard of in Alaska.

The average price of a new home is $20,000 to $25,000, which is roughly equivalent to $13,000 to $17,000 in Seattle."

Construction costs in Alaska range between $20 to $30 per square foot. Since most two-bedroom homes should contain at least 1,000 square feet, Alaskan builders thus far have been unable to provide housing in the most needed and most wanted price bracket: about $15,000 to $17,000 for two-bedroom homes; and about $18,000 to $21,000 for three-bedroom homes.

Clifford Cernick, editor of the Fairbanks *News-Miner*, one of the best-informed journalists in Alaska, said, "An Anchorage builder has announced that he will build thirty three-bedroom houses in a suburban area and sell them for about $20,000 each, with a $1,000 down payment. If he does not change his mind on the price, the houses will be snapped up before they are half completed."

In 1954, near Anchorage, some 150 one-family frame houses, occupied on a rental basis, were sold to the occupants following a mortgage foreclosure. The purchase prices—considered a bargain—were $13,990 for two-bedroom models, and $14,990 for three-bedroom homes. The dimensions were 25' x 30' and 30' x 30'—but all were without basements.

In the used-home category, prices are lower. But "quality" may range from homes with shack-like appearance and conveniences to homes of decent size and good construction, in the same price range. What you get for your money depends, as in any other state, on time, place and circumstances. In most out-of-town areas in Alaska, it is possible to purchase used one-bedroom homes of decent quality for about $10,000 to $12,000, and two-bedroom homes for about $13,000 to $16,000. But in the urbanized areas anything below these prices is apt to resemble a shack more than a home.

Generally, a home of "decent quality" in Alaska is one that has been constructed on a concrete or cement block foundation, and has sheet-rock walls, modern bath fixtures, a modern kitchen, and good insulation; but it would not necessarily include a garage of any sort, central heating, or a basement. A house with all the features you might find in any moderate-priced housing development in other states would be deemed "superior quality" in Alaska.

It should be noted, however, that many Alaskans, even those in the upper-income brackets, are passionate do-it-yourselfers. It is also common to see Alaskans sharing their skills, helping each other build or improve houses. In Fairbanks, I saw a civil engineer help build a bridge over a creek on his neighbor's property; his neighbor, a pipefitter, helped the engineer build a basement bathroom. Often, savings on labor costs can be substantial in Alaska. Thus many Alaskans will buy lower-priced new and used homes, hoping to make improvements as they go along.

Money to finance homes is generally available from the banks and savings and loan associations, as in other states. But FHA-insured loans are the most sought after because interest rates cannot legally exceed 5¾ per cent, plus ½ of 1 per cent for the mortgage insurance premium; whereas conventional loans usually carry eight per cent charges. Also, conventional mortgages are usually short-term, ranging from five to ten years. But FHA-insured mortgages can be carried up to thirty years. As a rule, banks will lend up to 75 per cent of the appraised value of the home. An expert in these matters, Robert A. Baker, one of Alaska's leading bankers, told me:

"It is relatively easy to obtain a loan in Alaska to build or improve a home. Most new homes are built on FHA commitments. FHA improvement loans are also quite easily obtained, and several of the banks in the territory have their own improvement loan programs with the loans *not* insured by FHA."

A mortgage insured by the FHA in Alaska, as elsewhere, may not exceed 97 per cent of $13,500 of the property value as appraised by the FHA, plus 85 per cent of the next $2,500 in value; plus 70 per cent of the remaining value.

As in most American communities, new homes in Alaska can be purchased with comparatively small cash down payments. But closing costs may be somewhat higher. Generally, the buyer of a $25,000 home in Alaska can expect to pay $700 to $800 in closing costs, *after* a down payment of about $3,000.

BUILDING LOTS

"Free" land in the form of homesteads in Alaska has been widely publicized. This subject is discussed separately in Chapter Seven because it is entirely different from land for conventional housing. Homestead land is "raw" land, whereas a building lot may be "improved" land, with roads and sewers nearby and utilities readily available.

There is a plentiful supply of building lots throughout Alaska. Prices of these vary considerably from town to town and are quite responsive to speculation. Since statehood, building lots have greatly increased in value around Fairbanks, Anchorage and Juneau.

A standard lot is about 50 x 150 feet, but it is impossible to report even a range of prices due to the almost week-by-week fluctuations of speculators, a situation that is apt to remain as long as Alaska's population continues to grow at a greater than average rate and cities continue their outward growths, as has been occurring in recent years. I have seen transactions in which building lots were sold for $500 on the outskirts of Anchorage, then at three to four times the price within a few weeks. In contrast, I have seen much smaller lots—75' x 80'—sell at $2,000 to $3,000 per lot. As a matter of fact, so far and wide has the post-statehood news of real estate speculation spread that "investors" from as far away as Japan have flown in for a week or so just to see what they could pick up in the way of land to "sit" on.

It is possible to obtain a bank loan for erecting a home, or business, on a building lot, but in almost all cases you have to pay a minimum of 8 per cent on the loan while construction is underway, even if an FHA-insured loan has been arranged and approved in advance.

THE ALASKA STATE HOUSING AUTHORITY: READY TO HELP YOU

One of the best-known builders in Alaska, Walter J. Hickel, who has been described as a "millionaire several times over," arrived in Alaska in 1940 with less than one dollar in his pockets. Mr. Hickel represents one of Alaska's many paradoxes, proof that those with talent, enterprise and tenacity can strike it rich, in spite of a widespread fear that capital invested in Alaska may not prove rewarding. In working toward an improved housing picture, the State Housing Authority has found that one of its greatest difficulties has been to induce Outsiders to invest in Alaskan housing.

Yet the State Housing Authority is itself proof that housing investments in Alaska can prove profitable. The Authority was established in 1945 by the Territorial legislature. It was authorized to plan and *operate* housing to help reduce shortages and generally improve housing standards.

As a state agency, the Authority today is a unit of the State Department of Commerce. It may operate housing projects of its own or borrow money to be re-loaned to builders under terms that would provide incentives for private construction. The Authority has been self-sustaining. It pays its own way, including salaries, entirely from the profits of its own ventures into housing. The only time the Authority has had to ask for money from the government was about ten years ago, when it needed $30,000 for unexpected administrative problems.

The Authority's main office is in Anchorage; branch offices are in Fairbanks, Juneau and Ketchikan. The executive personnel are youthful Alaskans, well informed, professionally trained, dedicated, and enthusiastic about the future of Alaska and Alaskan housing. One of the Authority's principal objectives now is to attract Outside investments in Alaskan housing. Toward this goal, it offers substantial technical assistance and guidance and helps builders cut red tape.

However, as a special service, the Authority will advise Outsiders on where and how to obtain housing in various parts of Alaska.

Said an Authority official: "Anyone who wants to be fairly certain of finding a place to live in Alaska would be wise to write in advance to the Alaska State Housing Authority, Box 179, Anchorage, specifying the type of housing desired and the maximum rental or price that can be paid. It's also a good idea to send a month's rent in advance, so that upon receipt of the money the Authority can make the necessary arrangements for the family to move right in, without going through the agonies—as so many do—of trying to find a place to live."

PROBLEMS AND THE FUTURE

The Alaska State Housing Authority recently has launched a more intensive urban renewal program. This is now one of its principal activities.

But urban renewal can create problems of its own in housing. Its objective is primarily to "prettify" cities by encouraging builders to raze slums and replace the slums with something modern. The something modern is not always a housing project pure and simple. It may be a "development" or a "center" containing offices and business places as well as apartment houses. More often than not, however, the number of dwelling units erected in the "center" is not equal to the number of dwellings that had originally existed in the removed slums. Consequently, housing is compressed. An urban renewal program in Alaska, as elsewhere, may *add* to the number of people in search of housing.

Some housing officials in Alaska predict that in the long run urban renewal, even if it has a compressing effect, will help increase the availability of housing in Alaska because modernization will make it easier for the state to attract investors.

By and large, builders have been wary of investing in Alaskan housing because of: (1) the relatively high cost of construction; (2) the short construction season; (3) permafrost; (4) the lack of a secondary mortgage market, and (5) uncertainty of Alaska's economic future.

These problems do, in fact, exist. But they are more of a challenge to ingenuity than barriers to success. Accordingly, the opportunities for financial rewards in Alaskan housing are fertile. It has often been said that the builder who can create "Levittowns" for Alaska is the one who will become Alaska's next great hero, and millionaire. Perhaps one reason Alaska has not given rise to its own great builder of low-cost, mass-produced houses is the simple fact that the overwhelming number of builders in Alaska are not really housing experts. Many are heavy construction specialists who will attempt a housing project or a few houses while "between" defense contracts in order to capitalize on fixed operating costs.

But few builders, even knowledgeable Outsiders, are optimistic with respect to Alaska's housing future.

Mr. Herman B. Sarno, president of the Alaska Housing Corporation, told me at his New York City office: "The housing shortage in Alaska will remain critical for a long time. The costs of construction are too high. They are about 45 per cent above those in the New York area, which is high.

"The high wages paid skilled craftsmen in Alaska are an important factor in construction costs. Commercial building construction at this time is not feasible in Alaska."

Nonetheless, Mr. Sarno did admit that his company has been "stockpiling" land in the Anchorage area, "just in case."

The Alaska Housing Corporation, perhaps the only large private housing investor in Alaska, is obligated for several millions of dollars in mortgaged loans. These mortgages are held by the Federal National Mortgage Association (popularly known as "Fannie May") and the New York Life Insurance Co.

But all the mortgage loans are covered by FHA insurance and

therefore interest payments are limited to the legal limit of about six per cent. However, not to be dismissed lightly is the fact that a New York Life Insurance Co. investment, about $1,000,000, has been committed to Alaskan housing. A company the size of New York Life Insurance does not make its investments without careful investigation and consideration. It is equally significant that New York Life is reinvesting its earnings in Alaska.

For the time being Alaska's housing future will continue to rely on Outside investments. Unfortunately, many Outside bankers and financiers know little or nothing about Alaska and because of this have remained aloof with their capital. A number of Alaskan bankers told me that every time they go Outside, they have to "educate" their banking colleagues about conditions and prospects in Alaska.

The outlook is for continued housing shortages, continued challenge and opportunities for builders and investors, and continued problems for those who may be foolish enough to arrive in Alaska with aspirations for settlement but without having made some advance arrangements for housing.

CHAPTER 7

A PICTURE OF HEALTH: DOCTORS, FEES, HOSPITALS, PUBLIC HEALTH—AND BITING INSECTS

> *"It is apparent that there are [in Alaska] unique conditions of living and health . . . which must be solved to attract . . . permanent settlement and economic development."*
> Ernest Gruening, U.S. Senator, Alaska

THE GENERAL PICTURE OF HEALTH IN ALASKA IS BETTER THAN passable. It is fairly good.

There are definite health problems among the natives (Indians, Eskimos, and Aleuts) but other Alaskans manage to live robust, healthful lives and—when all the extenuating circumstances are balanced—receive adequate medical and hospital care. There are no serious health problems unique to Alaska, although a high rate of tuberculosis among natives is perhaps one of the least-known scandals of American history.

Perhaps the most authoritative summary of Alaska's health was reported by the noted public health expert, Dr. Thomas Parran, who led a special investigation of health problems in Alaska. Said Dr. Parran: "The health conditions of Alaska's white population are comparable to those of whites in the United States, their problems being of no greater magnitude than those of the whites in the States."

For the most part, Alaskans have no difficulty in obtaining essential medical and hospital care. Largely, this is due to Alaska's youthfulness. There is no great need for doctors and hospitals. Nu-

90

merically there appears to be a greater shortage of doctors in Alaska than there is in most other states. As we shall note later, however, the nature and causes of the shortage are different from those of doctor shortages in other states. For example, there is throughout Alaska (except in the Anchorage area) a lack of medical specialists. And the complete absence of general practitioners in certain areas is largely due to socio-economic factors, not Alaska's notorious "isolation."

While there is a higher incidence of certain types of illness in Alaska, only the incidence of tuberculosis among the natives is deemed serious, if not critical. But in the general area of public health—communicable disease and sanitation—Alaska has made great progress in recent years, thanks to the intensified (and better-financed) efforts of the U. S. Public Health Service and the Alaska State Department of Health.

Alaska's progress in health is reflected in a steadily declining mortality rate. In the past decade, the mortality rate has fallen from about nine deaths per 1,000 population to 4.5 per 1,000. The mortality rate in Alaska is now about half the national average. Taken alone, mortality-rate indicators are not necessarily criteria of a good or poor health picture. But when studied together with a host of complex statistical factors, including growth and composition of population, mortality rates can have meaning. Not long ago, such a study was made by experts of the Metropolitan Life Insurance Company, and they concluded that "Alaska has improved its health record measurably in the past decade."

DOCTORS AND THEIR FEES

The doctor-to-population ratio in Alaska is, as anyone might expect, low: about one physician to every 1,500 persons, compared with one to 760 for the U. S. as a whole.

There are about 125 private licensed medical practitioners in Alaska (a 40 per cent increase over 1954). Most are in the major cities: Anchorage, Fairbanks, Juneau, Ketchikan and Sitka. In Anchorage alone, however, there are about 50 physicians, more than half of whom are qualified specialists (3 obstetricians and gynecologists; 3 general surgeons; 8 internists; 3 pediatricians; 3 psychiatrists; 1 pathologist; 1 anesthesiologist; 1 ophthalmologist; 1 neurosurgeon; 2 orthopedists; 1 urologist; 1 thoracic surgeon; and 2 EENT specialists).

Yet in many communities in Alaska there are no physicians what-soever.

It would seem from these figures that there is a grave shortage of doctors in Alaska, or that Alaska could use at least twice its present number of doctors just about anywhere except in Anchorage. But if many more doctors were to set up practice in Alaska, they'd per-haps have to take part-time jobs to support themselves.

Alaskans are too young, hence comparatively healthy, to support a much greater increase in physicians. In the continental U.S., the average American makes five calls per year at his doctor's office. In Alaska, the annual average is two calls.

In most cases, Alaskan communities without doctors now could not generate enough "business" to support a physician. Since the end of World War II, the town of Valdez (pop. 750) has had a turnover of at least twelve doctors, all of whom had left because it was economically difficult for them. In one south central Alaskan community the only reason the town has a physician—an experienced surgeon at that—is because he and his wife happen to like the town and their seashore home, which is ideally suited to their first love—boating! On more than one occasion patients have had to pay a visit to the doctor's "office" by going out in their boats or calling him over radio.

Several doctors in Alaska told me that they are "not getting rich" and often were compelled to return at least 40 to 50 per cent of their incomes toward the maintenance of their practice. Several old-timer doctors are known to be quite wealthy, but few know that their wealth was actually accumulated almost entirely through real estate investments.

Other factors contribute to the economic difficulties of private physicians. For one thing, the natives receive free and rather ex-tensive medical care from the Federal government. This rules out more than 30,000 prospective patients. Also, many military personnel and their dependents, as well as Federal civilian employees, take advantage of the medical facilities provided for them at their respec-tive bases. Finally, Alaska's physicians, faced with the same high cost of living and "business" as other Alaskans, must maintain their practices against fees that are, as a rule, similar to fees charged in other states.

Physicians' fees range from $5 to $10 an office visit. But some doctors in Alaska still cling to an earlier and almost traditional fee of $2.50 per office visit!

Presently, Alaska's real need is not for more doctors but more specialists. In this regard, only the Anchorage area is well provided for. However, in order to help offset the high cost of maintaining a practice, Alaskan doctors have grouped in "medical buildings," sharing offices and other facilities. There are several such groups in Anchorage and Fairbanks. As a result, doctors are often able to consult each other freely on medical problems. Patients benefit because there are usually no extra charges for such informal consultations.

There are about fifty licensed dentists in Alaska, and as might be expected most of them are in the Anchorage-Fairbanks area. Elsewhere, dental appointments must be made weeks in advance. Dental fees vary, but a $50 charge is not uncommon for two "routine" fillings, a full-mouth X-ray series, and a cleaning.

HOSPITAL IN ALASKA

There are three distinct types of hospitals in Alaska: hospitals for natives, who can obtain free care; hospitals for military personnel and their dependents; private voluntary hospitals for the general population.

There are no veterans' hospitals. Veterans entitled to hospitalization or medical care are treated at Air Force hospitals or by private physicians under special contractual arrangements with the Veterans Administration.

Of a total of 32 hospitals (see appendix for complete list, location and sponsorship), 18 are private voluntary general hospitals for the public, either church or community supported. There are no county hospitals. All private hospitals, however, are required to admit indigent patients and are reimbursed by welfare agencies, or the government. Private patients are charged an average of $30 to $35 per day. In view of high fixed operating expenses, the charge is reasonable. But no comparison with Outside hospital charges is possible or fair, since nearly all hospitals in Alaska lack the medical-specialty services that may characterize comparable hospitals in other states. Only one private hospital, the Catholic-sponsored Providence Hospital in Anchorage, maintains a staff of radiologist, pathologist and anesthesiologist.

The private hospital bed ratio is low, about 3 beds per 1,000 civilian population, which compares with a national average of 9 per 1,000. The total number of beds in private hospitals is about 500, and nearly half of these are in three hospitals! Providence, the only private hospital in Anchorage, has 70 beds for a civilian population in excess of 60,000. A U.S. Public Health Service hospital for natives in Anchorage has 340 beds.

Ironically, the smaller hospitals, some with only a few beds, are rarely troubled by over-crowding. Occasionally, however, the nuns at Providence Hospital have given up their rooms or offices to accommodate an overflow of patients or for patients in need of isolation. But in an emergency, any hospital—military or native—will accept a civilian patient. The civilian population also can almost always count on the armed forces, especially the Air Force, to get emergency cases to hospitals in a hurry.

PUBLIC HEALTH: FACTS, MYTHS, PROBLEMS

Using the ten leading causes for death as a reliable yardstick of public health, Alaska fares about the same as the rest of the nation, except for accidents, tuberculosis and suicides, all of which show substantially higher rates in Alaska than elsewhere in the U.S.

The suicide rate is more than double that of the national average.

Many inferences may be drawn from this. It may reflect, as some say, a high incidence of depression, "cabin fever." Some public health officials, however, insist that it simply reflects Alaska as some sort of last-resort refuge for those seeking a fresh start, but failing to find success, solace or hope in Alaska, many end their lives there, rather than return to the same old "rat race."

The incidence of tuberculosis in Alaska is one that reflects disgrace for Uncle Sam.

Tuberculosis is found largely among the native population, whose health for many years had been ignored by Congressional largesse, although medical care of natives has always been a moral obligation of the U.S. ever since we bought Alaska from the Russians.

A former Public Health Service doctor, tears in his eyes, told me that he had to quit the Service because "I couldn't take it, year after year, going back to the same native village to treat TB-crippled children, offering nothing but hope, then returning again to make out death certificates for the same children while their parents looked on."

In 1954, Dr. Parran's study team reported that the incidence of

TB among the native population was 6,474 per 100,000 population. The incidence among the non-natives was 222 per 100,000, more in keeping with the average rate of TB in the U.S.

Since Dr. Parran's report there have been dramatic reductions in TB cases and deaths. Largely, this has been due to the introduction of new "miracle" drugs. But it also has been the result of special efforts by the Alaska State Department of Health and the two agencies representing the U.S. Public Health Service in Alaska—the Arctic Health Research Center and the Alaska Native Health Service.

On a number of occasions doctors and assistants in the Public Health Service have worked around the clock for days in order to diagnose and treat native children brought in by special air round-ups from all parts of Alaska. Once, several commercial airline operators complained that Air Force airplanes should not have been used in the round-ups, not with taxpayers' money! What the commercial critics did not know was that without the aid of the Air Force the round-ups could not have been accomplished and many lives would have been lost. There was no money in the Public Health Service to pay for airplanes or for the tremendous amount of overtime put in by PHS volunteers who worked on the round-ups without pay.

But the existence of TB among the natives is still a serious problem and one that requires constant vigilance, more especially so if Alaska's population is to grow and there is to be increasing contact between newcomers and natives. This was observed in the Parran report which said, "The problem is essentially a 'native' one, but we cannot say that it is or will be limited to this group and will not affect the white population should closer contact be established."

One of Alaska's most revered leaders, Sen. Ernest Gruening, himself a medical graduate of Harvard (but never a practitioner), said in April, 1959, at a medical school dedication in New York, that the high rate of TB among Alaska's natives was a "great and smoldering danger." He placed the blame on "nearly a century of colonialism."

Alaska's third "public health" problem, the high rate of accidents, reflects the vigor of a young state that is constantly fishing, hunting, hiking, camping, climbing, building and flying. About 70 per cent of the accidental deaths in Alaska occur "off the job," mainly in flying accidents. One official of the Federal Aviation Agency in Alaska has written a compendium of flying accidents, and his what-to-do-about-it advice has become a veritable best-seller among pilots and would-be pilots in Alaska.

Disease and "Frozen Lungs"

Many apocryphal tales have been told of Alaskans afflicted with an infirmity known as "frozen lungs," supposed to be caused by the constant breathing of frigid air. But if there is such a condition in Arctic or sub-Arctic land, it is not known to a man who should know, Dr. A. B. Colyar, medical officer in charge of the Arctic Health Research Center. Dr. Colyar told me, "We do not know of the occurrence of such a condition. True, legend has it that the lungs become frost bitten or frozen in persons who exercise vigorously in the winter at extremely low temperatures. This supposedly occurs when the individual breathes rapidly by mouth.

"Among Norwegian skiers there is a condition which has been referred to as the cross-country cough. I do not know the exact cause of this condition but suspect that it is merely an irritation of the vocal cords by rapid breathing of extremely cold air through the mouth."

There are, however, certain diseases which do occur with a somewhat higher frequency in Alaska. These are chicken pox, measles, mumps and diphtheria. Now almost unknown in other states, diphtheria still occurs in epidemic proportions from time to time in Alaska.

The Problem of Biting Insects

Many Alaskans claim that they have developed a social, physiological, and psychological immunity to mosquito bites and to the fierceness of tiny flies they have aptly named the "no-see-ums," sometimes called "punkies." Those who have developed the "immunity" are fortunate. Biting insects plague the Alaskan countryside—including towns—everywhere during the warmer months.

The season for biting insects ranges from about May 15 to July 30 in northern and interior Alaska and from about April 15 to September 15, sometimes longer, in the southern portions.

As possible carriers of disease, the biting insects of Alaska are innocent. If anyone is guilty of making it uncomfortable and possibly hazardous for Alaskans, it is the private bush pilots who, for fun and profit, engage in sometimes promiscuous spraying of insecticides to kill the biting insects. After some such sprayings, Alaskans have been known to groan that *they'd* rather be dead.

Generally, Alaskans living in or near the larger population centers experience the least discomfort from biting insects (and over-zealous sprayers) because these areas benefit from more organized anti-insect control. Civilians living near the military bases derive added comfort from the massive DDT spraying by large bomber planes during June and July. But in smaller towns the problem of biting insects on occasion has been formidable. One public health official said that at times the no-see-ums had invaded Valdez in "veritable clouds" and Valdez had to close down. He said, "Even ship unloading was delayed."

Alaskans, individually, combat biting insects through the use of smear-on repellents and aerosols, the former said to be more effective. Many wear head and bed nets when camping, fishing, hunting, hiking, or gardening during the no-see-um season.

Public health authorities and scientists who have studied the biting insects of Alaska believe that not enough has been done to combat the problem. In their view, Alaska needs "abatement districts, to be organized by people who are not apathetic and to be paid for by local taxation." They believe, however, that abatement districts, like school districts, will be formed and supported by local taxes. Thus the task of fighting flies and mosquitos in Alaska will not be left to hit-or-miss methods.

THE PROBLEM OF SANITATION

In most areas of Alaska, adequate facilities for reliable water supply and sewage disposal are sorely lacking.

I saw one report, dated December, 1959, which disclosed that in the city of Fairbanks and its environs only 30 per cent of the residents were on the city sewer system; 53 per cent relied on septic tanks; and 17 per cent used chemical disposal tanks.

Of the septic tanks in use, only 25 per cent had met the standards of the State Health Department; and an overwhelming majority of the residences obtained their water from wells which were labelled "unacceptable."

"The use of shallow wells as a source of water and the use of seepage pits for sewage disposal on the same lot is not a safe practice," said an Alaskan public health official. "All too commonly," he said, "this is the practice in Alaskan cities and towns."

In recent years considerable progress has been made, notably in Anchorage, toward linking more and more residential areas with community-operated water and sewage lines. But public health officials generally are unhappy that there has been little or no improvement in the *final* disposal of waste. There is in all of Alaska not one municipally operated sewage or garbage disposal plant. The final disposal of waste is usually in a stream or tidal flat, and garbage is unloaded in outlying dumps.

To some extent, neglect of Alaska's sanitation problems may be attributed to its long period of territorial status and Congressional disinterest in promoting the welfare of the "colonists."

The high cost of digging deep wells, sometimes through permafrost, compels many Alaskans to accept the "economy" of relatively shallow wells as a calculated risk. Also, substandard sanitation has been tolerated because there have been few laws requiring compliance to standards, and the few laws themselves have not been effectively enforced.

There also has been a general reluctance in cities and towns to increase taxes in order to install community-operated water systems and modern waste-disposal facilities. Under Federal Public Law 660, for example, it was possible for any organized community in Alaska to receive a Federal grant toward the cost of installing sewage treatment plants. But in order to obtain the grants, Alaskans had to contribute a percentage toward construction costs. In recent years Alaska's share of Federal grants under the law, $1,250,000, had been allowed to lapse because no community in Alaska had applied for the Federal aid.

Nonetheless, most public health officials in Alaska are optimistic that better sanitation practices will increase in the near future. As one of them said, "Gradually, as the operation of local government becomes more effective and cities are able to establish ordinances requiring high standards for water supply and waste disposal, people will meet the standards. Property owners in Alaska, as elsewhere, do not hasten to spend money for costly improvements until urged or forced to do so by community pressure, and laws."

THE FUTURE

As a force in opening new frontiers, the science of public health has been one of the truly great weapons of modern times.

In this respect, the type of research conducted at the Arctic Health Research Center in Alaska, while unique to America, has not been unique to the world. In the Soviet Union, public health scientists have contributed greatly to the settlement and development of vast Arctic and sub-Arctic areas similar to Alaska.

To improve Alaska's position as a possible defense bastion, the 49th State will require more than a fresh Klondike of adventure-minded, success-minded, pioneer-minded settlers. In the words of a Department of Health, Education and Welfare report, "Alaska will require standards of housing, waste disposal, water supply, heat, food, insect control, general sanitation and health and medical services comparable to the standards enjoyed in [other parts] of the United States."

Toward such goals, a good start has been made with the establishment of the Arctic Health Research Center. As chief medical officer Dr. Colyar said, "Ten years of work of the Arctic Health Research Center have produced a great amount of knowledge concerning health and disease in Alaska and in the arctic. Many of the original staff are still with us. They constitute our most valuable asset. It is in the national interest to preserve this investment in arctic health research and the future of Alaska."

Alaska needs technical breakthroughs in the economic design and construction of wells, especially in permafrost areas. Also needed is more scientific and technical information on septic tanks and seepage systems for disposal of household wastes. Finally, more scientific information is needed regarding the effects of low temperatures on organic waste in Alaska.

For the most part, Alaska will continue to rely on the Arctic Health Research Center to develop the technical and scientific knowledge needed to define and encourage the acceptance of improved sanitation. But for years the Center has operated under severe handicaps. Its staff is scattered in 23 different office and research buildings. It needs at least $6,000,000 to construct central, permanent quarters. The Center also requires a basic staff of 55, but from its Federal appropriations it has been able to employ only about 40.

Alaskans are not now adversely affected by a serious *numerical* shortage of doctors. But as population increases there may well be a serious doctor shortage which could hinder rapid and permanent settlement. The 49th State will have to exert greater and more organized efforts not only to attract more physicians to practice in the state, but to make it easier for physicians to remain. The state will have to expand and improve hospital and clinic facilities, and perhaps extend some tax-exemption incentive to encourage physicians to work and stay in Alaska. Most Alaskans are not quite aware of the fact that the over-all U.S. population is also growing and against this there is a declining rate of medical school graduates. If Alaskans overlook these facts, it may be a lamentable case of too little and too late for their own doctor-shortage ailment.

Nearly all of Alaska's hospitals now barely meet their operating expenses. Little has been done to accumulate capital funds for the expansion and maintenance of plant and facilities. Hospital funds in the future will have to be substantially increased through voluntary community support, or taxes. In this regard, Alaska's comparative youthfulness has been somewhat of a handicap. A relatively healthy population tends to ignore its future health problems and needs; and there is in Alaska no large segment of older people to exert effective counter-pressure in the community for a politically mature attitude toward hospital and clinic support.

But now that the State of Alaska is represented in Washington, the task of obtaining increased Federal assistance for the Arctic Health Research Center, and possibly for hospitals, should not prove as difficult as in the past.

Nevertheless, medical administrators, community leaders, and social workers with a crusading spirit should find Alaska an interesting challenge to their respective talents.

CHAPTER 8

OPERATION UPLIFT: EDUCATION IN ALASKA

"One thing that surprises a visitor is to learn that Alaska has one of the best school systems anywhere." U.S. News & World Report

RUTH MATSON, A SWEET, EVER-SMILING, CHERUBIC-FACED, greying woman, came to Alaska thoroughly prepared not to like the place. In her mind, Alaska was an uncivilized wilderness peopled by a handful of social misfits, renegade illiterates and Philistines who'd rather hunt and fish or dig for gold than help a town put up a schoolhouse. But Ruth, who had never before lived in the country, educated at the University of Seattle, daughter of a doctor father and schoolteacher mother, decided that she simply had to do something to keep busy in Alaska. She had married a man who had been to Alaska and was eager to return to take a crack at fishing in the Territory. Matt, her husband, a quiet industrious man, liked to do things for himself, especially build boats. Matt had chosen to settle in a tiny and isolated community, Gustavus, where he could stake a homestead, raise his own food, cut timber to build a boat, and have access to fishing waters, although Matt knew Gustavus only from maps and charts.

So, on an impulse, but with a feeling of complete despair, Ruth wrote a letter to the Commissioner of Education, asking whether there might not be a need for a schoolteacher in Gustavus. *How completely stupid,* Ruth thought. *The Commissioner will probably*

*think I am utterly naive and ill-informed. I suppose there aren't more
than a dozen families at Gustavus.*

Actually, Ruth didn't know it, but there were at the time only
two families!

The reply was prompt. Yes, indeed, they could use a schoolteacher
at Gustavus and Ruth could come anytime, the sooner the better.
As part of her salary, she'd be furnished with quarters and fuel. She
and Matt soon set sail for Alaska. The year was 1930. She has been
there ever since and has only recently retired as schoolteacher at
Gustavus, where there are now perhaps a score of families and many
children, and where the comparatively modern schoolhouse doesn't
even resemble the one room with adjoining quarters in which Ruth
originally started teaching. Then there was no electricity, no running water, wood-burning stoves for hot water and heat and cooking,
and kerosene lanterns for illumination; and her "home" was a small
room that opened from the classroom, her "bedroom" a folding bed,
and her library a bookcase in the corner of the room.

And her only contact with "civilization" was the mail boat, which
came once a month with a standing order of groceries to unload for
Ruth. But if Ruth needed something different, such as a pair of
shoes, or a blouse, she'd have to be extremely careful and exacting
in her mail-ordering, for if the apparel were to return a size too small
(larger would be manageable), it would be three or four months—
what with re-ordering and a few more round-trips of the mail boat—
before she'd receive the correct fit.

But Ruth and her husband quickly learned to love Alaskans and
their tremendous zeal for education, as exemplified by the great expense and effort taken to bring her to Gustavus just to teach three
isolated children.

Her husband built his boat and was successful in salmon fishing.
Together, they also built their homestead, near the school. As a
matter of fact, Matt, now past sixty, is building another fishing boat
—a 30-footer!—all by himself, scheduled for 1964 completion and
launching. The sight of the massive boat going up, plank by plank,
each painstakingly cut, shaped, and fitted by hand, underneath a
huge shed erected from trees felled by hand, is almost unbelievable.
But quite credible and quite plain is the enormous joy, the deep satis-
faction, Ruth and Matt virtually radiate for having chosen their way
of life in Alaska.

The saga of the Matsons may not be epic in scope, but it is a vivid, moving historical vignette of education in Alaska—a portrait of teachers and parents who by concept, devotion and tradition are bound to support education.

Today Alaskans reflect such a passion for learning that a library dedication is a major event, not an irksome social or political obligation to which the mayor sends the town clerk around to say a few words. Teachers in Alaska are often regarded as community leaders, and sometimes literally so.

Consider, for instance, the story of the teacher who was assigned, some twenty years ago, to a native school about fifty miles west of Fairbanks, where he (and his wife) had found deplorable conditions —impoverishment, hunger, illness, and alcoholism, and a widespread feeling of hopelessness. The teacher promptly became an acknowledged one-man force for betterment. He organized a local government, a post office, a law enforcement squad, a drugstore, a general store, a new well (to replace one that was obviously contaminated) and instilled a voting consciousness among the natives, so that they could make their voices felt where it would do the most good.

Before long, the teacher had created a new village of humans. Infant mortality fell sharply; population doubled during the twenty-year period of the teacher's presence, a monumental achievement among natives, an unforgettable reward and a memorable experience for the teacher and his wife.

Miss Ethyl Peasgood, a teacher in one of Fairbanks' modern schools, recalls with feeling her experiences as a teacher in Alaska. Farm-bred in North Dakota, she began by teaching Eskimo and Indian children in a "one-room log hut out in the bush, at Takotna, 300 miles southwest of Fairbanks." In a small room attached to the school, she lived alone, but never frightened, cooking on a kerosene stove, chopping holes in ice to get drinking water, conducting a "churchy Sunday school" and sometimes funeral services.

What's it like to be a teacher in Alaska? In a word, Miss Peasgood replies, it's "thrilling."

"People have misconceptions about life in those remote areas," she said. "The people read avidly. You have to read to hold your own with them. Life can be enriched in so many ways. You sort of do your own thinking, and there is something to be said for that, too."

There is no doubt that if Alaska chose to do so it would have a pre-eminent right to adopt as a state motto, "49th State, State of Education." The people support their schools. Alaska spends about 40 per cent of its budget on education, which compares with an average of about 30 per cent in other states. Not long ago, when a plan for a Methodist College in Anchorage was announced, Alaskans of *every faith,* organizations and individuals, pitched in to help raise some $750,000 for the college—an enormous sum for a city the size of Anchorage.

It is no accident, therefore, that Alaska's schools and standards of education are among the finest and most highly regarded in the U.S., a fact which continually surprises visiting educators.

A variety of surveys has shown that students in Alaska's schools are generally above average in grades, IQ, and work accomplished, and there are fewer high school dropouts. By way of explanation, Dr. William K. Keller, director of the Department of Education at the University of Alaska, said, "Alaska's school system is conservatively run. We stick mainly to the three R's and we don't go in for the frills that have become the fashion in the States. Students in Alaskan schools get more homework to do than is the general practice in the States."

Not to be overlooked in explaining Alaska's dedication to and high standards of education is the state's youthful population, among which is a high ratio of school-age children and a higher proportion of high school graduates and college-educated people than in any other state.

THE SCHOOL SYSTEMS AND STANDARDS

The elementary and secondary schools of Alaska are similar to systems in other states: eight years elementary; four years high school. In most instances, there is also one year of kindergarten for children between the ages of five and six, although a child may enter kindergarten usually at the age of four years, ten months; first grade at the age of five years, ten months. Kindergartens are generally on a half-day basis. From age seven through sixteen, school attendance is compulsory.

School normally begins immediately after Labor Day and the school "year" is 180 days, which includes five legal holidays and a few days set aside for teacher conventions. The schools are required to operate a minimum of 172 days of actual school during the school year, which extends over nine calendar months. In almost all areas, pupil transportation is provided, and in those areas which are too isolated for regular schools parents may obtain free correspondence courses for their children.

The general standard for class size is 25 students in elementary school, 22 in high school.

There is no separation of the sexes nor of the races in schools. There are schools only for native children, however, because these schools are built and operated with Federal funds to accommodate the natives living in the remote and isolated areas, where almost all the children are natives anyway. Non-native children may attend native schools whenever other facilities are not available.

There are three distinct school systems: (1) unincorporated; (2) incorporated; and (3) schools for natives.

There are also private schools, which include a few boarding schools, administered by five different religious groups. A denominational school is usually an elementary day school only. One of the denominational schools, operated by the National Board of Missions of the Presbyterian Church in Sitka—the Sheldon Jackson High School and Junior College—is an accredited high school and the oldest school in Alaska.

Unincorporated schools. Schools beyond the political jurisdiction of organized communities are in the "unincorporated" system. This means they are administered directly by the State Board of Education, under the Commissioner of Education. There are slightly more than 100 unincorporated schools, including "on-base" schools established to serve the armed forces. About half the schools in the unincorporated system are one-teacher, one- and two-room schoolhouses; but there are a number of larger schools, some employing up to 25 teachers per school. In most cases, youngsters going to high school in an unincorporated school system have to go to one of the "on-base" high schools.

Special schools may be established by the state whenever there are ten children between the ages of 6 and 16 in any community, provided the local citizens furnish a building which meets requirements of the State Department of Education.

A school is established by the state in any community, however, where there are at least 15 children between the ages of 6 and 16.

In the larger communities, many of the unincorporated school buildings are quite new, well equipped, and of modern decor. But in the more isolated areas school buildings range in age from 10 to 25 years and some are log cabins erected by local residents.

Incorporated schools. The incorporated school system consists of 28 organized-community school districts. As in most other states, the school districts function by legislative mandate and are semi-autonomous. The largest school districts are Anchorage, which employs approximately 450 teachers; Fairbanks, 175 teachers; Ketchikan and Juneau, about 90 teachers each.

Most of the school buildings are new and extremely well designed, perhaps more so than those in many other states. The interiors are attractive and colorful and show little of the spartan institutionalism characteristic of many recently built schools in other states, where constant emphasis on cost-saving has created a simple, cement-block approach to school design.

Native schools. There are about 80 schools in the native school system. Most of these schools are administered directly by the Bureau of Indian Affairs, an agency of the U.S. Department of the Interior. Some native schools are administered by the State of Alaska for the Federal government under special contractual arrangements authorized by a law known as the Johnson-O'Malley Act. Sometimes a school is called a "Johnson-O'Malley" to indicate a state-operated native school.

In most native settlements, the school is also the community center, and the teacher may be the only link between the people and the government and the outside world. Some teachers also operate the communications equipment. More than one teacher has had to play "doctor" for ailing natives, using short-wave radio to contact physicians, describe symptoms, and carry out prescribed treatments.

How Teachers Are Employed

The Bureau of Indian Affairs employs teachers through the Federal Civil Service. But those interested in obtaining teaching jobs in the Alaskan native school system may receive detailed information and assistance through the Personnel Officer, Bureau of Indian Affairs, Box 1751, Juneau, Alaska.

Teachers in the unincorporated schools are employed through the Commissioner of Education, Box 1841, Juneau, Alaska; and teachers for the military schools are employed through the Director, On-Base Schools, Elmendorf Air Force Base, Anchorage.

Teachers in the incorporated school system are employed through the respective school district boards of education. Applications for employment should be directed to either the Superintendent of Schools or to the Clerk of the School Board in whatever town a teaching position is sought. (See appendix for list of schools by location and grades.)

Additional information regarding schools and teaching in specific districts may be obtained from the various Chambers of Commerce; and in Alaska, as in the continental U.S., almost every town of any consequence has a Chamber of Commerce (see Chapter 14). General information regarding schools and education in Alaska may be obtained from the Commissioner of Education, Juneau.

Salaries for teachers. The minimum salaries for teachers are prescribed by state law; in 1959, salaries ranged from $4,500 to $7,600 per year.

As a rule, salaries tend to increase as the geographical location of the school becomes more remote and isolated. Principals receive at least $600 above a teacher's base pay. The minimum salary for superintendents is from $5,300 to $9,400. As in most other states, minimum salaries depend on a teacher's total higher education and previous experience as a teacher. Teachers employed for the first time in Alaska may apply four years of their Outside teaching experience toward their placement on the minimum salary scale in Alaska.

Teachers employed from the Outside usually have no difficulty in obtaining housing. Nearly all schools have some system, such as a parent-teacher committee, to assist Outside teachers in obtaining housing, and in getting generally settled in the community. At most small schools (one to three teachers), the schools provide relatively low-cost housing for teachers. At on-base schools, teachers may obtain housing on the base on the same terms as Federal Civil Service employees, but generally such housing is provided only for single teachers, except in cases where civilian housing for families may not be available.

Only teachers employed by the Bureau of Indian Affairs for native schools receive reimbursement for round-trip travel from the continental U.S. to their teaching posts in Alaska. Other teachers must pay their own way to their destinations in Alaska.

COLLEGES AND UNIVERSITIES

Hardly a generation ago, a 28-year-old former gold miner turned college instructor stood at a small building on the outskirts of Fairbanks to greet six young men who were about to join the first class in the first college to be established in Alaska. It was the fall of 1922, and burning black powder, to keep the mosquitoes away, sent thick, pungent clouds of smoke swirling about his head.

"I thought it was a joke when I was offered a job as a mining instructor for a proposed college that wasn't even built," the same man, Ernest N. Patty, recently recalled. "But I finally agreed to come up for two years, at a starting salary of $3,750 annually. The first three months we didn't get paid, and the staff owed everybody in town."

But this time as he spoke, Dr. Ernest N. Patty, president emeritus of the University of Alaska, stood before a new $3,000,000 administration building, where once there had been a few decaying shacks. He could glance lovingly at a modern $750,000 dormitory, observing scores of students strolling blithely toward their beautiful student hall and spacious cafeteria. And this time Dr. Patty could speak with justifiable pride of the big "joke" that has become the world's northernmost university, 120 miles below the Arctic Circle, famed for its faculty and research in sciences.

It was on July 4, 1915, that the legendary Alaskan pioneer, Judge James Wickersham, laid the cornerstone for a building that was to have many heartbreaking ups and downs before it could open for business in 1922 as the Alaska Agricultural College and School of Mines. In 1935, the Territorial Legislature voted to make it a university.

But things seemed to go from bad to worse. "After World War II," said Dr. Patty, "we were about as low as you can get. We had only twenty or thirty students. The old buildings were obsolete. There had been no new construction. We had to do one of two things—quit or build."

But Dr. Patty and his fellow Alaskans and colleagues in Alaskan education would have nothing to do with "quit." They knew only how to build. The spirit of Alaska! They fought to keep the University going and pressured Congress for money until at last they succeeded in getting more than $6,000,000 for new buildings and faculty salaries.

The *modern* University of Alaska, therefore, has had a comparatively short but spectacularly successful existence, and an even brighter future, with new buildings (including a $1,000,000 gymnasium) yet to come. It is already accredited to offer degrees, including doctorates, in a wide range of curricula: liberal arts, biology, chemistry, physics, geophysics, mathematics, anthropology, social sciences, history, economics, political sciences, business administration, education, agriculture, wildlife management, geology, mining and metallurgy. It also has three branches of engineering: civil, electrical, chemical.

In addition, the University offers a degree in one of the newest branches of medical science, "medical technology." It is a unique program under which qualified graduates receive BS degrees and professional recognition as medical technologists. Under this program, students spend six semesters at the University of Alaska and then one year of internship at St. Luke's Hospital School of Medical Technology at Spokane, Washington.

Since statehood, enrollment of students at the University has almost doubled, and the University is planning for substantial increases in enrollment over the next decade. At present, there are over 800 students, who come from all over Alaska, from other states, and several foreign lands. The faculty is equally diversified. At the time of my visit, there was a professor from Japan. Male students usually outnumber co-eds by more than two to one.

The University is tuition-free to Alaskan residents. Outsiders pay $100 tuition per full-course semester. Students living on campus pay about $512 for lodging in a double room. There is a modern cafeteria where students may take their meals at comparatively inexpensive prices. Co-eds who do not obtain "approved housing" off campus must live at the University. The housing capacity of the University includes: 390 in men's residence halls; 104 in women's residence halls; 24 married students' apartments; 25 married students' trailers; 29 houses for faculty.

Generally, male students who want to work to help support themselves find no difficulty in obtaining jobs, either at nearby Ladd Air Force Base, on construction projects, in mines, or in the city of Fairbanks to which there is a good scheduled bus service, about a 15-minute ride one way.

University officials say that off-campus jobs for women are rather difficult to obtain. But the dean of students will advise Outsiders, prior to enrollment, as to their employment possibilities if they will send outlines of their experience or skills together with some indication as to the type of employment they prefer.

Faculty pay, said Dr. Patty, has increased by about "50 per cent in the last six years," and now ranges from $6,500 to $12,000. Dr. Patty has estimated that "fees, books, room, board, and laundry" runs to about $1,150 per year at the University. However, according to Dr. Robert Wiegman, the University's vice president, students "can clear $2,000 in summer employment," working at one of the many scientific and defense construction projects around Fairbanks and Ladd Air Force Base.

The University has acquired world-wide fame for its School of Mines and its Geophysical Institute, which often receive important research contracts. The Geophysical Institute participated in the International Geophysical Year and has gained considerable recognition for its contributions to the field of cosmic radiation and studies of the strange but beautiful *aurora borealis,* "northern lights," which is a frequent and dazzling sight above the University.

The University also works closely with the Alaskan branches of the U.S. Department of Agriculture, which has several experimental research and administrative offices and facilities on the campus.

The University also sponsors two-year community colleges and many adult education courses in key cities, namely Anchorage, Juneau, and Ketchikan.

The Alaska Methodist University. At the time of this writing (1960), the Alaska Methodist University was scheduled to have construction well underway and to be almost ready to open its doors as Alaska's second institution of higher education.

The University will have a 470-acre campus, located on a high bluff in Anchorage, overlooking the majestic snow-peaked mountains of the Chugach range. It will be principally a liberal arts school, but an expansion program calls for the eventual construction of 30 buildings in which will be housed a medical school, a school of fine arts, a school of theology, and a hospital. Also to be built is a $700,000 dormitory.

For the present, the University will have ten classrooms, ten administrative offices, a library, laboratory, cafeteria, lecture rooms, art facilities, and a student lounge.

The Future

Alaska's school problems are similar to those of schools elsewhere —increasing school-age population, rising enrollments, rising costs. But in Alaska pupil enrollments have been increasing at a far greater rate than in other states. In the decade following World War II, Alaska's pupil enrollments in the elementary schools and high schools increased more than 250 per cent. In the rest of the U.S., the average increase was 33 per cent.

Alaska's growing school-enrollment rate, as in other states, is due to a higher birth rate. But a significant factor in Alaska also is the influx of young families with school-age children.

At present, some elementary schools in the more populated centers of Alaska are on double sessions and there are overcrowded classrooms in some high schools. But for the most part Alaskan communities have maintained school construction at a pace sufficient to meet the need for additional classrooms.

However, there is no doubt that the problem of providing for additional schools will become increasingly serious in the 49th State. The flow of incoming families consists largely of job seekers, who bring no capital with them to start new industries by means of which the state and school districts may acquire larger revenues without materially increasing taxes on property. Unless there is substantial Federal aid in the future, newcomers in Alaska can expect to pay for increasing school needs through some form of increased direct taxation. But Alaskans generally are optimistic that school expansion will meet no serious wall of tax resistance. Their tradition of education is too strong. They hope only that newcomers will not dilute this tradition.

It is not likely, however, that the 49th State will have the same teacher-shortage troubles plaguing almost every other state in the nation. Apparently the lure of Alaska is as strong among teachers as it once was for gold-obsessed Klondikers. Alaska is perhaps the only state that receives more applications for teaching jobs than there are available positions. (Almost always needed, however, are teachers to staff the small schools in isolated areas.) Consequently, Alaska will be able to maintain high standards for teachers, which, after all, is worthy of the 49th State—State of Education.

CHAPTER 9

HOW TO GET LAND IN ALASKA:
FOR HOMESTEADING, HOMESITES, BUSINESS,
HUNTING AND FISHING CAMPS

> *"There are few today . . . who will accuse Seward of folly in having bought this princely domain for one and nineteen-twentieth cents an acre."* Thomas A. Bailey, *A Diplomatic History of the American People.*

B EN CALDERON, A HEFTY HANDSOME BROOKLYNITE IN HIS EARLY forties, is the sort of man who likes to build and create, to look at a challenge and say, "O.K., you're on." At his cabin, a few miles from Anchorage, he placed his axe alongside the woodpile, wiped his brow, rubbed his tough, calloused hands on his work pants, then held his hands up and said, "A year ago these hands were soft. Look at them now." He spoke glowingly, proudly. Yet if he had wanted to have soft hands the rest of his life, it would have been easy. He had already met and successfully conquered a challenge in business.

In a few years following World War II, from a leathercraft hobby practiced in the rear of a barbershop, he moved into a large downtown New York plant, employing more than 150 persons. Calderon Belts & Bags, Inc., a family-owned business, is one of the nation's best-known producers of high quality fashion belts and handbags for women.

But while on a vacation trip to Alaska in 1959, he saw many young couples in the bush, working on their homesteads, clearing

112

land, burning brush, pouring concrete, painting, planting seed, carving pathways from wooded thickets toward winding, rough dirt roads. "The sounds and sights were thrilling," said Ben. "I could feel the spirit move me."

And it did. Ben went to the nearest land office, acquired some maps, made inquiries about choice homestead sites, borrowed a jeep and went into the bush to look over some land.

A few months later, back in New York, Ben sat behind the wheel of a new International Harvester "Travelall," loaded with guns, fishing gear, camping equipment, and two roomfuls of furniture. He and his wife, Sarah, took a last look at Calderon Belts & Bags, waved goodbye to a number of employees looking out of their factory windows, and rolled slowly through the streets of New York, heading for the Alaska Highway.

Like thousands of others, Ben Calderon, lured by the challenge of Alaska, has staked a homestead and is now a happy part of the "sights and sounds" that had thrilled him. He also hopes that some day in the near future he will help Alaska create a new industry based on one of Alaska's most prevalent natural resources, wildlife, for processing and manufacturing fur, skins and leather.

Pioneering has always been that way. People and land and challenge.

If the 49th State were not so far removed from the "other 48," the Alaska land rush would make the last Oklahoma land stampede seem like a trot in slow motion. Alaska is the last remaining part of the United States where, as in the days of the old West, it is still possible to obtain a sizable chunk of public land by entering the land, staking it out, and "proving up." By and large, this is what Alaskans call homesteading for "free" land.

However, homesteading is not entirely "free," nor is it by any means the only way in which you can get land in Alaska.

There are Federal land laws that make it possible for individuals, corporations, and associations of citizens to obtain land for homesites, business sites, vacation retreats, and hunting and fishing camps —with considerably less trouble than homesteading, and sometimes at less cost in time, money and effort.

However, to appreciate the vast opportunities—and challenges— of Alaska's land it is important to first understand the fundamentals of laws and procedures pertaining to the Federal public domain.

THE FEDERAL PUBLIC DOMAIN IN ALASKA

Land acquired by the United States of America, *after* the Union of the original thirteen colonies, became the Federal public domain. Over the years, more than one billion acres of public domain have been sold, leased, or granted to individual American citizens, associations of citizens, municipalities, states, and corporations under a great variety of laws and regulations. *Almost 5,000 public land laws and regulations remain in effect today!*

Acquisition of the Territory of Alaska added approximately 375,-000,000 acres to the Federal public domain. Under the Statehood Act, Alaska, *over a period of 25 years,* will acquire about 104,-700,000 acres from the Federal public domain. The balance of the public domain will remain under Federal administration and subject to Federal regulations.

Much has been made of the fact that with approximately two-thirds of the original Territory to remain in the Federal public domain, Alaska's claim to being the "biggest state" in the Union is more apparent than real. Yet of some 385,342,000 acres of public domain scattered throughout 29 other states, there are at least four states—Idaho, Nevada, Utah, and Oregon—in which the Federal public domain almost equals or exceeds half the area of the state. There are today, mainly in the western states, more than 167,000,000 acres of vacant, unreserved Federal public domain.

The Federal land to be chosen by the State of Alaska will be subject to disposition under state land laws. The first basic land act of this kind was passed by the 1959 session of the Alaska state legislature. Under this act, state lands will be administered by the Division of Lands in the State Department of Natural Resources. However, much of the land chosen by the state will be utilized as a source of revenue for the state. The state, for example, hopes to be able to lease or sell considerable land for oil and gas exploration, from which, like the Federal government, it will derive revenue through cash payments and royalties on production. It will perhaps also choose the most desirable and accessible lands for business and homesites and dispose of these lands under regulations designed to encourage settlement and yield revenue.

As the State of Alaska selects its lands from the Federal public domain, that land is immediately "closed" to homesteading, or any other form of acquisition, under Federal laws. In Alaska, as in the western states, however, a great deal of the public domain will remain Uncle Sam's land.

UNCLE SAM'S "LANDLORD"—THE BUREAU OF LAND MANAGEMENT

In Alaska, as elsewhere, the bulk of the Federal public domain is administered by the Bureau of Land Management, an agency of the Department of the Interior. BLM's headquarters are in the Interior Department Building, Washington, D. C. But it has "branch" offices throughout the public domain states, including Alaska.

Three BLM offices are in Alaska, under the over-all supervision of an "area administrator," whose office is in Juneau. The most active land offices are in Anchorage and Fairbanks, where sometimes lines form out into the streets.

Outsiders seeking general information about the Federal domain in Alaska should write to the Bureau of Land Management, Box 1481, Juneau. But if you want *specific* information regarding public domain in or near Anchorage or Fairbanks, you get faster and better service by writing to either office: Land Office, Bureau of Land Management, Box 1740, Anchorage; or, Land Office, Bureau of Land, Box 110, Fairbanks.

THE "LANGUAGE" OF THE FEDERAL PUBLIC DOMAIN

Officially, the BLM is compelled to employ certain terms in its land dealings with the public. Sometimes, the language is confusing, sometimes utterly obscure. For example, when you receive title to public domain land you get a "patent," which in effect is a deed. A settler on public domain is an "entryman" if he files his claim to *surveyed* land, but he's a "locator" if he files on *unsurveyed* land.

As a basic and indispensable guide to the Federal public domain in Alaska, you should understand four comparatively "technical" subjects: (1) land classification; (2) "vacant" public domain; (3) land records; (4) locating and identifying the public domain.

1. Classification

As a rule, in the "lower 48" states, under the Taylor Grazing Act of 1934 and other public land laws, public domain may not be leased, sold, or otherwise appropriated unless it has first been classified by a BLM expert as most suitable for the use to which it is to be put. For example, if you are seeking a patent to a homestead in Utah, you aren't even permitted to enter the land for that purpose unless and until it has been officially classified as suitable for agricultural purposes, which is the intent of homesteading laws. It has been many years since the BLM has classified land for homesteading anywhere in the United States.

In Alaska, on the other hand, there is no requirement for classifying land for homesteading—although for other land uses, the land may need to be classified first. Thus, if you happen to take a fancy to any 160-acre, vacant, unreserved tract of land in Alaska's Federal public domain, you can enter the land, "stake" it out, file a claim, and eventually—after fulfilling required residential and agricultural regulations—you get your patent to the land.

The patent makes the land yours, just as if you had purchased it privately; and thereafter you may do with it whatever you may care to do, even give up farming and just use the land as a weekend retreat. But until you receive the patent, you are either an "entryman" or "locator," and you must observe all the rules established for the privilege of entering and settling on the land. However, if the land should be known to contain valuable minerals such as oil or coal, or gold, you may *not* get a patent, or the patent may be issued to you with a clause reserving the mineral rights to the United States Government.

2. Vacant Public Domain

Periodically, public domain land will be "reserved" or "withdrawn" from the public domain, indicating that it has been set aside for some public or official use. Land may be reserved as a national forest or national park, or perhaps as a military reservation. It may be withdrawn for oil and gas exploration. Sometimes, reserved or withdrawn land is placed under the direct control of some other government agency, such as the Department of Defense, the Forest Service, the Bureau of Reclamation, or the National Park Service.

Of the 215,000,000 acres of Federal public domain in the Fairbanks district, for instance, some 56,000,000 acres have been withdrawn or reserved. Throughout all Alaska, about 92,500,000 acres of Federal public domain have been removed from public entry by withdrawal and reservation orders. The remaining land is the "vacant" public domain and subject to acquisition under various laws, such as homesteading.

But just as orders are issued to "withdraw" or "reserve" public domain, there are revocations. Most often, a revocation order will return the land to the "vacant" public domain. As a result, the total amount of land that may be "vacant" changes from time to time.

In 1943, for example, about 211,244 acres of public domain near Bethel, in western Alaska, were withdrawn for military use. In 1955, the withdrawal order was revoked and the land was opened to settlement for those seeking homesites or recreational sites.

All such orders—withdrawals, reservations, revocations—are published in advance in the *Federal Register,* a daily official diary of public activities and notices. The *Federal Register* is available in most large public libraries and may be purchased from the Superintendent of Documents in Washington.

In addition to notices in the *Federal Register,* the BLM sends press releases to the nation's newspapers so that the public may be informed; but usually news pertaining to the public domain is published mainly in western newspapers, because there is great interest in the public lands in western states. Alaskan newspapers almost always publish news affecting the public lands in Alaska. Land orders are also posted on the bulletin boards of various BLM offices. Many Alaskans visit BLM offices regularly, to check the bulletin boards, hoping to pick up in "advance" some news that might give them a jump on land in choice hunting and fishing areas or vacation sites, or in areas of prospective population and business growth.

In December, 1959, the BLM announced that it had published a "Technical Atlas of Alaska Federal Land Withdrawals and Reservations." The Atlas shows the location and boundaries of Federal public domain withdrawals and reservations as of June 30, 1958, and should prove valuable to all land hunters in Alaska. The Atlas may be purchased from the U.S. Government Printing Office, Superintendent of Documents, Washington 25, D. C. at $5.25 per copy.

Also available from the Superintendent of Documents at 45 cents per copy is a publication, "Orders Affecting Public Lands in Alaska," which is a chronological compilation of all orders, proclamations and official actions regarding public lands in Alaska from 1867 through June 30, 1958.

3. Land Records

Frequently, the BLM in Washington will receive a request for a map showing the exact location of the public domain. There can be no such map. As we have seen, the status of the public domain is subject to almost daily change.

The only accurate and reliable source of information regarding the public domain and its status at any given time is the public land records.

These records are vital to anyone concerned with the Federal public domain, whether that concern is for a homestead, a business site, or a hunting and fishing camp.

Each land office maintains a set of records pertaining to the public domain in its jurisdiction. Certain records will show whether a particular tract of land is "vacant" and other records will show when and to whom patents were issued, or whether certain lands have been entered and filed on. Plainly, it would be foolish for anyone to stake out a homestead that may have been entered already. As we shall see later, a homestead settler is required to "stake out" his land. But sometimes the "stakes" are not always seen on the ground and conflicting claims arise.

Once, near Fairbanks, three "locators" had reached the point of settling their conflicting claims by having a "shoot out." A tragic denouement was avoided only when one of the wives involved tearfully called a BLM official to help resolve the conflict, which he did by a compromise in which all claimants pulled in their stakes to avoid overlapping boundaries. However, had each claimant first consulted the records he would have discovered that a portion of his claim overlapped the boundary of an adjoining claim, even though the stakes were not visible to him.

In addition to the official records, each land office will often have available for public inspection a series of maps with overlays, so that while the map itself may be dated with respect to land status, the overlay, altered almost daily, may show the latest changes in land status, making it comparatively easy for a land hunter to locate "vacant" land or avoid possible conflicting claims.

4. Locating and Identifying Land

In dealings with the BLM, there is often a need to locate or identify land in terms of "legal subdivisions." Such subdivisions are based on a system known as the "rectangular" or "cadastral survey," which is unique to the United States and Canada and originates in one of the first laws passed by the Continental Congress. At first, the system seems inordinately complex, especially when a legal subdivision is seen for the first time in abbreviated form. Example: *Lot 1, SE¼, NW¼, Sec. 14, T2S, R3W, Seward Mer.* But as we shall see, the system is ingeniously simple and many nations envy us for having started the system more than 180 years ago because accurate identification of land is vital in nations where property lines are held in legal (and social!) esteem.

According to this system, land laid out on a cadastral survey map has the appearance of a checkerboard. Each box in the checkerboard pattern is known as a "township," which is a six-mile square, containing 36 square miles of land. Each township is further subdivided into sections, numbered one through 36.

The principal problem then is how to locate a particular "square." For this there are two intersecting reference lines, much like the street corner sign which tells you that you are standing at the corner of Maple and Vine Streets.

The two reference lines are known as *base lines,* and *principal meridians.* The base lines are horizontal, east-west. The principal meridians are vertical, north-south.

Vertical tiers of squares are called *ranges.* Horizontal rows of squares are *townships.* Abbreviated, *R* for range; *T* for township.

Consequently, the *third* tier of squares to the left (west) of a principal meridian is known as *range 3 west,* abbreviated *R3W.* The second horizontal row of squares below (south of) the base line is *township 2 south,* or *T2S.* Thus, a particular square may be identified as *T2S, R3W.* In plain language, this means: the land is in the square which is two rows down from the base line, in the third tier left of the meridian.

All cadastral survey maps show base lines and meridians. There are five principal meridians in Alaska, each bearing a proper name and located by latitude and longitude. These are:

> *Copper River Meridian:* 61° 49′ 21″ north; 145° 18′ 53″ west.
> *Fairbanks Meridian:* 64° 51′ 50″ north; 147° 38′ 26″ west.
> *Seward Meridian:* 60° 07′ 36″ north; 149° 21′ 24″ west.
> *Kateel River Meridian:* 65° 26′ 16″ north; 158° 45′ 31″ west.
> *Umiat Meridian:* 69° 23′ 30″ north; 152° 00′ 05″ west.

An example of land description may read, *Sec. 14, T2S, R3W, Seward Mer.* In everyday language, this refers to a piece of land known as section 14, located in the second township south of the base line, in the third range west of the Seward Meridian.

A *section* of land is usually 640 acres. But because it is often necessary to identify smaller parcels of public domain (a typical homestead is 160 acres), the sections are further subdivided by quarters, making each such quarter 160 acres. Consequently, a typical homestead is a quarter-section. But even these quarter-sections may be further subdivided, by quarters.

For example, if you were to quarter a 640-acre section, you'd have a northeast quarter, a northwest quarter, a southeast quarter, and a southwest quarter, each containing 160 acres. You may then subdivide each of these quarters by quarters, thereby dividing a 160-acre quarter into 40-acre quarters. Example: *SE¼ NW¼ Sec. 14, T2S, R3W, Seward Meridian.* Spelled out, this means: a 40-acre parcel of land located in the southeast quarter of the northwest quarter of section 14 in township 2 south, range 3 west of the Seward Meridian.

Sometimes, a parcel of land is too irregular to identify by legal subdivision. The BLM will then give it a "lot" number, but its particular location will be written down as: *Lot 1, SE¼, NW¼, Sec. 14, T2S, R3W, Seward Mer.*

There are numerous advantages to this system, most important of which is the fact that you can locate the boundaries of even the smallest parcel of land simply by drawing lines on a map. The best maps for locating and identifying the public domain are those showing the township-grid arrangement of the cadastral survey system. Such maps are readily available from any map office of the U.S. Geological Survey. In Alaska, there are USGS map offices at: 520 Illinois Street, Fairbanks; 204 Denali Building, Anchorage; 111 Federal Building, Juneau; and the Brooks Building at the University of Alaska.

There is also a main office in Washington, the Map Information Office, Geological Survey, Washington 25, D. C., where maps may be purchased. In other states, there are USGS public inquiry offices at: 468 New Custom House, Denver, Colorado; 504 Federal Building, Salt Lake City, Utah; 602 Thomas Building, Dallas, Texas; 1031 Bartlett Building, Los Angeles, California; and 232 Appraisers Building, San Francisco, California.

GENERALIZED DIAGRAM OF
THE RECTANGULAR SYSTEM OF SURVEYS

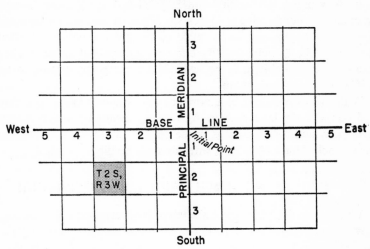

- TOWNSHIP GRID -

TOWNSHIP 2 SOUTH, RANGE 3 WEST

SECTION 14

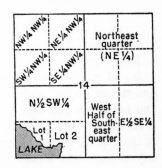

Each of the USGS offices has a library of publications and maps pertaining to Alaska which are sold over the counter. However, the same publications and maps may be purchased by mail from either the Washington, Denver, or Fairbanks offices.

To make selections and purchases by mail, you may obtain, free of charge, a complete "List of Geological Survey Publications" and an "Index of Maps in Alaska."

In November, 1959, the USGS published a six-page mimeographed brochure entitled, "MIO-35, Maps of Alaska," which is a highly informative and useful guide to the great variety of Alaskan maps and charts published by different government agencies. The brochure, if available, may be had without charge by writing to the USGS office in Washington.

With this background, it is now possible to understand, appreciate and consider the land rush in Alaska, the means by which Americans today and tomorrow—as in the days of the Last Chance Saloon —may help Uncle Sam part with his land holdings in Alaska.

HOMESTEADING—FREE LAND FOR THE ASKING!

Within months after the hullabaloo over statehood for Alaska, newspapers everywhere were filled with such headlines as: 'FIFTY-NINERS' LEAVE DETROIT ON TREK TO ALASKA HOME-STEADS; ANCHORAGE HAILS CARAVAN OF HOMESTEAD-ERS.

Not since the days of the Pony Express has there been anything like homesteading in Alaska to excite the imagination. Come and get it! Free land for the asking! Just drive a few stakes into the ground, and 160 acres can be all yours.

It's all true. There are "wagon trains" and "caravans" and trucks and station wagons and house trailers, laden with uprooted families, and household pets and furnishings that could not or would not be sold, Alaska-bound, for a chance at a new way of life; and the lure is land which, except for nominal "proving up" fees, is free. Almost anyone can stake a claim to as much as 160 acres of vacant public domain for a homestead, provided the land is unreserved, and provided no one else has filed a prior *valid* claim on the same land, or on any portion of it. But it isn't easy.

Homesteading in Alaska, as it was in Kansas and Oklahoma and California in Pony Express days, is truly pioneering, which means *work,* hard work and lots of it. Also, it means that you must comply with certain regulations and then prove that you have complied before you can get a patent to the homestead from Uncle Sam.

The first Homestead Act, signed by Abraham Lincoln, was designed to encourage *agricultural* settlement in the West, not to give land away. In other words, Lincoln wanted Americans to establish farms in the West and did not want the price of land to be a barrier to prospective farmers. The intent of homestead laws today is the same. In other public land states, for example, not only must the land first be classified as suitable for agriculture, but on the rare occasions when choice homesteads become available—usually as a result of a reclamation project—those receiving homesteads must *prove in advance* that they have the *means and capability* for successful farming.

But it is not the same in Alaska. The homesteader needn't wait for land to be classified; he needn't prove that he has means or capability. He can move onto the land with a jeep or a mule, with a tractor or an axe, with or without overwhelming ambition to become a farmer in Alaska. But if and when he is ready to ask Uncle Sam for a patent to the homestead, he must prove that he has actually lived on the land for a certain minimum period and that he has tilled a minimum acreage of soil. Uncle Sam cannot question his intent, nor his past experience as a farmer. Some of the most successful farmers in Alaska today had never been near a plow prior to their arrival in Alaska; and some of the most dismal failures were among men who had been bred on a farm. The odds against a successful homestead in Alaska are great (see Chapter Eleven). Success in homesteading in Alaska, that is, creating a going farm, not a rural residence, is a badge of courage and enterprise and sometimes ingenuity. Those who wear the badge are usually the sort who thrive on battling the odds.

To stress the ruggedness of homesteading in Alaska, the Bureau of Land Management has come up with some interesting data: out of more than 327,000 acres patented in Alaska under the Homestead Act, only about 22,000 acres are being farmed today!

What of those homesteads that were patented but not successfully farmed? Some were abandoned. Some are used today as rural residences, or as weekend retreats and vacation sites. Some have been sold outright or subdivided and sold.

It is no secret, in fact, that many Alaskans have obtained homesteads without having had any intent whatsoever to farm the land, a statement that causes some officials to shudder. But under the law, there's nothing officials can do about it. If you want to obtain a homestead for real estate speculation, BLM officials have no effective means to prevent you from doing so. In this regard, the Homestead Act, as it applies to Alaska, is sterile.

In Anchorage and Fairbanks, I met a great number of Alaskans who didn't even attempt to conceal their intent to obtain homesteads for speculation. One young man, who had settled in Anchorage shortly after World War II, told me how he had staked a homestead at an exquisite site known as "Big Lake," about 80 miles north of Anchorage because he knew that someday "Big Lake" would become a popular recreational area and land there would be valuable. He fulfilled all the requirements for homesteading and finally obtained a patent. His cost for clearing the land and putting up a house, and planting, came to $2,350 over a period of four years. The shack he built on his homestead is now his weekend cabin, where he goes to fish and hunt. After having set aside 7½ acres for himself, he subdivided the remainder and is now selling it at prices ranging from $2,200 to $3,000 per acre!

There are numerous examples of former homesteads closer to Anchorage and Fairbanks which have been subdivided into parcels selling at thousands of dollars per acre, or per lot. It is safe to say that 90 per cent of all business and residential sites now being sold in or near major population centers throughout Alaska are former homestead lands; yet as recently as eight or ten years ago some of these homesteads were described as "bush" lands, remote, isolated, inaccessible.

Incidentally, whenever it seems as though a new road is to be built, especially into previously "isolated" but picturesque areas, perhaps where there are good fishing lakes, there is a sudden flurry of interest about homesteading in those areas, and not all the interest is motivated by a desire to farm. One Alaskan, for example, told me how he keeps close tabs on highway construction news. As soon as there is the remotest chance that a road may be built in a certain area, he said, he will stake a homestead there and eventually sell the land for cemetery plots.

Qualifications for homesteading.

Generally, homesteading is open to any American citizen who is at least 21 years of age. The minimum age requirement is waived for anyone who is married or is serving, or has served, in any branch of the armed forces. A non-citizen may claim a homestead if he has declared his intention to become a citizen, although he cannot receive a patent to the land until he becomes a citizen.

No one, however, may claim a homestead if he has already received a patent to a previous homestead of 160 acres. But a homestead patent received in the continental U. S. is no bar to a homestead patent in Alaska.

The rule of thumb is one 160-acre homestead to a customer. It is possible, nonetheless, to obtain several homesteads, provided the total does not exceed 160 acres. But a married couple is looked upon as a "single" customer, meaning that a married woman *not* separated from her husband cannot apply for a homestead while her husband has a homestead. On the other hand, any child that is otherwise eligible (for example, a 21-year-old son, or a younger *married* son, or a son serving in the armed forces) may obtain a homestead in his own right.

On the outskirts of Fairbanks, I met a civilian employed by the Army in Alaska; his son also happened to be serving in the Alaskan Air Command. Between them, they claimed two adjoining homesteads, for a total of 320 acres.

How to "stake" a homestead.

Only "vacant" public domain may be claimed or entered as a homestead. In short, it must be land that is unappropriated, unreserved, and not withdrawn from public entry. It is up to the settler to determine whether the land is "vacant." A wise homesteader will check the land office records to be certain there are no prior claims to the land and no official acts which may have caused the land to be withdrawn, reserved, or appropriated for some other purpose.

A homestead claim filed on reserved or withdrawn land will not be allowed to patent. A claim that conflicts with another homesteader's claim results in a legal contest between the conflicting parties. The BLM does not enter into the case. It can be troublesome as well as costly.

A homestead entry or location begins the moment you obtain an official entry allowance, or after you stake out the boundaries of your homestead and through "personal" acts show your intent to settle on the land. Obviously, a homestead cannot be obtained by "remote" selection. There are no mail-order homesteads, in spite of the young man who called the BLM director long distance from New York to Washington to ask for a homestead and driving instructions to get to it.

As a minimum personal act, you are expected to place conspicuous stakes, or mounds of stone, or both, at the four corners of the land, and to post notices to the effect that "this is a homestead claim." In Alaska, homesteaders can purchase simple printed posters to "claim" homesteads.

Alaskan veterans have found that the best way to stake the land —to avoid intentional or unintentional claim jumping—is to (1) run a bulldozer around the boundaries, or (2) place a single strand of wire around the perimeter of the land, and then (3) clear a substantial patch of land where the house or shack may ultimately be erected, *in addition* to posting the usual notices.

Filing notices on the homestead.

To obtain a patent eventually, you must prove you have met the minimum legal requirements of residence and cultivation.

In general, you have about five years in which to "prove up." The date the proving up period begins depends on whether your homestead claim is on unsurveyed or surveyed land. Although less than 5,000,000 acres have been surveyed in Alaska, the survey program has been substantially accelerated since statehood in order to assist the new state in its own acquisition of Federal public domain lands.

However, if you enter a homestead on *surveyed* land, in addition to the payment of a nominal filing fee (about $16 for a 160-acre tract), you must file an application for a "Notice of Allowance." The application must be filed within 90 days of your settlement on the land. After this application is received and accepted as a completed application, the BLM will have the land investigated to determine whether it contains valuable minerals. If the land is determined to contain valuable *metalliferous* minerals (such as gold, silver, lead) the application will be disallowed, saving you the trouble and expense of putting up a shack, assuming you weren't foolish enough to do so before receiving notice of approval of your application.

If the land is determined to be valuable for what the law calls "leasable minerals" (oil, gas, coal) the application will not be allowed unless you sign a waiver reserving these minerals to the Government.

If all goes well, your application is approved and you receive a "Notice of Allowance," and your five-year proving-up period begins from the date of the "Notice of Allowance." To avoid wasting time and effort, a prudent homesteader will also: (1) check the land himself for evidence of mineral deposits, especially making certain that there is no sign of a prospector's diggings or mine on the land, and (2) write to the Regional Director, U.S. Bureau of Mines, Box 560, Juneau, inquiring as to whether anything is known of the potential mineral value of the general area in which the homestead claim is being made.

The BLM's mineral investigation of the land is usually based, not on a personal investigation of the land, but on the known records of the U.S. Geological Survey. Thus, an additional source of information may be the nearest USGS office, where various reports may be available for public inspection. A vastly useful source of information is the USGS "List of Publications," which is available free of charge upon request from the USGS. By consulting the List's index under "Alaska" a number of appropriate and sometimes revealing reports may be located. These reports may then be purchased or consulted at a USGS office. As a matter of fact, professional prospectors often go to the "List of Publications" is search of clues for potentially valuable mineral areas in which to prospect.

On unsurveyed land, a homesteader is not required to file an application for allowance. But he is required to file a "Notice of Location," also within 90 days of settlement on the land, in which case the five-year proving up period begins on the date of settlement, *not* the date on the "Notice of Location." In effect, the proving up period can begin on the very first day you enter and stake out the land. But a "Notice of Location" protects you against future claim jumpers in the event a conflict of claim dates arises. Accordingly, homesteaders like to file their "Notice of Location" immediately.

But "staking out" alone is not usually considered a bona fide attempt at settlement, which the law requires. You are expected to follow this up with a series of personal acts, such as clearing the land for a road or for a *permanent* home within a "reasonable time" after settlement or staking out. The cultivation of the land may come later.

Work begun on the construction of a permanent home is generally accepted as proof that you intend "faithfully and honestly" to comply with all the requirements of homesteading. In Alaska, many homesteaders build a basement first and live in the basement while the rest of the home is being erected. In some areas, it is almost startling to see kerosene lanterns burning in a series of "basement" homes, almost as though a housing developer had sold a colony of concrete-block basements.

In choice homestead areas it is also considered a wise move to establish your residence as soon as possible as insurance against claim jumpers and "contestants." Some in Alaska have refined "contesting" to an art. It works this way: you stake out a homestead, and that's all you do for a time. But suddenly the area becomes the target for a land rush and everybody wants a homestead there. Along comes Mr. Big Red Wolf, disappointed. All the good homestead lands are taken. But suddenly he notices your homestead, the only one without any "personal-act" evidence of settlement. Mr. Big Red Wolf rushes to the nearest BLM office and contests your right to the homestead. He can prove, he says, that you have no legal right to the homestead because you were not a bona fide settler. Result? A contest, between you and Mr. Big Red Wolf. Maybe he gets a lawyer; maybe you do, too. But whatever happens, if Mr. Big Red Wolf wins he gets a prize—your homestead! That's the law.

"Contesting" in Alaska has become increasingly popular and is expected to continue in popularity as population expansion pushes the cities and towns farther, making "remote" homesteads more desirable, and as new highway construction makes them more accessible.

Residential requirements for "proving up."

Under the law, you must establish a residence on your homestead within the first six months of the "Notice of Allowance," or the legally acceptable date of settlement. The residence must be a "permanent" one; permanence usually means "a home to the exclusion of a home elsewhere."

But the law recognizes that sometimes illness, climatic conditions, or some "unavoidable cause" may prevent you from establishing a permanent residence during the first six-month period. Consequently, a six-month extension may be obtained upon the filing of a proper application at the land office. The application requires payment of a nominal fee ($5) and a statement of cause, supported by two witnesses.

The home you build must be a "habitable house," which, based on experience, is just about anything with four walls and a roof and is fixed to the ground. Sometimes, what has passed as a habitable house on a homestead would have been thrown out as a coop by a New Jersey chicken farmer.

You must also maintain your residence on the land for at least three years before applying for a patent, or "proving up." But you are allowed to be absent from the homestead for a five-month period during each of the three years. The five-month period of absence may be broken into two separate occasions, such as a three-month absence in the early part of the year, then a two-month absence in the latter part of the year. In any event, you must allow a substantial period of time for residence on the land between any two five-month periods of absence. For example, you cannot space your permissible periods of absence so that you are away from the residence ten consecutive months, even though, strictly speaking, the ten-month total may fall during two separate years.

In most cases, because homesteads are usually in isolated and remote country, the BLM, understaffed as it is, may never dispatch an official to check up on your house and term of residence. It would seem comparatively simple, therefore, to evade the residential requirements of the law. Some do and get away with it. But when "proving up" time comes, you must take an oath, certifying that you have met all the requirements of the law. Thereafter, it is entirely possible that the Government may nullify your patent on the grounds of fraud, which is just about the only way the land can be taken from you after patent. Also, if a Mr. Big Red Wolf should come along seeking to contest your claim, evasion of residential requirements provides him with excellent grounds for doing so, successfully! A cautious homesteader, when absent from his homestead, takes pains to notify the land office.

Another "fine" point of law generally overlooked is the fact that the three-year *residence* requirement begins from the "date the actual residence is established," which may or may not coincide with the date of "Notice of Allowance" or "Notice of Location."

Veterans' exemptions.

The law allows all honorably discharged male and female veterans with more than 90 days service in World War II, the Korean war, or

World War I, to receive special "credit" toward residential requirements in accordance with length of service.

Veterans with *less* than 90 days service may receive credit for two
years of service if they were "discharged on account of wounds received or disability incurred in the line of duty," or if they were
honorably discharged and "subsequently furnished hospitalization or
awarded compensation by the Government on account of such wounds
or disability."

The "credit" is a reduction in the minimum time required for
residence before filing application for patent. For instance, a veteran
entitled to a credit of 19 months or more of military service may
apply for patent after only seven months of residence during his
first homestead year, assuming he has met also the minimum requirements for cultivation, discussed later.

The chart below shows the exact residence "credits" for qualified
veterans having three to 19 months service.

MINIMUM RESIDENTIAL HOMESTEAD REQUIREMENTS FOR VETERANS,
IN ACCORDANCE WITH LENGTH OF MILITARY SERVICE

No. of Months Service Credit	No. of Months Residence Required First Year	No. of Months Residence Required Second Year	No. of Months Residence Required Third Year
19 or more	7	0	0
18	7	1	0
17	7	2	0
16	7	3	0
15	7	4	0
14	7	5	0
13	7	6	0
7 to 12	7	7	0
6	7	7	1
5	7	7	2
4	7	7	3
3	7	7	4

Qualified veterans of World War I may "prove up" (apply for
patent) after only seven months of residence on the homestead during the first year of residence and *need not meet any of the cultivation requirements*. In short, a qualified veteran of the First World
War can obtain a patent to a homestead simply by living in a habitable house for seven months during the first year of his "claim,"

without bothering to plant a seed. Perhaps the underlying assumption of this largesse is that the average World War I veteran is too old for the rigors of farming in Alaska.

Special reduction in residential requirements.

If you are hampered by extreme climatic conditions, which make it unusually difficult if not impossible for you to remain on your homestead for seven months each year, you may apply for a special reduction in residential requirements as follows: six months in each year for a period of four years; or five months in each year for a period of five years. In effect, a one-month reduction in residence per year extends your "proving up" period a year. To obtain the special reduction, you must file an application, for which there is a nominal fee ($5).

Leave of absence.

You may also file a special application for a leave of absence from your homestead for a year, in the event some unusual occurrence, such as illness, accident, or destruction of your crops, makes it necessary for you to leave the homestead. The "unusual difficulty" must be of such a nature as to prevent you from supporting yourself through cultivation of the land.

Requirements for cultivation.

To fulfill the agricultural intent of the homestead law, you are required to perform a *minimum* amount of cultivation of the land. Cultivation, under the law, is defined as "tillage of the soil." You must also make a bona fide *attempt* at producing a marketable crop, but you are *not required to be successful* at the attempt. Many homesteaders who really have no intent to farm in Alaska have succeeded in meeting the cultivation requirements merely by planting oats.

Normally, the minimum cultivation requirements are: *first year,* no cultivation necessary; *second year,* you must have one-sixteenth of the total homestead land area cultivated, which, on a 160-acre homestead, would mean ten acres have to be cultivated; *third year,* you must have one-eighth of the land under cultivation. If you enter a fourth or fifth year of homesteading, as a result of special permission, you must continue to keep one-eighth of the land cultivated.

In addition to the exemption for World War I veterans, there are two other possible exceptions to the cultivation rule: (1) If you discover *after* having established a residence that certain portions of the land are not practicable for cultivation, making it impossible for you to meet the minimum requirements, you may apply to have the minimum reduced according to circumstances. But you must be able to show that this condition was not apparent at the time the land was first taken up. (2) In the event of a personal mishap, such as a disabling accident or illness, you may also receive a reduction in cultivation requirements for the period of your disability by filing a special "Notice of Misfortune" within 60 days of its occurrence.

How to "buy" the homestead.

There is an exception to the residential requirements which is known as "commuted proof" or "commuted homestead." The rule applies to veterans and non-veterans alike. In effect, it makes it possible to "buy" your homestead for $1.25 per acre and obtain your patent in less than half the three-year minimum period of residence. To be eligible for a commuted homestead you must show that: (a) you have resided continuously on the homestead for a period of 14 months; (b) you have cultivated at least one-sixteenth of the land if your application for commutation is made during the second year of entry or one-eighth of the land if it is made during the third year; and (c) you have constructed a permanent, habitable dwelling on the homestead.

"Proving up" for a patent.

When you have met all the minimum requirements of residence and cultivation and are prepared to prove it, you may apply for a patent. You obtain "proving up" forms from the land office. These forms include an oath and corroborative testimony from two witnesses to the effect that you have complied with the homestead requirements. In addition to the payment of nominal "final proof" fees (totaling $11 for 160 acres), you will be required to publish a "notice of final proof" in a local newspaper designated by the land office and to pay for the cost of the advertisement. The period of publication may be five or nine weeks, depending on whether the land is surveyed or unsurveyed.

The following illustrates a typical public notice for final proof in claiming Federal public domain land in Alaska. Note how description of land is given in terms of "legal subdivisions" or rectangular survey "code."

LEGAL NOTICES
UNITED STATES
DEPARTMENT OF THE INTERIOR
BUREAU OF LAND MANAGEMENT
Land Office
334 East Fifth Avenue
Anchorage, Alaska
Aug. 25, 1959.

NOTICE FOR PUBLICATION

Notice is hereby given that Rodney Spendlove, entryman, of Anchorage, Alaska, together with his witnesses,

Donald L. Fohaley of Anchorage, Alaska and

Kenneth Perkins of Anchorage, Alaska, has submitted final proof of his homestead original and additional entries, Anchorage Serial Numbers 028736 and 028736-A, for a tract of land described as

Lots 2 and 3, Section 30, Township 12 North, Range 2 West; N ½ SE ¼ NE ¼ , SW ¼ SE ¼ NE ¼ , N½ SE¼ SE¼ NE¼ , Section 25, Township 12 North, Range 3 West, Seward Meridian,

containing 98.09 acres, and it is now in the files of the Land Office, Anchorage, Alaska. Any person, corporation, or association, having or asserting any adverse interest in, or claim to the tract of land or any part thereof sought, may file in the Anchorage Land Office during the period of publication or within 30 days thereafter, under oath, an adverse claim setting forth the nature and extent thereof, and such adverse claimant shall, within sixty days after the filing of such adverse claim begin action to quiet title in a court of competent jurisdiction within Alaska.

Signed.
ALFRED P. STEGER
Chief, Lands Adjudication Unit
Pub: Aug. 27; Sept. 3, 10, 17, 24, 1959.

After the required period of publication, you have to file an "Affi-davit of Publication" (a form usually obtained from the newspaper). Then a "field investigation" by an employee of the BLM is made to see whether you have met all the requirements. If the field investiga-tion confirms your application of "final proof," and if no protest is received within 30 days after the publication of the "notice of final proof," the land office will send a "final certificate" to BLM's Wash-ington headquarters where the patent is prepared and issued. How-ever, if your homestead is on unsurveyed land, the patent will not be issued until *after* the land has been surveyed. The survey will be done by the government, free of charge. After you receive your patent, you must record it at the office of the local United States Commis-sioner.

Thereafter, the homestead belongs to you and you will have no further dealings with BLM. But you may receive a notice from the tax office. As a private landowner, you may, like others, have to start paying real estate and other community taxes.

Adding to the original homestead.

Sometimes, after a homesteader settles on his land and has estab-lished a residence on a homestead of *less than 160 acres* he finds that he would like to have additional land. In that event he may claim an additional amount of *contiguous* vacant land, provided the combined total of land does not exceed 160 acres. But he must do this before filing final proof.

Moreover, the additional entry cannot be commuted and the home-steader must retain his residence on the original land; also, he must cultivate one-eighth of the additional entry or one-eighth of the com-bined acreage.

You may also make an additional entry on non-contiguous land but the same limit applies: no more than 160 acres for the combined homesteads. However, you may make an additional entry on non-contiguous land after final proof has been filed on the original home-stead, provided you fulfill all the requirements for residence and cultivation on the additional land just as though it were your first and only homestead. In effect, you may have two homesteads on non-contiguous land for a combined area not in excess of 160 acres.

HOW TO GET LAND FOR HOMESITES, BUSINESS, OR
RECREATION

Shortly after the Korean war, a pair of discharged Army buddies decided to strike out together for Fairbanks, Alaska, to build a new future for themselves, a future in which there would be some fun and excitement, but also peace of mind. They had selected Fairbanks because they had learned that it was not quite as urbanized and as developed as Anchorage. But they never reached Fairbanks. On the way, via the Alaska Highway, they passed an exquisite glacial lake deep in a verdant pine forest. They pulled off the road, unpacked their fishing gear and within a few hours their creels were loaded with trout in sizes they had always read about but had never seen. True enthusiasts of the outdoor life, they were thrilled and decided that here, at last, was really a place to live!

After a few days of camping at the lakeside, they learned from a passing Alaskan that they were encamped on Uncle Sam's land, the Federal public domain. They repacked their gear in the car and detoured to the nearest Bureau of Land Management Office, where they were informed that the land around the beautiful lake was up for lease or sale under the Small Tract Act. They applied for a lease, with option to purchase the land, and eventually obtained between them ten acres at a total cost slightly above $100. Meanwhile, they erected a shack and went into business selling groceries, souvenirs, sandwiches, gas, and auto accessories to passing motorists. Now they are successful businessmen, not rich, not even moderately well off, but successful because, as they say, they are doing what they have always wanted to do, fishing, hunting, and occasionally working —in their own backyard.

Because the story of these ex-Army buddies can be told many times over with as many different variations in Alaska, the Small Tract Act has been aptly labelled "jackrabbit homesteading."

Compared with other land laws, the Small Tract Act has had a comparatively recent and unique history. It began in the early 1930's, when a BLM official in California was sent to public domain land in the desert to investigate settlers who had filed for conventional homesteads. The settlers were mostly ailing World War I veterans who had found the desert land personally salubrious but unyielding to their efforts at agriculture. But the veterans were tanned, healthy, and happy. Legally, however, they were not entitled to the home-steads.

The BLM official decided that something ought to be done about it. Over a few years, at his own expense, he made several trips to Washington, pressuring Congressmen to pass a new law that would make it possible for ordinary Americans, like the veterans in the desert, to obtain small tracts of public domain land as home, vacation, and convalescence sites. On June 1, 1938, the official's seemingly hopeless hegiras to Washington were climaxed when the Small Tract Act went into effect, the first land law of its kind in history.

Today, the Small Tract Act, as subsequently amended, is perhaps the best and most popular means for obtaining land in Alaska at reasonable cost, with least effort. In contrast with homestead lands, usually remote from organized communities, many areas of public domain have been set aside for disposition under the Small Tract Act in and around major population centers.

In 1958, for instance, the BLM's Juneau office started selling large maps, at $2 each, showing highly desirable Small Tract lands near Juneau, Ketchikan, Wrangell, Sitka, Haines, and Petersburg. Some of these tracts were on wooded islands, others were alongside lakes or at the edges of mountains that were beautiful enough to have been made part of a national forest or national monument.

Under the Small Tract Act up to five acres of land may be leased, purchased outright at a public sale (auction), or leased with an option to purchase.

The rental and purchase prices are set by BLM at "fair market appraisals," which generally are quite reasonable, if not bargains. When purchased at a public sale, the land goes to the highest bidder; but bids may be submitted by mail no matter where you live.

One of the most scenic plots I saw in Alaska, the future site of a businessman's hunting and fishing lodge, was a five-acre tract just off the Anchorage-Seward Highway, almost on the shores of beautiful Knik Arm (part of the Cook Inlet), less than an hour's drive from Anchorage. The businessman, a New Yorker, had purchased the land for less than $700, having been the high bidder at a public sale. His bid was submitted by mail.

Getting land under the Small Tract Act is catching on fast in Alaska, and will undoubtedly become the most popular means of establishing suburban homes and weekend or vacation retreats as population expands.

In the fall of 1950, for instance, the BLM made 48 parcels of land, ranging from one to five acres, available in the beautiful Nancy Lake area some 40 miles from Anchorage. The land was classified as extremely well suited to recreational purposes and was appraised to sell under the Small Tract Act at about $35 an acre with a slightly higher price for lakefront acreage. As the area proved popular, other small tracts were made available. By 1957, the appraised price was increased to about $50 an acre, but a year later, when the land office held a public auction for a few sites that had been abandoned by original Small Tract Act leaseholders, bidders went as high as $150 to $225 per acre because a new road had made the area more accessible than ever. Recently, land in the same area has been selling according to lakeside front-footage, at $8 to $10 per foot and at $500 and up for small lot-size parcels.

Before land is sold or leased under the Small Tract Act, it must first be classified as suitable for home, business, or recreational use. When the land is classified, the land office will issue an announcement specifying the terms, conditions, and manner in which the land will be disposed. The announcements are posted on land office bulletin boards and are invariably published in Alaskan newspapers as news of great public interest.

It also has been the practice of some land offices to maintain mailing lists of those requesting notification of Small Tract Act disposals. It has been largely through such mailing lists that Outsiders have been able to participate in land auctions, for which, unlike homesteading, personal inspection of the land is not required. A Small Tract land-disposal notice will usually carry a brief description of the land to be sold, its exact location, size, and "minimum acceptable bid" if there is to be an auction.

It is BLM's policy not to put Small Tract land up for auction unless it is located within an organized community, in order to be sure that some form of orderly land-use rules (zoning) will prevail, protecting the best interests of the community as well as Small Tract purchasers. If the land is in an outlying area, the policy is to offer the land only under terms of a lease with an option to purchase, in which case the application for lease, when signed, becomes an agreement to pay a stipulated annual rental for the land, an agreement to maintain certain conditions for erecting a home or cabin on the land, and an option to purchase the land at a price based on a fair appraisal. The purchase price is pre-fixed in the lease, based on the "unimproved" value of the land, and cannot be changed even when, at the time the option is exercised, the land may have gone up in value.

The usual annual rental is about one-twentieth of the purchase price, payable in advance for the entire term of the lease, but the minimum is $5 per year. The maximum term of the lease is three years, and in all cases the purchase option may be exercised any time after the improvements and conditions set by the terms of the lease have been met.

Almost always, the lease specifies that before you can exercise the purchase option you must have put up a habitable house with suitable facilities for sanitation. Whenever the purchase option is granted, the unearned rental is applied toward the purchase price. A lease is usually renewable if you can show that your failure to construct the necessary improvements was due to unavoidable circumstances and that not obtaining a renewal would create a "hardship" for you. But sub-leasing is not permitted.

One of the disadvantages of a Small Tract lease is that it is almost impossible to obtain a mortgage loan to erect a house or cabin because you don't have title to the land; and you can't get title until you have put up an approved dwelling.

Plainly, the lease-purchase technique makes it possible for BLM to prevent shanty-town developments and to insure safe sanitation for all. However, if several "jackrabbit homesteaders" want to organize a little community of their own, establishing reasonable conditions of sanitation and housing, and if each is willing to sign an agreement binding themselves "to observe, in the development of their leased tracts, standards of building, sanitation, and health requirements consistent with the terms of their leases," they may exercise their purchase options *without* first establishing the improvements required of others. This makes it easier for Small Tract owners to obtain building loans.

Land classified for business sites under the Small Tract are also made available under lease-with-purchase-option terms, except that the leasing period is usually for a longer term, frequently 20 years. The annual rent for a business site depends on the nature of the business, but is set as a percentage of the gross income. Many of the most successful gas-service stations and tourist cabins along Alaska's most-traveled roads have been established under Small Tract leases.

Of course, once a Small Tract is patented, the lessee, now owner, may do whatever he pleases with the land. But the same general rule of one-to-a-customer applies, although individually qualified members of the same family may each apply for Small Tract parcels in their own right.

Eligibility for Small Tracts.

Any American citizen, or person who has filed a declaration of intention to become a citizen, is eligible to participate in Small Tract leases and sales. Also eligible are: partnerships and associations in which each member is a citizen or has filed a declaration of intention to become a citizen; corporations, private and non-profit, organized under the laws of the United States, any of its states, or territories; any state, territory, municipality, or subdivision of government.

Priority rights for veterans and their dependents.

Under the law: "Honorably discharged veterans who served in the armed forces of the United States for a period of at least 90 days *after September 15, 1940*" enjoy certain priority rights for participating in Small Tract leases and auctions. The same rights are extended also to dependents and survivors of veterans.

In general, these rights consist of the privilege to participate in Small Tract disposals ahead of the general public, for a period of not less than 90 days. Suppose, for example, BLM announced a Small Tract disposal to which the public responds in great numbers, and there are more applicants than there is land available. Then for the first 90 days, only applications from qualified veterans will be considered. After 90 days, the general public's applications will be processed.

Priority for non-veterans, too!

A little-known aspect of the Small Tract Act makes it possible for *any* qualified American to obtain an absolute priority to a Small Tract site. In effect, the priority is a "reward" for locating land that may be suitable for classification under the Small Tract Act.

It works this way: You go land hunting and you find an area of vacant public domain that you think is ideal for a Small Tract site. You check with the BLM office having jurisdiction over that area to determine the status of the land. If it has not been classified under the Small Tract Act, or is not under consideration for classification, you ask for an application which in effect is a "petition" to have the land classified under the Small Tract Act. In your application, you specify the type of classification you want—homesite or business site, for instance—and you specify the amount of land you want (limit, five acres). Also, you agree to abide by the terms of lease or sale that may be established after the land is classified.

When the land is classified as per your petition, you receive, as your "reward," an absolute priority to your tract of land. If the land should subsequently be put up for public auction after it has been classified, you will be required to pay only a "fair market" value for the land and need not bid against others. Of course, if you are not satisfied with the final classification terms you needn't take the land.

Land auctions.

If you get on a mailing list to receive Small Tract land auction notices, each notice will contain specific instructions for bidding, such as how to submit your bid by mail, where to send it, and the cut-off date and time after which mailed bids will not be accepted. You may submit a bid on more than one tract, but as soon as you are declared a winner on one tract all your other bids are disqualified.

All bids must be at or above the established minimum. Many Outsiders have obtained Small Tract land in Alaska simply by submitting the minimum bid. Outsiders frequently do mail-bidding on land they are familiar with as a result of previous visits to Alaska, or after having received "tips" from friends and relatives in Alaska.

THE HOMESITE ACT: "JUNIOR HOMESTEADING"

For those who want to do their own land hunting and "claim staking" on the Federal public domain in Alaska, but without the rigors of making the land agriculturally productive, as in homesteading, it can be done, thanks to the Homesite Act of May 26, 1934, which authorized a "junior" version of homesteading for Alaska. Under this Act, the land is not free, but the charges are next to nothing, assuming you can be content with five acres.

As Alaska grows, this Act should prove to be one of the most popular means for obtaining residential land. As in conventional homesteading, you can obtain land simply by entering or locating on the land, staking it, filing a notice of location, or homesite application, and proving up, except that there is no requirement for cultivation. You can stake up to five acres of land. At proving up time, if you are entitled to patent, you pay $2.50 per acre (minimum $10) plus the usual homesteading cost of advertising the "final notice" in a designated local newspaper. There is also a nominal filing fee ($10) for the application to purchase. Unsurveyed land, as in a homesteading procedure, will be surveyed without charge by the BLM.

Otherwise, the same general provisions of homesteading apply. You must perform personal acts of settling on the land; you must establish a habitable, year-round house, and live on the land for a minimum of five months during each of the first three years, after which patent may be applied for. Qualified veterans of World War II and the Korean war may receive credit for their time in service toward a reduction in the residential requirements. It is entirely possible for a veteran with only 17 months of service to prove up after residing on the land only five months during the first year.

The Headquarters Site Act: A Place to Live and Work

In 1898, a public land law made it possible for any qualified person to claim and acquire land in Alaska for a trade and manufacturing site. But almost three decades later it was realized that there may be some who would like to claim land in Alaska as a place of residence and business combined, as for example: fishermen, trappers, guides, bush pilots, fur farmers.

The Headquarters Site Act of March 3, 1927, made this possible. You can claim up to five acres of vacant public domain as a headquarters site if you are engaged in, or "you are *employed* by someone engaged in trade, manufacture, or other productive industry in Alaska."

There are no residential requirements. You may prove up any time you can show that you are making continuous use of the land as a headquarters in connection with a "productive industry." But the usual five-year statutory limit applies. In other words, you must prove up within five years.

The cost of acquiring the land when final patent is issued is $2.50 per acre (minimum $10) plus the usual filing and advertising costs of "final notice." But there is one important exception. If the land claimed is on unsurveyed public domain, you must eventually pay the cost of survey. Under this law there is no provision for a free survey. A survey in Alaska for a five-acre tract may range from $300 to $600, depending on location.

TRADE AND MANUFACTURING SITES

In recent years there has been a great rush for land on which to establish a fairly large-sized business in Alaska, such as a service station and garage, a commercial hunting and fishing camp for tourists, or a warehouse. Nearly always this type of land, in outlying areas, has been made available to the public under the Trade and Manufacturing Site Act of May 14, 1898, which makes it possible to locate and claim up to 80 acres of vacant public domain in the name of an individual, an association, or a corporation.

The cost is $2.50 per acre, plus the usual costs of filing and advertising fees. The cost of a survey is paid by the claimant if the land is unsurveyed. The statutory limit for proving up is five years after the notice of location is filed, and the usual acts of settlement must be performed within a reasonable time after the land is staked and claimed.

But land under this law may *not* be claimed for a *proposed* business. Only land that is actually being used "for the purposes of trade, manufacture, or other productive industry" may be patented. If the land is claimed in the name of an association or corporation the application for patent will have to show that each member of the association is qualified (that is, a citizen or one who has filed a declaration of intent to become a citizen), and the corporation must show that its certificate of incorporation authorizes the holding of land in Alaska.

LAND FOR RECREATION AND PUBLIC PURPOSES

In April, 1958, the Secretary of the Interior, Fred A. Seaton, said: "For several years we [the Bureau of Land Management] have been following an informal policy and now we have it down on paper for all to understand clearly. It recognizes that recreational needs have been growing in step with the population increase and our increasing travel. Lands which years ago weren't even recognized as having recreational value are now developing extremely rich potentials for recreation."

This statement may be applied to Alaska as well as to any other part of the public domain in the United States.

Under the Recreation Act of 1926, amended in 1954, any recognized unit of government (state, city, county, township, village) and any recognized non-profit association may apply for the lease or purchase of up to 640 acres of public domain for a recreational or public purpose, for example: camps, schools, shooting range, golf course, beach, picnic grounds, historic monuments, cemeteries. The land will be leased or sold in accordance with terms to be established by the BLM. But the terms will vary with the use of the land. The greater the public purpose, the lower the terms.

The limit of 640 acres, however, is for any one calendar year. There is no limit on the number of calendar years in which 640 acres may be leased or purchased. It is entirely possible, for example, to lease or purchase a total of 6,400 acres over 10 years.

Any organization that applies for land under this law must be prepared to submit a concrete plan for use of the land and show that it has the means with which to carry out the plan. Land may not be obtained merely for some "future" use. There must be a specific plan to begin within a reasonable time after the land is obtained. In Alaska, thus far, several church-sponsored groups have applied for land under this law.

PUBLIC AUCTIONS OF LAND FOR BUSINESS OR HOUSING

From time to time, the Bureau of Land Management in Alaska will put up at auction tracts of land, not exceeding 160 acres, which may be classified as suitable for "industrial or commercial purposes, including the construction of multiple housing [apartments]." Individuals, associations, and corporations are qualified to bid and may request any BLM land office to have their names placed on a mailing list to receive notices of such public land sales.

Successful bidders may not acquire the land, however, until their plan for utilization has been approved. If the plan is approved, the successful bidder receives a "Certificate of Sale," which is assignable, if the assignee is also qualified and obtains approval of his utilization plan.

HOMESITES IN THE BEAUTIFUL NATIONAL FORESTS

Some of the most beautiful land in Alaska, as in other public domain states, lies within the reserved boundaries of the national forests. Because a national forest is reserved public domain, you can't "claim" any of its land. But there is an important exception in

Alaska. You may apply for a special "homesite use permit" in a national forest; and under such a permit you may settle on the land and establish a permanent home. After maintaining a bona fide residence there for three consecutive years, you may apply to have your tract of land "eliminated" from the reserved area and restored to the vacant public domain so that you may apply for a patent.

A permit costs $5 per year and may be issued only to citizens or those who have taken out their first papers and who show intent to complete citizenship within three years.

Most of the areas suitable for homesites in Alaska's southeastern national forests have already been returned to the BLM and may be obtained under the regulations of the Homesite Act. However, as of February, 1959, about 220 national forest homesite tracts were opened for special-permit homesite application in the Chugach and Tongass National Forests. These tracts average about two acres each. Needless to say, most of these homesites are in isolated areas where at times bad weather may prevent access to town. In many instances, the only means of access to the homesites are by boat or airplane. But homesites in the Chugach National Forest, on the Kenai Peninsula, south of Anchorage, are near forest service highways and development roads.

Application forms and procedural information for national forest homesites may be obtained from the Forest Service, United States Department of Agriculture, Box 1631, Juneau, Alaska.

"GAMBLING" IN OIL AND GAS LEASES

Perhaps the greatest spurt in public land activities since the purchase of Alaska has taken place in "wildcat" oil and gas leasing. Less than ten years ago, only about 20,000 acres were under oil and gas leases in Alaska. Then there was an oil strike on the Kenai Peninsula in 1957, and now more than 32,000,000 acres are held under "wildcat" oil and gas leases.

Whenever the Government is aware that certain lands may be potentially valuable for oil and gas, it may lease the land to the highest bidder, usually commercial oil and gas companies, and share in production through royalties if there is a successful strike on the land. However, in order to encourage the search for oil and gas on lands where there is *no known* potential for oil and gas, the Government will issue what are popularly known as "wildcat" leases.

Those who purchase wildcat leases are gambling on two counts: (1) That when they go exploring for oil and gas they may strike it rich, an extremely remote possibility but one that has been realized a number of times, as several millionaires in Texas and Oklahoma can verify; (2) That someone may make an oil and gas strike in an area near the land on which they happen to hold wildcat leases, in which case commercial oil and gas companies (or lease brokers) may come knocking at their door with juicy, profitable offers to purchase part or all interest in their leases.

It may be said, without exaggeration, that the overwhelming number of wildcat leases are held by individuals and groups who lack the means to explore for oil and gas. Their principal intent is to "sit" on the leases until such time as an oil and gas discovery is made on nearby land, after which they stand ready to negotiate with commercial interests.

Quite a few "promoters" have obtained wildcat leases in Alaska. Through advertisements in popular magazines and newspapers, they offer to sell small fractional interests in their leases (permitted by law) at prices ranging from $100 to $1,000, although their total cost for an entire lease may be only a small proportion of these amounts. In most instances, the advertisements are misleading, hinting at the possibility of "big strikes" and "fortunes to be made" when the probability of such strikes and fortunes is more in the realm of a dream than reality.

Nonetheless, sometimes wildcatters' dreams come true and the promoters will relate the exciting results among oil and gas leaseholders, inviting you to try your luck at becoming an oil and gas millionaire.

The laws and regulations pertaining to oil and gas leases are many and complex. A brochure explaining the regulations is available from the Bureau of Land Management, Washington 25, D. C. But those who have acquainted themselves with the rules have been known to profit in other ways. The *Wall Street Journal* once reported that an Anchorage barber, knowing that an oil company had inadvertently permitted one of its wildcat oil and gas leases to expire in Alaska, promptly filed for that same lease. After the barber received it, the company bought it back from him at a price said to be in excess of $100,000, although the total cost to the barber for obtaining the lease was under $100. The lease in question had become valuable as a result of oil and gas strikes on the Kenai Peninsula.

PROSPECTING ON PUBLIC LANDS

For many Alaskans, prospecting is a part-time avocation for fun and profit. The great lure, of course, is the chance of striking it rich overnight with a lucky find in gold, silver, lead, zinc, uranium, or in one of the many other valuable minerals known to exist in Alaska but largely unexplored.

However, prospecting in Alaska is not for sissies. It often means camping out in the bush for days or weeks at a time, although many Alaskans prospect by boat and airplane on weekends and holidays.

I met a young airplane mechanic in southeastern Alaska who, after three years of spare-time prospecting for gold, had accumulated enough of the yellow stuff from small diggings and pannings to purchase a $9,500 airplane, which he now uses for prospecting in some of the more remote areas. He lives with supreme confidence that one day his spare-time prospecting will make him rich. He frequently takes a friend on his camping-prospecting trips, and there's no doubt that he's having fun.

Nearly all prospecting takes place on the Federal public domain because it would be silly to prospect on private property or in areas where a strike could not be claimed. Generally, on the vacant public domain you may prospect to your heart's content and stake a claim, just as the Klondikers and Forty-niners had done. Prospecting is often permitted, too, on reserved and withdrawn lands, such as national forests, although it is always a good idea to check in advance with the land office.

The Superintendent of Documents, Washington 25, D. C., has compiled a number of government publications which are of great value to prospectors anywhere in the U.S., including Alaska. These publications discuss just about everything, from tips on how to prospect for gold, to laws pertaining to mining claims on the public domain.

Not to be overlooked, however, is the fact that 90 per cent of prospecting is the art of researching, knowing where to look in the first place. The days of the oldtime prospector wandering in tranquility but aimlessly on a burro have long since disappeared. Two government agencies are the principal sources of research information: the U.S. Bureau of Mines, and the U.S. Geological Survey.

Extremely important for Alaskan prospectors is the U.S. Geological Survey's *List of Publications*. Scanning the list under the indexed subject of "Alaska," for instance, you may come upon old or new professional geological studies and reports in which there may be clues to the potential discovery of valuable minerals. As a matter of fact, one of the purposes of Uncle Sam's geological activities is to make the studies that enable citizens to find clues. During the height of the mid-1950's uranium boom in the West many prospectors would conceal themselves in the hills to observe government geologists at work. Whenever a government airplane, containing Geiger counters and geologists, would circle an area more than once or twice, that area would soon be black with prospectors pouring out of the hills.

In Alaska, many spare-time prospectors have not fully exploited Uncle Sam's resources for their assistance, especially the USGS *List of Publications*. For instance, in the March, 1959, supplement to the *List*, which is always free of charge, an Alaskan prospector might open his eyes wide at the sight of a report entitled, "Bulletin 1058-B, Geology and ore deposits in the Reid Inlet Area, Glacier Bay, Alaska," which bulletin is described as a "mineral resources report" and states further: "Only two mines in the area have produced much gold, but other veins seem to be of sufficient size and grade to be potential ore producers." That may be enough to cause a would-be prospector in that area to purchase the full report at 65 cents, or to visit the nearest USGS office where he may be able to read the report "over-the-counter."

Many such reports have led prospectors to "interesting" discoveries.

CHAPTER 10

AGRICULTURE: NUMBER-ONE CHALLENGE IN ALASKA

*"Alaskans work hard . . . they are imbued,
consciously or unconsciously, with the challenge of their vast land."* James Warner
Bellah

BERT STIMPLE WRITES A FARM COLUMN FOR THE FAIRBANKS
News-Miner, and to read it week after week is to come away with
the impression that the farmers of Alaska are living off the fat of
the land. They must be. Otherwise, why is there so much gaiety
among them, so many social festivities, so much humor? Why is
there an optimistic, almost cheery note even to the hard and bitter
news? Or is Bert's column merely a reflection of himself, a robust
affable man in his forties, a man who carefully conceals his in-
stinctive intellectualism behind a captivating façade of unpretentious charm and the earthiness of a rube?

Actually, farm life in Alaska is rough. To live the life of a
farmer is to live, day by day, face to face, with the number-one
challenge that is Alaska. But Bert Stimple has no façade. He is a living
symbol of Alaskan farm life and perhaps more than most others
has earned the right to be their spokesman, their alter ego, their
one-man laugh against nature and all its ironies and ruggedness.

Bert Stimple arrived in Alaska during the worst possible time,
the depression-racked Thirties. Bert had seen his father's farm,
burdened by debt, taken away and vowed that he would never let

that happen to him. He, Bert, would always buy for cash. But when, at the age of twenty, he stepped off the boat that had carried him to Alaska via steerage passage from Seattle, Bert had all his worldly possessions with him: exactly $78, a bedroll, over-sized boots and coat, and a motorcycle.

He followed the Richardson Trail (now a highway) north from Valdez to Fairbanks and staked out a 160-acre homestead and began clearing the land by hand, with an axe. It must have been one of the strangest sights in Alaska, for Bert was (and is) a slender, dimunitive, almost frail-looking man. While laboring on the land, he worked at a variety of jobs in town and when his $78 ran out he sold his motorcycle.

Within a few years, he had obtained title to his homestead, and was producing and selling potatoes and making deliveries in a 1918 Model T, purchased for $20. In 1939, at a time when there were only four other full-time farmers in the entire area, he married Leah Harrington, a California schoolteacher who had been visiting her sister in Alaska. Even next to Bert, who seldom tips the scales at more than 130 pounds, Leah looks slight. But on the land the Stimples were giants.

Together, they worked the homestead and worked in town as janitors. What they could build with their own hands, they built and possessed. What they could not build or buy for cash, they went without. Every spare dollar was invested in the homestead. From potatoes, which they now farm exclusively, they went to other row crops: turnips, radishes, celery, and lettuce. Gradually, they purchased machines and equipment to make work less burdensome and home life more comfortable.

By 1942, income from the farm was sufficient to enable them to quit their jobs. In 1946, they sold their homestead for $6,000, admittedly a low price, but they were anxious to have the cash to buy another tract which they felt was better for potatoes. The Stimples had to learn everything the hard way; how to deal with the problem of permafrost, for example, and what sort of fertilizer, if any, to spread over the soil. There was then no Soil Conservation Service in Alaska, as there is today, to advise them.

But their farm today has been valued conservatively at about $100,000. They have a lovely home, a two-row planter, a two-row tractor, a two-row cultivator, a two-row tiller, a digger-harvester, a baler, mower and hay conditioner, plus adequate storage space, automatically refrigerated, and machinery for processing potatoes.

The Stimples have leased some of their land and generally lead a relaxed, semi-retired life. Bert is always busy helping other farmers, attending to all sorts of farm meetings, Chamber of Commerce, planning and promoting parties, and occasional practical jokes. Leah, artistically talented, paints. She can always be seen with oil colors, brushes, and easel in hand. Together, Bert and Leah have taken many trips Outside and indulge jointly in a hobby, pampering their first car, the 1918 Model T, aboard which they ride proudly around Alaska during the warmer months.

The story of the Stimples of Fairbanks serves to illustrate two vital aspects of agriculture in Alaska. It's a long, slow hard road to success. And the road to success needs to be chosen with care and negotiated with enterprise, tenacity, courage—and a sense of humor.

There is considerable land suitable for agriculture in Alaska. According to official but perhaps conservative estimates, there are about 1,000,000 acres of arable land, which can be cleared for crop, or dairy farming and livestock. Presently, however, only about 22,000 acres have been cleared; and of these about 15,000 acres are in actual farm use.

But this vast gap between available farm lands and land in use as farms is not a void waiting to be filled to overflowing with farming successes. Those seeking to become bona fide farm-homesteaders in Alaska would be wise not to burn their bridges behind them. In this regard, we shall report here on the various farm land areas, the products grown in Alaska, specific farm problems, greenhouses, and how Alaskans view the future in farming. But first a glimpse at Alaska's relatively brief farm history and a look at some economic and social aspects of farming in Alaska are in order.

In all the time Alaska was in Russian hands, and during much of the time it was a Territory of the U.S., farming in Alaska was considered an occupation to be dreaded. Those who had attempted serious farming could be counted on one hand. Few knew what could be grown commercially in Alaska; fewer cared. Even during the Klondike era, when "imported" eggs were selling at $5 each, not many took up the challenge to try poultry farming as a more glittering and reliable source of income than gold.

The first serious attempt at farming began in 1935, when a colony of some 200 families was settled in the lush Matanuska Valley, about an hour by highway north of Anchorage. The colony, born of misery and depression, was one of President Franklin D. Roosevelt's pet relief and rehabilitation projects, to aid farmers in the western states as well as to prove that it was possible to colonize Alaska. Today, the Matanuska Valley, an astonishing untold American drama, an epic tale of incredible struggle, of anger and jubilation, of men with and without faith, of Herculean achievements and failures and betrayals, is Alaska's largest agricultural community, a community of rich green slopes and picture-postcard trimness, producing substantially more than half the agricultural products raised and sold in Alaska.

There are now in Alaska about 350 commercial, full-time farms and approximately 900 part-time farms. The full-time farms are classified as "commercial" because they usually represent the sole source of income for farm families, not because they are exceptionally large.

By western farm-state standards, almost all commercial farms in Alaska are small. The part-time farms are mainly homesteads in varying stages of transition. Some are on their way toward becoming commercial farms, but most will probably remain part-time operations, to augment family incomes or as profitable avocations.

As in other farm states, the economics of farming in Alaska is influenced by marketing facilities and distances to markets. But in Alaska these economic factors are uniquely influenced by an additional fact: *Alaska is a one-state market.* Farmers in Alaska must either sell their products to Alaskans or "dump." They aren't large and efficient enough to seek markets in Canada or other states. The cost of transportation is prohibitive for them. Actually, due to the high cost of transportation and competition with "imports," most commercial farmers in Alaska are limited to the markets of their immediate population areas, mainly Anchorage, Fairbanks, Ketchikan, Juneau.

It is the consensus of Alaska's expert agronomists that Alaskan farms can provide 25 to 50 per cent of the state's current consumption of agricultural products. Yet farms in Alaska now supply only about one-tenth of this consumption. Almost 90 per cent of the meat and fresh produce and about 70 per cent of the milk consumed in Alaska is "imported." Mechanization and the efficiency of larger farms in Canada and western states makes it possible for Outside farmers to compete with Alaskan farmers.

Clearly, there is room for expansion of agriculture in Alaska. But in order to compete with "imports," Alaskan farms must be extremely well managed; farmers must work hard, saving on labor, making use of family labor whenever possible.

"With good management, Alaska farmers realize $6,000 to $8,000 net cash income," said Mr. C. F. Marsh, of the Agricultural Experiment Station at Palmer, one of the most reliable and most important sources of farm information and farm assistance in Alaska. However, the average net farm income in Alaska is about $4,000 a year. A few farmers earn about $10,000 net. But this net income, as Mr. Marsh has noted in many of his published reports, does not account for expenditures of farm families on their own living costs, debt, retirement, and reserve for future investment in farm equipment and expansion.

Practically no one farms in Alaska with the hope of getting rich, or even with the hope of amassing a nest egg for retirement. Most believe that farming has a bright future in Alaska, but for the time being it remains strictly *a way of life,* to be chosen for the sheer social rewards of living among neighbors who have deliberately made the same choice—to pioneer. If farmers elsewhere may be thought of as rugged individualists, the same may be said, but with special emphasis, of farmers in Alaska. As pioneers in Alaska, however, they share a bond that yields many profits in intangibles—a close, happy, active community life.

The farmers of Alaska enjoy a sense of common destiny, a sort of "national purpose" for which Americans elsewhere seem to be groping. They leave a visitor with the feeling that they are extracting from their lives in Alaska what no computer has ever produced, a sense of fulfillment.

You are left with this feeling when you talk with the farmer whose nine children have grown up in Alaska, then went to live Outside, then one by one returned to live in Alaska—except the ninth, who is still struggling to make up his mind.

You get the feeling when you meet the farmer who, during the long and relatively inactive winter months, works busily at his hobby of building furniture and then gives it away to his neighbors. You also grasp the sense of a wondrous life when you look at some of the many paintings Alaskan farmers have produced, depicting their life in Alaska, or when you visit the farmers' wives at their clubs and you hear a familiar complaint, "I have no time, so much to do . . ." and you wonder where is this thing called "isolation" in Alaska?

The true wonder of farm life in Alaska is not that so few homesteads have been commercially farmed but that so many have succeeded at it in the face of the direst warnings from nature and man.

FARM LIFE

There are three principal areas in Alaska where agriculture has proven commercially feasible and where farm land is available: (1) Matanuska Valley, near Anchorage; (2) Tanana Valley (pronounced TAN-a-naw), near Fairbanks; (3) Kenai Peninsula, also near Anchorage.

There is some farming in the Panhandle, near Juneau, Sitka, and Ketchikan. But much of it is on an extremely small scale—truck, dairy, or poultry farming—because a great deal of the land in southeastern Alaska, where topography is almost vertical, is unsuited to large-scale farming and the competition with "imports" from Vancouver and Seattle is particularly keen.

Some farm land is also available on islands along the southern shores of Alaska, but mainly these lands have been found best suited to raising livestock for beef, or sheep for wool.

MATANUSKA VALLEY

The Matanuska Valley lies about 50 miles north of Anchorage, bounded by the Talkeetna Mountains and the Chugach range. The head of the Valley is Cook Inlet, and the principal town is Palmer, which connects by a branch rail line and roadways to Anchorage.

Transportation to, from, and within the Valley is the best of any farm land in Alaska. The main rail line runs through the western part of the Valley and almost every farm has access to a network of roads which connect with the Richardson Highway, Glenn Highway, and the Alaska Highway. There also are several well-kept airstrips for light aircraft, all near good roads.

The total population of the Valley is about 3,500, although nearly one-third live in or near Palmer. The Valley is serviced by its own rural electric cooperative and the farmers are highly organized through the Matanuska Valley Farmers Cooperating Association, founded shortly after its colonization, to provide farmers with marketing assistance and facilities. The cooperative maintains a modern and large general store in Palmer, a dairy plant, produce department, garage, warehouse, and cold-storage plant.

Homestead lands are still available in the Valley, but the best farm lands are now in private hands as established farms, selling (when available for sale) at more than $200 per acre. Uncleared, tillable land, privately owned, sells for $15 to $50 per acre. There has been increasing demand in the Valley for uncleared land as rural homesites. Land for farming or homesites in the original Colony, which was established by the Federal government as a non-profit organization called the Alaska Rural Rehabilitation Corporation, may still be purchased through the Corporation, which maintains headquarters at Palmer; but no land within the original Colony may be purchased without the presence of the buyer in Palmer for an interview.

The farm products.

The total cash received by all farmers in the Matanuska Valley for all livestock and vegetable products is about $1,900,000 a year. The principal product is milk, which accounts for about $1,500,000 of the total. Milk is sold at about $11 per hundredweight (four per cent milk), produced at an average cost of about $6 to $7 per hundredweight.

The second most important cash product is potatoes, for which Matanuska farmers receive about $250,000 annually, at $80 to $100 per ton, U.S. No. 1 grade. Many farmers in the Valley average 12 tons of potatoes per acre.

Other cash products are: cabbage, lettuce, carrots, celery, radishes, eggs, poultry, beef, and pork. Farmers in this area can also produce oats, wheat, barley, hay, and Canadian field peas. For hay, silage, and pasture they grow brome grass.

Home gardeners manage to grow such typically "cool season" vegetables as beets, brussels sprouts, kohlrabi, parsnips, kale, and rhubarb. Some have succeeded also in growing strawberries, raspberries, and currants. A hybrid strawberry has been found to be peculiarly suited to large-scale production in the Valley but is not grown commercially due to the high cost of labor. A number of farmers also grow tomatoes and cucumbers in greenhouses for their own use.

Soils and climate.

A U.S. Department of Agriculture research report has said that "location, transportation, climate, and soils combine to make the Matanuska Valley the most promising for agriculture of any area in Alaska." With respect to climate and soils, this is true largely because the farmers of Matanuska Valley have had many years with which to experiment, making the most of their climate and soils. The farmers of Matanuska Valley are "experiment-minded to an unusual degree," said one farm expert.

Because the climate in the Matanuska Valley is comparatively mild, the outstanding feature of the soils is that they are almost free of permafrost. For the most part, the tillable soils have developed from "silty and very fine sandy materials laid over a base of water-sorted glacial drift." According to the U.S. Department of Agriculture, the soils in the area "on the whole, are responsive to good soil management" but usually require intensive use of commercial fertilizers even after clearing, for profitable yields.

The growing season in the area is slightly more than 100 days. However, because there is almost no darkness and an intensive amount of sunshine between June and July, farmers have been able to produce spectacularly over-sized vegetables. At farm fairs, it is not unusual to see cabbages the size of basketballs.

The average annual rainfall in the area is about 15 inches; average temperature in July is about 58° F. and about –12° F. in January. The extremes of temperature range from about 90° F. in summer to –40° F. in winter.

Tanana Valley

Agriculture in the Tanana Valley, experts agree rather enthusiastically, has a "promising future." With Fairbanks as its major trading center, its future rests primarily on continued population growth around Fairbanks and continuance of active military installations nearby. At present, most of the successful commercial and part-time farms, about 150 in all, lie in a northerly direction outside Fairbanks. But at least 300,000 arable acres available for homesteading lie in a southerly direction, bordered by Big Delta on the east and Nenana on the west.

Of the farms now operating in the area, however, perhaps no more than a score may be considered commercial; of these, only two are large dairy farms.

Most of the available farm lands are at least 2,500 feet to a mile from the nearest access road. Consequently, every newly built road, even a dirt "trail" leading off a secondary black-top, causes a rush for homesteads.

Many homestead farms in the area, however, were obtained long before there were roads near them. Those with true pioneering spirit and a strong desire to farm in Alaska do not mind clearing their own roads to their homesteads. It is not unusual on weekends to see entire families of homesteaders swinging axes, using chain saws, some with bulldozers, building roads to their homesteads. Once, a former U.S. Army civilian engineer stationed near Fairbanks staked a homestead in order to have some "fun" as a part-time farmer and eventually have a rural residence. With the help of his wife, he began by bulldozing a road of more than three miles to reach his homestead. He enjoyed the work so much that he ultimately resigned his Army job and became a full-time farmer. Incidentally, after he had built the road, others rushed in to claim adjacent homesteads.

The products.

Farmers in the Tanana Valley area have earned a total of about $525,000 annually from all their livestock and vegetable products. As in the Matanuska Valley, they rely heavily on milk and potatoes for cash products. Average total annual income for milk is about $152,000, and about $230,000 for potatoes. Also, as in the Matanuska Valley, other cash products consist of: cabbage, lettuce, carrots, celery, radishes, eggs, poultry, beef, and pork.

Generally, whatever can be grown in the Matanuska Valley can be grown in the Tanana. But experts believe that a real potential for the Tanana lies in the production of cereals. This potential is said to exist because it may prove easier, hence less expensive, to grow and harvest cereals in the Tanana Valley, and with improved transportation these cereals may be sold to other farmers in the Matanuska and Kenai areas.

Soils and climate.

One of the principal features of climate in the Tanana Valley is the almost complete absence of wind at any time of the year, particularly during the winter and summer. It is, however, a comparatively dry area, with an average annual rainfall of less than 12 inches;

consequently, farmers have to practice their best techniques for conservation of water. The growing season is about 100 days. But during the summer the Tanana, as is the Matanuska, is blessed with continuous sunshine, day and "night," accelerating growth enormously.

Average temperature in July is 60° F., −12° F. in January. The extremes of temperature range from over 100° F. in summer to −40° F. in winter.

The soils range from coarse sand to very fine sand, and the hills near the valley are composed of silt loam. As a rule, farmers employ commercial fertilizers intensively to get their best yields.

Many farmers maintain livestock in the Tanana, but it is tough and costly because the winters are longer and by far more sereve than those of south central Alaska. Tanana farmers must put in large quantities of winter feed. This accounts for the fact that the cash crop of potatoes is more important than milk.

THE KENAI PENINSULA

Compared with the cash products of Matanuska and the Tanana, the Kenai Peninsula is agriculturally insignificant. The population of the Peninsula is small (about 5,000) and there are relatively few farms. The exact number of farms is not known, but there are perhaps no more than 100, most operating on a part-time basis and nearly all of them very small. The total acreage cleared for agriculture has been estimated at 2,000.

But the future of the Peninsula is bright because it has become increasingly popular for summer residences and there is a good chance for population and industrial growth stimulated by recent oil and gas explorations, discoveries, and pipeline installations. In addition, it is less expensive to clear land on the Peninsula because much of it is low, open land with a good grass cover; and the area has only begun to feel the benefits of the recent opening of the Sterling Highway, which connects the Peninsula with Anchorage and has made it easier for Peninsula farmers to compete in the Anchorage market with Matanuska farmers.

A highly significant tribute to the future and potential of the Kenai is the fact that the State of Alaska has "selected" all the Federal public domain land there, which means that the entire Kenai public domain is closed to all forms of settlement, including homesteading, under Federal land laws. Eventually, formal title to Kenai land will pass to the state and the state will dispose of land in accordance with its own programs and policies. Most likely, choice lands will be offered at public sales, auctions, or through some form of "controlled" homesteading, to be certain that only bona fide farmers get the arable lands.

Just before statehood, the Interior Department's Office of Territories published the following pertinent report on the farm land potential of the Kenai:

> Some of the better potential agricultural lands of Alaska are situated in the western portion of the Kenai Peninsula, between Kachemak Bay and the Kasilof River. On the basis of reconnaissance surveys it has been estimated that 204,708 acres of bench and bottom land in the Kenai lowland are sufficiently smooth and well drained to be used for crop. Lands best suited for general crop production, totaling 41,415 acres, are mainly north and northeast of Homer, north and south of Ninilchik, south and southwest of Kasilof, and south and southeast of Kenai village. Areas suitable for limited general crop production and livestock farming, totaling 90,760 acres, are distributed irregularly through most of the western coastland belt.
>
> Tracts suitable for forage crop production and grazing, totaling 72,533 acres, comprise mainly range lands in the Caribou Hills to the south-central portion.

Dairying and raising of beef cattle are said to represent the best potential for agriculture on the Kenai Peninsula, especially in view of the great rate of growth anticipated for Anchorage.

The products.

Farmers on the Kenai are able to raise the same cash livestock and vegetable products as those in the Matanuska and Tanana valleys. The annual average cash yield for all products has been less than $150,000, with milk accounting for $20,000; potatoes, $20,000; eggs, $60,000.

One enterprising couple has found that berries grow extremely well on the Kenai and have a unique flavor. In fact, over the years they have created a sizable mail-order business, selling Kenai berries to thousands of customers in every state and some foreign lands.

Soils and climate.

Of all the agricultural areas in Alaska, the Kenai Peninsula enjoys the most moderate climate. Temperate extremes range from 70° F. in summer to –7° F. in winter. The growing season is about

110 days. During the growing season, daily temperatures, thanks to maritime influences, do not vary much, ranging from a low of about 40° F. to 60° F.

Prevalent soils are silt and fine sandy loams, which produce good crops of potatoes, hardy vegetables and hay without the intensive use of commercial fertilizers. Land near Homer, however, has been evaluated as "only fair to good" for crops and as best for stock raising and dairying.

SOUTHEASTERN ALASKA

Opportunities for large-scale farming and homesteading are most limited in southeastern Alaska, especially near comparatively populous areas. The chief handicap to farming in this area is a lack of good highway transportation. Transportation, being mostly by air or water, or a combination of both, is now costly or time-consuming.

The number of farms in southeastern Alaska is not known, but most are small, part-time truck farms and quite a few are said to be unprofitable. According to the U.S. Department of Agriculture, "There were several large and long-established dairy farms near large towns [in southeastern Alaska] but they faced increasing Stateside competition. Dairies are now found only near Juneau and Petersburg."

At one time, fur farming was a thriving agricultural enterprise in southeastern Alaska but competition from Canadian and Great Lakes fur farmers has all but killed it.

Anything grown in other parts of Alaska can be grown in southeastern Alaska. However, this is the only known area where it is possible to grow tomatoes and peppers outdoors, as well as cherries and cane fruit. Southeastern Alaska's strawberries are also known for their unique flavor and color, and abundant yield; but no significant attempt has been made to produce strawberries commercially, probably on account of the high costs of harvest labor, storage, and transportation.

This area has the longest frost-free season in Alaska. In some places the growing season ranges from 150 to 200 days; the average is about 120 days. But there is a great amount of rain. There may be as much as 35 to 40 inches of rain during the growing season alone. There is also persistent fog and cloudiness, which materially reduce the amount of sunshine during growing periods.

Although there is much optimism regarding the future for agriculture in other parts of Alaska, there are few who hold high hopes for farming in southeastern Alaska. Until southeastern Alaska develops an extensive network of highways, perhaps linked with a ferry network, there is no reason to expect any significant growth in farm opportunities in this area.

THE ISLANDS

When speaking of agricultural opportunities on the islands, Alaskans refer to islands in the western portion of the Gulf of Alaska, in the Alaska Peninsula, and in the Aleutian chain. The largest of these islands, Kodiak Island, on Shelikof Strait east of the Alaska Peninsula, and some smaller islands in the Aleutians, have recently attracted attention as possible ranching sites. On these islands, there have been several small but successful cattle and sheep ranching enterprises.

Ranchers have been selling beef, slaughtered locally, to markets in nearby villages and small towns and to the armed forces. They also have been selling beef in the Anchorage market, in spite of the complexities and high cost of transportation. Sheep ranchers have been shipping wool to Oregon, also at a profit; the type of wool produced is said to be very much in demand.

The total population of all the islands is estimated at no more than 10,000. The U.S. Department of Agriculture reports that ranchers on these islands have about 14,000 sheep and 1,700 cattle.

Most of the cattle are on Kodiak and are grassfed. On other islands, livestock are fed at beach sites on kelp, which has proven to be a nutritious roughage. However, most of the islands from Kodiak westward have growths of grass and plants deemed ample and suitable for livestock grazing. Nearly all experts agree that the development of a large efficient slaughterhouse and cold storage on Kodiak, plus improved means of transportation, could open the island to large-scale commercial cattle ranching with profitable beef markets in Anchorage and possibly Fairbanks. Presently, the naval base on Kodiak is the ranchers' number-one beef customer.

Grazing land on these islands is available on a lease and permit basis from the U.S. Bureau of Land Management; the BLM will negotiate long-term (twenty-year) leases, with grazing charges based on what the BLM calls "economic and physical factors commensurate with the animal-carrying capacity of the lands within the lease

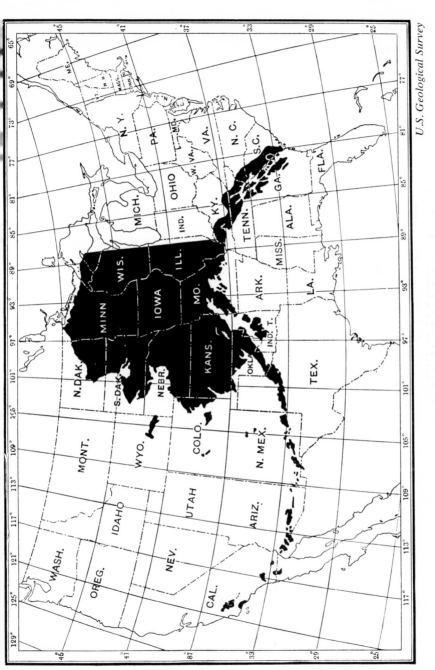

Map showing the relative size of Alaska and the United States.

U.S. Geological Survey

Anchorage, Alaska's largest city, with the beautiful Chugach Range in the background. A busy, modern city, with more airplanes per capita than any other in the world, and Cook Inlet's forty-foot tides washing its front door, it is also headquarters for the Alaska Railroad, for the building of which the town was established in 1914.

Division of Economic and Tourist Development

Ward W. Wells

A fur auction in the streets of Anchorage.

Private housing development, typical of recent construction, financed by First National Bank of Anchorage.

Mac's Foto Service, Anchorage

Alaskan Air Command

Lake Hood, foreground, and Lake Spenard, the famous seaplane base at the Anchorage International Airport. More than 200 planes use these lakes as their base, using floats in summer and skis in winter. There is also a landing strip (alongside the canal) for planes on wheels. A separate tower (right of landing strip) controls traffic on the two lakes.

Eskimos have some fun with a blanket toss during a holiday in Anchorage.

Ward W. Wells

Ward W. Wells

A dog-sled race in the streets of Anchorage. For the event, the snow had to be carted in and laid down.

Serrated mountains of the Chilkat Range — Seen from the Haines Highway along the Chilkat River in Alaska, this highly mineralized country is beautifully spectacular with peaks and glaciers. The Haines Highway connects with the Alaska Highway.

Division of Economic and Tourist Development

Upper Russian Lake, typical of the many scenic lakes on the Kenai Peninsula just 45 minutes from Anchorage by small plane. Trout, rainbows and Dolly Vardens are found in abundance.

Taku Glacier is an interesting spectacle even to ships' officers who see it often.

Modern gold dredging near Fairbanks, Alaska. The giant dredges scoop up gravel, extract the gold and deposit the tailings as they ear their way up the creeks. Here, a hydraulic giant is directed against the overburden of frozen muck which must be washed off ahead of the dredge operation.

Division of Economic and Tourist Development

Aerial view of University of Alaska. It has a 2,200 acre campus, and is co-ed.

University of Alaska

Two ships work cargo at Skagway's terminal, the White Pass and Yukon Route motorship *Clifford J. Rogers* and the Alaska Line motorship *Susitna*.

Almost to the summit of Deer Mountain, near Ketchikan. Hikers and mountain climbers find an infinite variety of terrain in Alaska.

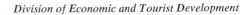

Alaska's first pulp mill—the multi-million-dollar plant just six miles north of Ketchikan, has been operating since 1954. The plant is one of the most modern in the world and produces a basic pulp for rayon products. Alaska's thickly forested islands and mainland areas make lumbering and pulp a major industry in the 49th State.

Timber and fishing provide the economy of Ketchikan, Alaska. Most of this southeastern portion of the state is incorporated in Tongass National Forest, and under the supervision of the U.S. Forestry Department the dense crop of trees is harvested for pulp and lumber. Part of Ketchikan's fishing fleet is visible in the foreground.

Division of Economic and Tourist Development

The prosperous fishing port of Wrangell is seen through the spars of the Alaska Steamship Company motorship *Susitna* as she approaches for a port landing.

Fishing craft loll in the sun in Wrangell's small boat harbor.

Edwin Crittenden

Modern church architecture in Alaska. St. Mary's Episcopal Church, Anchorage.

An elementary school at Inlet View.

Phil Fein & Associates

Edwin Crittenden

House of the president of the University of Alaska.

"Knobhill," the home of Bob Atwood, publisher of the Anchorage *Times*.

Mac's Foto Service, Anchorage

Cleaning day's catch taken from icy Naknek River at Alaskan Air Command Recreation Camp near King Salmon. G.I. fishermen land grayling, rainbow trout and Dolly Varden, while furnishing the U.S. Fish and Wildlife Service with much valuable information.
Alaskan Air Command

A 3,400-pound load of jade, worth thousands of dollars, arrives at Pier 42, Seattle, Washington, home of the Alaska Steamship Company. These man-size gems, from Kotzebue, Alaska were cut down to sizes suitable for commercial use.

Alaska Steamship Company

These little seaplanes provide the only transportation available for many communities in Southeastern Alaska. They move everything that is moved—children to school, the sick and injured to hospitals, hunters and fishermen to hidden places where game and fish are there for the taking, as well as equipment and supplies of every kind.

Division of Economic and Tourist Development

area." In short, BLM's rates for grazing leases are generally designed to provide incentive for the economic development and utilization of the islands. Free-use permits are also issued to those who may want to maintain livestock for domestic use.

A major problem on Kodiak, however, is the prevalence of a notorious, aggressive, voracious predator, the Kodiak bear. These predators kill many cattle in spite of protective measures by ranchers. But the ranchers are forbidden to use guns. They are not permitted to kill the bears for any reason, even if a bear should be caught in the act of ripping cattle to shreds. The situation has become a source of friction, almost bordering feuding, between ranchers and agents of the U.S. Fish and Wildlife Service, who are as determined to preserve the Kodiak bear as some other Americans are devoted to the preservation of our national symbol, the bald eagle.

Climate on the islands is under maritime influences, of course, and is therefore mild, as well as wet and foggy. But many islands are treeless, bare, rugged, and windswept. Some islands in the Aleutian chain lay bare to the most severe windstorms known in North America.

There is some truck gardening on a few of the larger islands, including Kodiak. But as a rule the soils on most of the islands contain considerable raw organic matter. Crop farming is considered difficult, sometimes impossible.

At one time, about thirty years ago, it had been proven possible to graze reindeer on the islands, as well as in the more northern Arctic regions of Alaska. The noted explorer, Vilhjalmur Stefansson, once said that Alaskans could readily pasture great herds of reindeer, which would make excellent meat and might prove popular with epicures in other states. But plans to experiment more extensively with reindeer grazing never materialized. No one knows why. As is the story for many aspects of Alaska's history, objective evidence is lacking. But Stefansson provided a hint in an obscure reference to political influences. He said, ". . . attempts to popularize Alaska reindeer meat in the States . . . promising some success, met with violent opposition from the cattlemen of the northwest and therefore were abandoned." Stefansson gave no further explanation. Under Federal law, today, however, only natives of Alaska (Indians, Eskimos, Aleuts) may pasture reindeer. Some experts in Alaska still feel that reindeer ranching may have a commercial potential for Alaska, assuming Federal permission to graze reindeer commercially is given to those who may have the capital and knowledge to popularize reindeer meat, like the Alaskan king crab, as a uniquely Alaskan delicacy for gourmet restaurants and households in the U.S.

GREENHOUSES IN ALASKA

There are numerous greenhouses throughout Alaska, but very few, perhaps no more than a dozen, may be called "commercial" in that the products are sold profitably on a large scale. Most of the greenhouses range from about 50 to 150 square feet and are concentrated among farmers in the Anchorage and Fairbanks area.

Heating of greenhouses is unduly expensive. Artificial lighting is necessary during the long periods of darkness in the fall and winter, and electricity rates are usually high. Most greenhouses are operated as hobbies, to start flowers, or to raise cucumbers and tomatoes for domestic use; but in these instances no consideration is given to costs.

The use of greenhouses in Alaska for large-scale commercial production is largely unexplored. With one or two notable exceptions, greenhouse owners have done little or no experimenting in commercial greenhouse operations, such as finding ways and means to reduce costs and promote markets for greenhouse-grown vegetables. Tomatoes and cucumbers, for instance, are fairly expensive in Alaska, and the market for these is extremely limited. But there is some evidence that a market can be created with a greenhouse product.

One man whose greenhouse success has attracted attention is Harley D. Hurst, a Federal employee recently turned farmer, near Fairbanks. Mr. Hurst has a homestead potato farm on which he has built his own one-third acre, plastic-covered greenhouse, the largest in Alaska. He raises nothing but tomatoes in the greenhouse, and everything he has learned about greenhouses and growing tomatoes came from his persistent trips to the library. But he has actually created a market for tomatoes in Fairbanks and he told me that he manages to sell at a profit every tomato he can raise.

Two excellent booklets have been published by the University of Alaska Extension Service on the subject of planning and managing greenhouses in Alaska. These are: *Bulletin 804, Bulletin 801,* published in 1958 and 1955, respectively, available without charge from the Extension Service, University of Alaska, Fairbanks.

THE PROBLEMS

In addition to the problems specific to the various farm areas of Alaska, certain problems are basic to the future of all Alaskan agriculture.

The economics of marketing is perhaps the most basic problem. When you consider, for example, the vast amount of still-unfarmed arable land in Alaska and the fact that Alaskans still import most of their agricultural products, you are apt to conclude that Alaska abounds in farming opportunities. But agricultural experts in Alaska do not think so. They believe that Alaska cannot economically support many more farmers because the markets for Alaskan-grown products have not been fully developed, and the techniques of marketing have not been efficiently exploited.

Alaskan farmers could easily triple their present production. But they can't and won't. Speaking of this, Mr. H. P. Gazaway, head of the marketing and economics unit of the Alaska Experimental Station at Palmer, said:

"Production is no longer the major problem of Alaskan farmers. There are now enough farms, cleared land, machinery and equipment, production experience, and know-how to produce a $10,-000,000 crop rather than the $3,000,000 one.

"Adequate performance in purchasing, processing and marketing are now more of a limiting factor in agricultural expansion than production."

As a matter of fact, due to undeveloped markets, Alaskan farmers have been known on occasion to "over produce." In recent years, there have been potato price wars between the major farm markets, Matanuska and Tanana. During these wars the farmers of one group would attempt to "dump" their products in the markets of the other. Potatoes have been practically given away or destroyed.

Politically, no real effort has been made to control production and Alaskan farmers do not participate in any price-support programs, nor do they seem to desire price support. "The Alaskan farmer," said Bert Stimple, "is fiercely independent. If he weren't, he wouldn't be here. He'd be an Oklahoma farmer."

Another major problem in developing Alaska's markets is the nutritional habits of Alaskans.

Getting people to change habits of diet is difficult anywhere in the world. It is no less difficult in Alaska. At one time, Alaskans did not drink much fresh milk because it was expensive. Fresh milk is still comparatively expensive, but ever since the last war Alaska has managed to increase its consumption of milk—but largely of the processed variety, powdered, concentrated, and condensed. Consequently, Alaskans have cultivated a taste for processed milk and they turn to it even when prices of fresh milk are competitive. As a result, more than 70 per cent of the milk consumed by Alaskans is still "imported"—although Alaskan farmers could easily step up production of fresh milk and reduce prices further as a result of increased production.

A "political" problem that may have more significance for the future than the present, although it is now a source of difficulty, may be the homestead laws. Federal homestead laws in Alaska are outdated. In many instances it is not economically feasible for a farmer to establish a successful enterprise on the 160 acres which are legally allowed to homesteaders. Farmers who need to expand usually have to buy additional land privately, sometimes from an adjoining homesteader, at a greatly inflated price. Considerable friction is generated when it develops, as it often does, that the adjoining homesteader is not truly a farmer and never intended to become one, but is going through the motions of farming in order to fulfill the minimum legal requirements under which he may obtain title to the land.

Sorely needed in Alaska is a revision of the homestead law to compel the classification of land as suitable for agriculture, and then to permit the disposal of such lands only to genuine farmers possessing the desire, know-how and capital to create a successful farm out of raw land—as is done in the "lower 48" under a program of homestead disposals of the Bureau of Reclamation. However, the probability of such legislative reform seems remote. There would be a political storm. Homesteading, as a lark or adventure, or as an opportunity to get some of Uncle Sam's land for speculation or rural residences, is far too popular among far too many Alaskan voters.

THE FUTURE AND THE HOPES

In sum, farming in Alaska today is not for the timid, the weak, the cynical, skeptical and despairing kind, nor for those who want to strike it rich overnight, nor for those without vision and imagination.

Newcomers who want seriously to farm in Alaska are most welcome and will find a cordial, hospitable reception awaiting them among their farm neighbors. But as one of Alaska's agricultural leaders has said, "If you can't make a success of farming in your own backyard, you'd better not try it in Alaska."

Plainly, those who come to farm in Alaska should come prepared to work hard and to invest cash as well as their own labors. It has been estimated that a successful commercial farm in Alaska entails an investment of about $10,000 for each 1,000 hens in poultry farming; $2,500 per cow in dairy farming; and $2,000 per acre for potato farming. These investments would represent the cost of obtaining land, buildings, equipment, livestock, and supplies. Included in the cost of land would be about $100 to $200 per acre for clearing.

On the other hand, such investment costs should not appear too awesome because Alaska is still the land of the pioneer. A farm may be developed gradually, and investments may be made gradually and costs may be reduced by those who are prepared to do much of the clearing and construction work themselves.

The economic, social, and political problems of Alaska's farmers —their marketing obstacles, their homesteading difficulties, their battle with soil and climate—are neither permanent nor insoluble.

Every passing year brings new knowledge, new people, new capital, new ideas, new industrial potential—all part of Alaska's constantly changing society. The process of change will create new agricultural opportunities, incentives, and techniques. The great influx of newcomers may very well bring not only new markets for Alaska, but changing markets—a market, for instance, in which there may be greater consumption of fresh milk, thus stimulating greater production of fresh milk and perhaps new opportunities for dairy farming.

There will surely be investments in processing plants and storage, for potatoes, for eggs, for beef, and grains, and with these changes there will be new markets and new opportunities for increased production.

Much of Alaska's present farm success may be attributed to research and experimentation. In the past, a good deal of this research and experimentation was empirical, or hit and miss. Today, Alaskan agriculture benefits vastly from scientific research and experimentation, which is being conducted at an increasing rate by state as well as Federal agencies.

There is now a veritable library of informative booklets, reports, and brochures on almost every conceivable phase of farm life in

Alaska. There are booklets offering advice on soil, on what can and should be grown, what cannot be grown, on problems of farm sanitation and construction, and farm financing. There are even recipe booklets for farm housewives, passing on cooking tips and recipes for dishes that are uniquely Alaskan. Typical is a booklet, *Getting a Start in Dairying in Alaska,* which tells a prospective dairy farmer all but how to scramble his eggs in the morning.

Most of these extremely useful and important research publications are available without charge to anyone, whether within or without Alaska. A list of the publications available may be obtained free of charge from the Alaska Agricultural Experiment Station and Extension Service, University of Alaska, Fairbanks; the Extension Service will also answer specific questions regarding farming or farm problems in Alaska and will refer information seekers to authoritative sources.

Finally, there are several state and state-Federal agencies which offer financial assistance to farmers, but much of this assistance is based on loans for farm residences, farm equipment and supplies, and farm expansion. Virtually all loans are made only to those who have established themselves as farmers or farm homesteaders. Official loan aid is rarely given merely for the purpose of starting a farm, or buying a farm. Many Alaskan farmers have had financial aid, and this can be expected to increase in the future.

Generally, Alaska's farmers are filled with much hope for a better future. Most see not only an opportunity for an expansion of Alaskan agriculture to satisfy domestic consumption, but also opportunities to develop products which are distinctively Alaskan, to be sold to newly developed markets in other states, as, for example, Long Island ducklings and Idaho potatoes have found lucrative markets everywhere.

But to all would-be farmers in Alaska, the farmers of Alaska now speak as one in saying:

Don't uproot yourself entirely from your present home or job. First, visit Alaska to talk with farmers, to talk with experts at the Soil Conservation Service, to visit the Research and Experiment Station at Palmer, to see farm lands for yourself and, in general, to be reasonably certain you can be happy in Alaska and can make a go of farming. The farmers of Alaska welcome you to share the future with them; but they believe that as a minimum you should not arrive in Alaska without a return ticket and a home to go back to.

CHAPTER 11

BUSINESS OPPORTUNITIES IN ALASKA

"The oldtime Alaskan who made the country what it is was a man who made business where there had never been business before."
Bob Reeve, President, Reeve-Aleutian Airways

IT HAS BEEN ESTIMATED THAT ONE-FIFTH OF ALL AMERICAN families change their places of residence each year, usually moving to another state. Traditionally, the movement has been westward and more recently south (Florida). But in the past two decades a northward movement has been added to the pattern—Alaska. Between 1940-1960, with respect to net population increases resulting from migration, only four other states (California, Arizona, Nevada, Florida) have exceeded Alaska in the rate of population gain.

But there is a significant *difference in the nature* of Alaska's net population increase. Nearly all who settle in Alaska are comparatively youthful and have come to the 49th State, not to bask in warmer climate while collecting pension checks, but to grow with the state, to seek new opportunities. Those who remain learn that the streets of Alaska are not paved with get-rich-quick schemes, nor are they listed in the "business opportunities" section of classified newspaper advertising. An opportunity in Alaska has to be hunted down, or built up from an idea, sometimes "stumbled" over.

In any event, those who have made their fortunes in Alaska have worked hard and have often endured personal sacrifices; and those who seek to make their fortunes in Alaska can expect more of the same—hard work, sacrifice, enterprise, ingenuity, tempered by a sense of destiny and a sense of humor.

Well known to Alaskans is the story of a former "bush pilot," tough but cheery and friendly Bob Reeve, who arrived in Alaska about a generation ago, while in his twenties, with barely enough cash to pay for a week's lodging. In a small rented airplane, he started flying passengers and cargo into areas as yet unopened by commercial carriers. To do so, Mr. Reeve often had to risk his life, making landings and takeoffs where only dog sleds had travelled before, to prove that it could be done. Today, Bob Reeve owns an airline and is one of Alaska's upper-income entrepreneurs. His struggle against adversities, however, lasted more than twenty years.

On a somewhat less spectacular scale is the story of a prosperous Anchorage retailer who said that he and his family lived in a one-room log cabin and subsisted almost exclusively on canned K-rations for more than a year while he made the transition from wage earner to businessman.

As a new state, a dynamic state, Alaska's needs for goods and services are constantly changing or expanding. Sometimes it takes a little imagination to discover a business opportunity in this changing pattern. More often than not such discoveries are made by comparative newcomers, people who arrive in Alaska and have fresh perspective.

In 1953, Mrs. Jane Reed, a former Californian, had settled in Anchorage after accompanying her construction-worker husband to several small towns in Alaska. The sight of a large and new library in Anchorage suddenly reminded her that Alaskans are among the most avid readers she had ever known. She decided to open the kind of bookstore that is seldom seen these days in the U.S. —a real book store, *sans* drug counters, *sans* greeting cards—nothing but books!

She began with a very small shop in the heart of town, around the corner from the library! In other American cities, opening a bookstore near the town library might seem about as enterprising as trying to sell green stamps in front of a supermarket giving them away. But now Mrs. Reed owns two book stores. Her second one is directly across the street from the library, almost as large as the library itself, certainly as large and as modern as any to be found anywhere in the U.S., including New York's Fifth Avenue.

In fact, the last time I saw Mrs. Reed was in the huge sub-basement of her second store where she was busy—in her own ultra-modern office, complete with electric typewriters and streamlined steel office furnishings—laying plans for an additional expansion, converting the sub-basement and stocking it, too, with books.

A few years ago in Fairbanks, Miss Doris Dooley, fresh from her home in the State of Washington, was surprised to find no popcorn vending machines in the movie houses, bus terminals, and other public places. She ordered some machines and popcorn from the Outside and went into business, even to the extent of learning how to service and maintain the vending machines herself. Within a relatively short time, her business expanded substantially in other directions, *e.g.,* soda-dispensing machines. Today, she is one of the busiest business people in Fairbanks and has several full-time assistants.

A former aircraft assembly-line worker from California, while on a vacation trip to Alaska, was tremendously impressed by the growth of suburbs around Anchorage and was equally impressed by the apparent lack of private garbage-collection services in the suburbs. He returned to California, sold his home, went back to Alaska with his family, made a small bank loan, and started a garbage-collection business. Within a year, his enterprise expanded threefold.

Perhaps most typical is the story of Keath and Peggy Heathley, a charming, amiable young couple with three lovely, blonde school-age daughters. Keath, originally from St. Louis, had been stationed in the Aleutians with the Navy during World War II. After his discharge from service, he met and married Peggy, from Tucson, Arizona, and lived in California for awhile. But Keath longed to return to Alaska, where he had fallen in love with the outdoors, especially Alaska's plethora of hunting and fishing opportunities. A building contractor by trade and experience, Keath went into business in Anchorage, on a small scale, building custom homes, while Peggy took a job as an accountant.

One day, about six years ago, the Heathleys took one of their customary Sunday family auto trips to see the sights. This time they went down to Portage Glacier. They had been there many times before, but always found the glacier an intriguing sight. The children—like many adult visitors—loved the idea that they could walk up to the glacier and chip off a piece of ice that may be tens of thousands of years old, beautifully aquamarine in color. But on this particular trip the Heathleys suddenly realized that it was a comparatively static experience. There was nothing else to do but look at the glacier. There was no place to buy a picture post card, no place to browse among souvenirs, no place to sit down and relax with the family, have a cup of coffee, a sandwich, an ice cream; no place to mingle with other visitors, get friendly, ask where they're from—an Alaskan social tradition. But why couldn't there be such a place at Portage, perhaps a lodge?

The Heathleys investigated and learned that through the Forest Service they could apply for a lease of land facing the glacier, where they could set up a combination coffee and souvenir shop. (Portage Glacier is in a national forest, and in many other national forests throughout the U.S. many Americans have obtained a variety of business concessions, which attract millions of travellers every year.)

Before long, the Heathleys obtained their lease, under which they were required to pay an annual retnal of $50 for the land, plus ½ of 1 per cent of the gross income of their business. They gathered their savings, obtained a small loan, and went to work. Together, working themselves, stone by stone, sometimes with the aid of their children swinging paint brushes, they erected a lovely, colorful coffee bar and souvenir shop. They also placed on sale picture post cards of the glacier and representative products of authentic Alaskan handcrafts. (Among their first customers were Groucho Marx and Bob Hope.)

To be sure, the Heathleys had their troubles. In fact, one trouble almost proved disastrous. An unusual windstorm had swept their structure away before it had been completed. They had to start from scratch and with a new loan. But when they finally opened for business in 1957, they served 20,000 customers. In the following years, business increased at the rate of 20 to 30 per cent annually. Their establishment today has been valued at a minimum of $500,000, and already they have launched plans for expansion, an overnight lodge.

Watching the Heathleys operate their business, with their vivacious blonde daughters behind the counter, serving coffee, selling souvenirs, blithely mingling with customers, is to see a portrait of human happiness in motion. To top it, Mr. Heathley has been able to return to his principal occupation, building custom homes in Anchorage.

His wife runs the business but has four full-time employees to assist her.

These contrasting vignettes serve to illustrate what is perhaps the most distinctive feature of Alaska's business world—namely, that a person with little more than nerve and enterprise, and the willingness to withstand personal hardships if necessary, can strive for success in Alaska and can do so without having had previous business experience and without the social pressure of trying to keep up with the Joneses. If you want to try to make a go of it, even while living on K-rations in a one-room log cabin, Alaskans will say, in effect: *Go ahead! Good luck. More power to you.*

But those concerned with a business future in Alaska, or doing business from the Outside with Alaskans, should be familiar with the industries and resources of Alaska and the problems of doing business in Alaska. Such familiarity is indispensable to an objective and balanced appraisal of business opportunities, business ideas, and Alaska's business future. But first it is important to review two basic influences on Alaska's present and future business opportunities: (1) Population growth, and (2) Alaska's economic geography.

POPULATION GROWTH—A BASE FOR BUSINESS

In almost any state, a growing population stimulates new business and industry. This has been consistently true of Alaska.

Historically, the volume of business in Alaska has expanded in almost direct proportion to the growth in population. In 1952, when Alaska's population was about 190,000, the gross volume of business was approximately $322,000,000 for some 1,300 business establishments. Five years later when the population had spurted to 210,000 the gross volume of business climbed to more than $566,000,000 and there were more than 1,600 business establishments. This relationship between population growth and business expansion continues in Alaska and undoubtedly will continue for many years.

In terms of future business opportunities in Alaska, it is significant, therefore, not only that Alaska's population is still growing but that it is growing at a greater rate than that of the U.S. as a whole. It is equally significant that much of Alaska's population "explosion" has been largely due to an influx of newcomers, *cheechakos* and their families, seeking new homes, new services, buying more goods, anxious to remain in Alaska.

It is the consensus of official and private forecasts that by 1970 the increase in Alaska's population should exceed 50 per cent, more than double the 1950-60 rate of growth, almost triple the rate of growth for the U.S. as a whole.

Marketing experts of the well-known firm of Benton and Bowles, whose forecasts are bread and butter to their business clients, have estimated that by 1968 Alaska's population will be about 376,000, and by 1978 will be about 1,000,000. In evaluating Alaska's potential as a business market, Benton and Bowles indicated prospective business growth in the 49th State by equating Anchorage with Reno, Nevada, in 1958; with Fort Wayne, Indiana, in 1968; and with Providence, Rhode Island (or Denver, Colorado) by 1978.

It is also important to remember that Alaska is a youthful state and will remain that way. In an analysis of Alaska's population, experts of the Metropolitan Life Insurance Co. have concluded that by 1970 almost 70 per cent of Alaska's population will consist of people between the ages of 18 to 64, and there will be a *decrease* in the proportion of persons over 65; whereas, in the over-all U.S. population during the same period there will be a large increase in the over-65 group, and those between the ages of 18 to 64 will constitute only half the population.

Population growth in Alaska, therefore, quantitatively and qualitatively, is almost certain to generate many new business opportunities, particularly in the areas of consumer goods and services, housing, and recreation. With a substantially younger population than any other state, Alaska will perhaps have a special need for such businesses as: restaurants, bowling alleys, roller skating rinks, music schools, private nurseries for pre-school-age children, day camps, barbershops, beauty parlors, hotels and motels, gas stations, insurance and real estate agencies, investment brokers, travel agents, travel attractions, roadside refreshment stands, and appliance repair shops.

The do-it-yourself proclivities of Alaska's eager, youthful population should also create opportunities for establishments dealing largely in unfinished furniture, paints, hardware, and the rental of household and garden tools and equipment.

Opportunities will undoubtedly develop also for businesses that traditionally operate on low markups, volume production or rapid turnover, such as retail chain stores and large supermarkets. As a matter of fact, the F. W. Woolworth Co. and Safeway stores recently opened their first units in Alaska, and some discount stores have met with success in Anchorage.

HIDDEN VALUES IN ALASKA'S ECONOMIC GEOGRAPHY

Apart from predicting population growth, some Alaskan boosters have forecast great industrial growth on the basis of comparisons between Alaska and the highly industrialized countries of Scandinavia, *viz.,* Sweden and Norway. The comparisons are highly optimistic because Sweden and Norway have climates and natural resources similar to Alaska. But such similarities must be viewed with historical perspective because more significant are the *differences* between Alaska and Scandinavia.

To begin with, Sweden and Norway are more intensely populated than Alaska. Each country has only about one-quarter of the land area of Alaska. Yet Sweden has nearly 40 times as many people as Alaska, and Norway has almost 15 times as many. Also, Norway and Sweden have developed their natural resources and concomitant industrial capacities over a period of centuries, and each has had the tremendous eco-geographic advantage of being close to the "cradle of civilization," Europe, where there have been ready markets for the consumer and industrial products of Scandinavia.

It may be generations before Alaska becomes as intensely populated as Norway or Sweden. Further, it is highly improbable that industry in Alaska can be developed on the basis of adjacent markets in Canada or the continental U.S.

For the near future, industries in Alaska will have to rely largely on the *growth of markets within Alaska,* and population increase.

There is, however, a significant and generally overlooked "hidden value" in Alaska's economic geography. It is the simple fact that Alaska is much closer to important overseas foreign markets in the Pacific than any other state. The opportunity to establish in Alaska a business based on the manufacture or processing of goods for export to such markets as Asia, Australia, New Zealand, and the Philippines remains largely unexploited.

It is entirely possible, for example, to produce cement in Alaska. But nearly all of Alaska's cement—like many other products consumed in Alaska—is imported because the demand for cement within Alaska is as yet insufficient to support a large-scale processing plant in the 49th State. On the other hand, while the Philippines import large quantities of cement from California, no one has investigated the possibilities of invading the market in the Philippines with Alaskan-produced cement.

Another example is coal. Japan imports nearly 3,000,000 tons of coal from the eastern states, shipped via the Panama Canal. Yet there are huge deposits of this same type of coal in Alaska, and thus far only one company, the Jewel Ridge Coal Company of Tazwell, Virginia, has undertaken to investigate the possibilities of mining Alaskan coal for sale to Japan.

As we shall see, among the problems of doing business in Alaska are high production costs. Accordingly, anyone exploring export-business opportunities in Alaska must be concerned with determining whether the savings on shipping from Alaska can offset higher production costs. Yet, considering the large markets of Asia as incentives, Alaska's economic geography combined with efficient volume production may prove to be the formula of success for major business enterprises in Alaska.

Meanwhile, the Japanese have already "discovered" Alaska. Hardly a month passes that some Japanese business mission does not arrive in Alaska to investigate opportunities for business based on export from Alaska to Japan and other Asian nations. As one Japanese industrialist said upon his arrival in Anchorage, "The whole thing is economics and geography. Alaska is closer to Japan than California or New York."

In fact, one of the most significant industrial developments in Alaska came not long ago with the opening of a huge, modern $55,-000,000 pulp mill in Sitka, financed largely by Japanese business interests. A substantial portion of the Sitka mill's production will be shipped to the rayon and plastics industries in Japan.

Perhaps one major reason Alaska's "hidden values" have gone unnoticed in the U.S. has been Alaska's relative remoteness from the commercial and financial centers, especially Wall St. Unfortunately, it would seem that many of America's financiers and businessmen would actually need to visit Alaska in order to understand the state's potential, or merely to appreciate the fact that Alaska is not strange, foreign, or primitive and banks do not conduct their affairs around pot-belly stoves in log cabins.

A prominent Alaskan once met a well-known businessman Outside and discovered to his dismay that the businessman had hesitated to establish a branch in Alaska because he did not want to "get involved with foreign currency and export-import documents!" A banker in Alaska told me that he carries a wallet filled with photos of various Alaskan banks, in order to prove to his colleagues Outside that banks in Alaska are as modern in decor, techniques, and facilities as banks anywhere in the U.S.

Typical, perhaps, was the reaction of Arthur L. Wadsworth, vice president of Dillon, Read & Co., one of America's leading investment firms, which has been involved recently in some major industrial financing operations in Alaska. Referring to the time he had gone to witness the dedication of a pulp mill opening at Ketchikan, Mr. Wadsworth said:

> As part of a large group, I returned to Ketchikan for the dedication of the mill. This time, the representatives of three of our largest insurance companies, who had purchased Ketchikan's $36,000,000 bonds, were in the party—on their first trip to Alaska. It was a beautiful day and the mill was an inspiring sight.
>
> For all of us from New York, that was one of the most thrilling experiences we had ever had. We deal in millions of dollars and lengthy reports and documents every day, but it is very rare that we get the opportunity to see, in such tangible form, what we have helped to create.
>
> This story illustrates one of [Alaska's] greatest problems for large-scale financing of industry in Alaska. The problem is to get more people in American industry and finance to know Alaska much better.

ALASKA'S NATURAL RESOURCES

Much of any land's economic history and economic future is associated with its natural resources. In this regard, Alaska has little history but much future.

Only two of Alaska's best-known resources, gold, and fish—and more recently, pulp timber—have been exploited to any considerable extent, although the potential for mining other precious minerals and for expanding fish production is still great.

For a long time, and to some extent even now, the failure to exploit natural resources in Alaska has been attributed to the extremes of Alaska's climate and the political handicap of Alaska's Territorial status. But the latter is no longer true, and the myth of climatic extremes in Alaska is rapidly being dispelled. It is perhaps more accurate to place the blame on widespread ignorance of Alaska's natural resources. Yet it is important to understand these resources because such understanding breeds ideas not only for present business opportunities, but for future opportunities which may develop along with Alaska's growing population.

Investigation of the forest resources around Sitka, for example, gave rise to the pulp mill. Now, as the first major source of year-round employment in Sitka, the pulp mill will provide opportunities for such collateral businesses as housing, shopping centers, and service businesses (tailor shops, restaurants, recreation). Similarly the prospect of developing newly discovered oil and gas resources which, as we shall see, hold much promise for Alaska, should provide those with vision the ability to discern business opportunities on or near the Kenai Peninsula.

The report on Alaska's resources is presented here primarily as a general introduction, for the purpose of providing basic facts and perspective. A comprehensive survey of Alaska's resources would fill several volumes. Those seeking more detailed information, or answers to specific questions regarding natural resources, may find excellent and prompt assistance through one of the following: Alaska Resource Development Board, Box 2391, Juneau; The U.S. Bureau of Mines, and the U.S. Geological Survey, also in Juneau. (See also appendix.)

Mineral resources.

Although gold is one of Alaska's most celebrated mineral resources, the mining of gold is not an important activity in Alaska today. In recent years more income has been produced from Alaska's sand and gravel pits than from gold. Alaska's principal gold producer, the United States Smelting, Refining and Mining Company, actually the only large mining company in Alaska, has shut several of its gold-dredging operations in the Fairbanks area and expects to halt other operations elsewhere.

There is no doubt that more gold remains to be discovered in Alaska. Many Alaskans still prospect for gold, but usually in their spare time. However, because all gold has to be sold to the Government at a price that has remained unchanged for more than a generation, while costs and taxes have risen, there is practically no incentive to exploit Alaska's potential gold deposits. But if the price of gold should rise, it may well touch off another Klondike and with it many new collateral business opportunities in Alaska.

However, many other minerals are known to exist in Alaska. At least 31 of the 33 minerals on the Government's list of "strategic" minerals are part of Alaska's vast natural resources and are reported to exist in potentially large deposits. Among these are: oil and gas, coal, iron, lead, zinc, silver, uranium, nickel, chrome, cobalt, and copper.

In most instances, the proper exploitation of minerals involves an investment of time, money, and ingenuity not merely to locate them in commercial quantities but to extract them profitably. Except for gold, very little has been invested to mine and process minerals in Alaska, although oil and gas are now getting considerable attention, and it is possible that coal will be heavily exploited in the near future.

Professional and spare-time prospectors have staked many claims to a variety of mineral discoveries in Alaska. These same discoveries in other parts of the U.S. might be worth fortunes. But in Alaska— for the time being, at least—most claims are practically worthless, since the cost of mining ore and then shipping it Outside for processing is prohibitive. If ore processing should become a significant industry in Alaska, there will be many opportunities for prospecting.

Alert prospectors, miners, geologists and those interested in business opportunities associated with mining-town booms, would do well to watch developments in ore processing in Alaska. The establishment of major ore processing operations in Alaska could create virtually overnight the great variety of business opportunities generated by rapid industrial growth—and prospecting may well become one of the 49th State's greatest strike-it-rich lures.

Oil and gas.

The famous "black mineral" of America's rich southwest, oil, and its immediate by-product, natural gas, was first discovered in Alaska more than 25 years ago. Since then, the U.S. Geological Survey has reported indications of oil throughout Alaska. But it was not until recently that serious oil explorations began in Alaska. The first successful oil strike was made in 1957 on the Kenai Peninsula, within sight of Anchorage. Now, more than a score of American corporations have been supporting crews and equipment to wildcat Alaska's oil and gas resources, spending many millions of dollars on wages, supplies, equipment, and transportation. The impact of this spending has been felt in Anchorage and in towns on the Kenai Peninsula. Officials in Alaska are not quite prepared to call it a "boom" but it has all the earmarks of a boom lurking around the corner.

It is only a matter of time before oil and gas may do for Alaska what it has done for Oklahoma City, or Houston, Texas. In May, 1959, the Alaska State Commissioner of Mines estimated that about one-third of the 49th State is "geologically possible or favorable to petroleum development" which means refineries and pipelines for Alaska, as well as expanded over-the-road transportation. As we have noted (see p. 144) one of the most colorful and frequently profitable activities indulged in by Alaskans in all walks of life is trading in "wildcat" oil and gas leases on the Federal public domain.

Forest resources.

Alaska has two clearly defined forest areas, coastal and interior. The coastal forests, which range from southeastern Alaska (the Panhandle) to Cook Inlet, consist almost entirely of Western hemlock (about 70 per cent) and Sitka spruce (25 per cent); the remainder is mostly cedar.

The bulk of these forest lands are within the Tongass and Chugach National Forests, under the supervision of the U.S. Forest Service, which leases forest lands for commercial exploitation and also issues permits enabling settlers to obtain timber for residential purposes.

The interior forests, largely white spruce and white birch, cover an estimated 125 million acres of land under the jurisdiction of the Bureau of Land Management. Although never completely surveyed, the interior forests extend roughly from the Brooks range on the north to Norton Sound and Bristol Bay on the west, and east to the Canadian border.

The coastal forests have been commercially exploited but almost entirely for pulp, which is considered the principal economic use of these forests. Forest experts in Alaska anticipate further commercial exploitation of the coastal forests for pulp as the demand for newsprint in the U.S. increases. There may also be expanded pulp production for export to Asia, mainly Japan. New pulp mills always mean new jobs for many, stable employment, stable population— new business opportunities to service the plants and population.

Commercial exploitation of the interior forests has been negligible. The interior forests have been repeatedly ravaged by forest fires, still a major problem. Yet the potential for exploiting the interior forests for the production of finished lumber has been rated very high. Presently, almost all of Alaska's finished lumber is "imported" from the western U.S., although the white birch stands of Alaska's interior forests are considered ideal for furniture and other finished-lumber uses. A handful of sawmills has been operating in the interior forests, but most of these mills are small, individually owned and operated, sporadically employed, and inefficient. Mainly they produce rough green lumber which lacks manufacturing uniformity, and lumber dealers in Alaska are reluctant to purchase from them.

Tests made by the Forest Products Laboratory at Madison, Wisconsin, however, have shown Alaska's interior forest white birch to possess physical properties comparable with the well-known yellow birch of the East; it would make excellent lumber for fine-grade flooring, panelling, and small-dimension stock. According to a report submitted to the Secretary of the Interior as recently as 1958, a large percentage of the interior forest white birch "would be suitable for sliced or sawn veneer."

The establishment of highly productive, efficient sawmills in the interior forests would require a source of cheap power. Presently, such power is not available in the interior forests, although the potential for developing power from many streams and lakes in the interior forests is present. Some hydroelectric power has been generated through these forest water resources but chiefly for the domestic use of several small nearby towns.

State officials have been devoting considerable attention to the possibility of developing cheap hydroelectric power in the interior forests, in order to attract a sawmill industry. It is the consensus of experts that a sawmill industry could now find a considerable market for its products in fast-growing Anchorage and Fairbanks.

Fishery resources.

For years, salmon has been one of the most exploited natural resources in Alaska, although on a steadily declining level. According to a study prepared by the First National Bank of Seattle, the salmon peak for the five-year period 1953-57 was only 41 per cent of the previous five-year peak, 1934-38. In recent years, the dollar value of canned, packed, cured and frozen salmon caught in Alaska has been about $65,000,000 a year.

The other principal fish resources of Alaska are: carp, halibut, herring, clams, shrimp, sablefish, and lobster. The combined dollar value of these fish, however, represents only a small fraction of the total annual salmon product in Alaska.

Most commercial exploitation of Alaska's fishery resources takes place in Alaska's southern coastal waters by some 6,000 fishing vessels, many owned and operated by individuals. Commercial salmon fishing is permitted only in coastal waters, where it may be controlled.

Commercial fishing, especially salmon, is a volatile political subject in Alaska. There are many who believe that salmon is a dying resource and Alaska should encourage the exploitation of carp, halibut, and herring. They say these fish truly abound in the waters of Alaska and if properly exploited may well exceed by several times the total annual dollar value of salmon.

On the other hand, there is ample evidence to indicate that vast, untapped opportunities lie in the exploitation of Alaska's bottom fish resources, such as shrimp, clams, crabs, and abalone. George Sundborg, a noted authority on Alaska's resources, once told a U.S. Senate Committee on Interior and Insular Affairs (April 24, 1950): "In the categories of bottom fish, the opportunity for increased utilization is simply tremendous. We have hardly begun to utilize these fishery resources in Alaska."

This view has received further support more recently in a number of reports prepared for investment-minded readers. The *Magazine of Wall Street,* for instance, has said: "There is a great potential for the development of Alaska's other fishery resources. Varieties other than salmon have been neglected, especially bottom fish."

One man who has not neglected bottom fish, much to his firm's profit, is Lowell Wakefield, president of Wakefield's Deep Sea Trawlers of Seattle. He has promoted frozen Alaska king crab as an epicurean delight, now sold in thousands of restaurants and supermarkets throughout the U.S. The king crab, found in Alaska Peninsula bottoms and along lower Cook Inlet, ranges up to 18 lbs. and may have a five-foot claw-to-claw spread.

The Japanese have been known to fish for king crab in waters off Alaska, but the Wakefield firm was the first American commercial fishing company to explore the king crab potential, basing its efforts on research reports prepared by the U.S. Fish and Wildlife Service. Wakefield's catches, processes, markets, and promotes its own frozen king crab products. Its sales, according to a trade journal report, have "doubled" within one three-year period, "reaching 2.5 million pounds in 1957." (In 1956, a catch of 1,630,000 pounds of king crab was valued at $1,567,000.)

Hydroelectric resources.

There is no hydroelectric installation worthy of the name in Alaska. But the potential for hydroelectric power development in Alaska is staggering. Alaska can have all the electric power it will ever need. The proof lies in data gathered by the U.S. Army Corps of Engineers and the U.S. Bureau of Reclamation.

Electric power is perhaps one of Alaska's greatest needs, assuming continued growth of the state. Almost any adult who has lived a few years in Anchorage can remember when the shortage of power was so bad that auxiliary power had to be drawn from the generators of ships in the harbor. Most Anchorage residents can recall when there would be sudden brownouts, dimming of electric lights everywhere, and the standing joke was, "Well, it looks as if everyone is watching television again tonight."

No matter how much Alaskan officials may talk of the coming industrialization of Alaska, without some immediate and significant investment in electric power it is more apt to be a "creeping" industrialization than a rapid one. But developing Alaska's hydroelectric potential is no small undertaking. It would require an investment of tens of millions of dollars. There is also the problem of convincing Alaskans that such an investment will prove in the best interests of the entire state. The problem is posed as a chicken-and-egg proposition for Alaskans: Which should come first, the development of power in order to attract new industries, or the establishment first of new industries in order to have customers for the power?

Alaskan officials are confident an answer will be found. It may require, at first, Federal government financing, perhaps an Alaskan "TVA." But there are many who would prefer to see electric power developed as a private enterprise and therefore would resist "TVA" ideology.

On the other hand, a combination of Federal-state financing for hydroelectric power in Alaska may be inevitable, since private companies are not apt to invest heavily in providing a service for which there are few customers in sight, with only a hope and a prayer that customers may arrive after the power is available.

There is, however, a glimmer of hope which, if realized, may do more to hasten Alska's industrial revolution than anything now known. This is the possibility that a major aluminum company may develop a large hydroelectric installation of its own in Alaska for the purpose of making aluminum, which requires huge amounts of electricity. To do this, the company will have to import the raw material, bauxite, from which aluminum is made. The cost of shipping bauxite to Alaska, plus the generally high cost of production in Alaska, may be offset for the company by the availability of an inexpensive source of electricity. The company has been studying a tremendous amount of data and reports, but no decision has been made and may not be made for several years.

In any event, hydroelectric power is almost certain to be developed, whether by private industry or government. When this occurs there will undoubtedly be—as there was in the Tennessee Valley—many new business opportunities as a result of industries being attracted to the source of power and many new towns developing around the industries.

Another possibility, although remote now, is the development of atomic-generated power in Alaska. But in this regard, Alaska will have to await the results of continued experimentation in atomic power.

THE INDUSTRIES OF ALASKA

In order to evaluate opportunities for specific types of business in Alaska, it is important to know to what extent such businesses now exist. In this respect, however, it is equally important to remember that (1) Alaska is a growing state; (2) its natural resources remain largely unexploited; (3) generally, competition is either uninspired or non-existent.

For example: The fact that there is almost no manufacturing industry in Alaska should be related to the fact that Alaska's natural resources are almost entirely unexploited and that *future* exploitation may lead to many opportunities in manufacturing. And the fact that Alaska may seem to have many restaurants for a state its size should not deter those interested in retail and service industry opportunities, because in many of Alaska's cities and towns there may well be many opportunities for those with ideas for better or different types of restaurants.

With the above reminders, the following data on industries in Alaska should be useful.

MANUFACTURING AND PROCESSING INDUSTRIES

The closest thing to a manufacturing industry in Alaska are a few plants producing bricks and concrete and cement blocks. Almost all of Alaska's factory-type industry is engaged in the processing of "raw materials," such as the pulp mills, sawmills, and fish-canning factories. Three factors contribute to the absence of a manufacturing industry in Alaska: (1) a small domestic market; (2) the high cost of production in Alaska; (3) lack of investment capital within Alaska.

As a matter of fact, the bulk of the capital invested in Alaska's largest pulp mills and canning operations is Outside money, either American, mainly from the states of Washington and Oregon, or Japanese.

However, there is no doubt that opportunity exists for other manufacturing and processing businesses in Alaska, and the opportunity need not be hindered by the size or nature of Alaska's domestic market, nor by the high cost of production. In most instances, the high cost of production can readily be overcome by volume production and the use of modern, efficient machines and methods. New markets may be found within Alaska as well as overseas.

An example is the story of Alaska Concrete Products Co., which started in 1949 as a typically Alaskan enterprise—a small, almost one-man operation. Like other companies of its type, it used inefficient, outmoded equipment to produce blocks and pipes for wholesale and retail trade. Increasing volume often meant increasing production costs disproportionately. Consequently, it had to compete with concrete products "imported" from the West Coast. But not long ago, Alaska Concrete Products Co. managed to purchase modern machinery which made possible efficient volume production and lower costs. Today, the company employs an average of 50 people, which is big business in any Alaskan industry.

RETAIL AND SERVICE INDUSTRIES

Because Alaska is almost entirely a consuming economy, the number of business establishments in the retail and service industries is high in relation to its population. This is evident, for instance, in the fact that the number of persons employed in Alaska's wholesale and retail establishments is more than double the number employed in manufacturing and processing in Alaska; whereas for the U.S. as a whole the ratio of employment is almost the reverse.

Within the category of retail and service industries, the types of businesses proven most successful are those which deal directly with the consumer, such as restaurants, grocery stores, clothing stores, jewelry shops, hairdressing and barbershops, automobile service stations, liquor stores, furniture and appliance stores, and cocktail lounges. In most instances, stores which specialize in a product or service do well only in the major population centers of Anchorage, Fairbanks, Juneau and Ketchikan. In outlying areas, Alaskans tend to support the general-store type of business.

Some indication of the "spread" of business opportunities in the retail and service industries may be gleaned from the latest census of such businesses in Alaska:

> Food and drink stores, 300.
> Grocery stores, 102.
> General merchandising stores, 88.
> Clothing stores, 75.
> Gas stations, 41.
> New and used car dealers, 36.
> Liquor stores, 34.
> Furniture and appliance stores, 32.
> Beauty parlors, 25.
> Barbershops, 21.

There are also about 40 hotels with a total accommodation of 9,500 beds; and 18 trailer camps and motels.

To support these retail and service establishments, there are about 100 wholesale businesses. But most of the wholesale businesses are small, utilizing small warehouses and a handful of employees; and more than one-fourth of them handle only high-volume, high-turnover lines such as food and drinks.

The wholesalers' problems are that they frequently must absorb the cost of transportation to Alaska in order to compete with suppliers in Alaska's traditional "warehouse," Seattle. Food and drink wholesalers in Alaska can fare better because their volume and turnover is such that they can obtain larger discounts and prepaid shipments from Outside suppliers.

However, now that Alaska's population is growing and is becoming more stable, there is a definite need for more wholesale businesses, especially in the drug, chemicals, industrial and office equipment lines. In a recent study of Alaska's economy and market potential, the U.S. Department of Commerce's Office of Distribution said, "Prospects for the successful wholesaling of a wider variety of items [in Alaska], particularly in non-food categories, appear more promising."

It should be noted, however, that most businesses in Alaska's retail and service industries are conducted along fairly "traditional" lines. Streamlined techniques of merchandising, promotion, advertising, and publicity are virtually ignored. As a result, many of these businesses are quite vulnerable to the competition of businessmen with imagination. In Alaska's most prevalent type of business, restaurants, for example, the greatest concentration is in Anchorage. A walk down Anchorage's busiest street, Fourth Avenue, might indicate to the casual observer that there simply wasn't room for another restaurant. But a more knowledgeable observer might notice that most restaurants in Anchorage are small, inefficient, not particularly attractive, nor dedicated to serving unique and exotic foods. Accordingly, when a rather modern cafeteria-type restaurant—the kind that might be found on almost any business street of any large city in the U.S.— opened for business recently, in the heart of the most-crowded restaurant block on Fourth Avenue, it did a thriving business from the start. A visitor would have no trouble locating this new restaurant on Fourth Avenue because at dinner time it is the only one with a line of customers outside waiting to enter.

Tourism.

Perhaps the greatest promise for retail and service business in Alaska lies in the development of tourism. In 1960, tourism resulted in more than $100,000,000 income for Alaska, thus, for the first time, creating a single source of income larger than the total income from salmon sales.

This great surge of travel to, from and within Alaska has created new opportunities for motels, hotels, trailer camps, restaurants, gas stations, roadside dining and souvenir shops. Generally, Alaskans have hesitated to exploit their opportunities in scenic attractions because there has been a fairly widespread feeling (without any apparent justification) that the great increase in Alaska's tourism is temporary, due largely to the interest generated by statehood publicity.

There is, of course, no way of knowing whether Alaska's tourism boom is temporary. But there is substantial evidence in favor of its continued growth. In the first place, tourism has increased and continues to increase at a time when there is only one highway into Alaska, and not a very good highway at that. Tourism has increased:

in spite of a shortage of moderate-priced accommodations; in spite of the lack of attractive summer or winter resorts; in spite of the comparatively high cost and difficulties of travel within Alaska, which for most tourists means travel by air.

With the state now in control of its own future, there is no doubt that travel facilities to and within Alaska, especially highways, will be improved and increased at an unprecedented rate. Nor is there any doubt that a state government—as opposed to a territorial government—will continue to promote tourism through intensive publicity campaigns.

Alaska is blessed with one of the most impressive natural resources in the world, scenic attractions of unmatched magnificence. Many of these attractions represent potential business opportunities, which may be exploited and investigated through negotiations with the state government, the Bureau of Land Management, or the U.S. Forest Service. There are endless opportunities for mountain-top vacation retreats, hunting and fishing resorts, skiing resorts, and roadside dining and souvenir shops adjacent to well-known scenic attractions.

Construction and housing industries.

The principal source of income for the construction and housing industries has been government spending on facilities and housing directly or indirectly related to defense activities. As such, opportunities for business in the construction and housing industries have been confined largely to a small number of general contractors and architectural firms.

But generally needed in Alaska are real estate and insurance brokerages, also real estate developers who are capable of devising plans for shopping centers and housing developments and then organizing investor syndicates to finance construction. As Alaska's population grows, there will also be an increasing opportunity for construction specialists in recreational facilities (movie houses, bowling alleys, skating rinks) and office buildings.

Transportation industry.

Perhaps the most limited business opportunities in Alaska are to be found in the transportation industry. The air, land, and ocean transport companies now providing freight and passenger service for Alaska are more than adequate for the state's present and immediate needs.

The transport companies now doing business in Alaska will undoubtedly benefit from the growth in Alaska's population, tourism, and new industries. Newcomers will find it difficult to compete with established companies, which over the years have accumulated the vast knowledge and experience required to operate barges, ships, trucks, and airlines efficiently in Alaska.

As Alaska builds more highways and as tourism grows, however, there will be opportunities for establishing vehicle renting businesses and intra-city bus services. But the latter is more apt to be limited to high bidders for bus-service franchises issued either by the state or local governments.

Presently, there are opportunities for over-the-road guided-tour businesses in Alaska because most tourists arrive in Alaska without automobiles and the cost of hiring and operating an automobile is relatively high. The few guided-tour businesses now operating in Alaska are conducted with a deplorable lack of publicity, with unappealing tours, and uncomfortable as well as colorless vehicles.

In southeastern Alaska, there is a pressing need for ferry services. This need was described in comprehensive detail by a prominent New York firm of consultants, W. C. Gilman & Co., employed by the new state to study the feasibility of a ferry system. Gilman & Co. concluded that a commercial ferry operation in southeastern Alaska was desirable and feasible. In any event, it will require an investment of millions of dollars. If some investment syndicate or corporation should come forth with a plan for a private ferry business, especially one that may be underwritten by a public issue of securities, it can be assured of a sympathetic hearing by state officials. But the odds are in favor, eventually, of a state-owned ferry business.

PROBLEMS OF DOING BUSINESS IN ALASKA

In discussing the problems of doing business in Alaska, the purpose here is not to discourage those with ideas for business, but to provide a balance of all possible factors. Indeed, it may well be that some of the problems reported here may be seen as challenges, giving rise to business ideas. For example, while some may view the inventory problem in Alaska as an absolute barrier to establishing a certain type of business, others may see in it an opportunity to start a new type of business, perhaps a unique warehousing system designed to alleviate the need for many Alaskan merchants to carry heavy inventory.

The High Cost of Doing Business in Alaska

Many Alaskans insist that the only real problem for business in Alaska is high cost. The costs of transportation, labor, storage, rents, maintenance, and insurance are higher than similar costs in other states. It is quite true. The costs are high. But that isn't the entire story. As in the matter of the cost of living, there is a major compensating factor: *selling prices are high, too.* Just as a worker receives higher wages to offset his high cost of living, most Alaskan businesses receive higher prices for their goods and services.

For most types of business, the high cost of doing business in Alaska is not a serious problem, if indeed it is a problem at all. It is definitely a problem to be carefully weighed by any business seeking, with Alaskan products, to compete in Outside markets. But it is scarcely a problem for a business which has its markets *within* Alaska.

On the other hand, it can become quite a serious problem for a businessman who suddenly finds that he is unable to pass on high costs, either on account of new competition or unexpected consumer resistance. As a matter of fact, some Alaskan merchants tend to resent the influx of newcomers because they are bringing with them an unprecedented resistance to Alaska's relatively high cost of living. Interestingly, one hardware merchant said: "There was a time when a man would come in, pick up a hammer and ask how much. Now, they come in and ask how much do I get for a hammer and then they go down the street to see what my competion is getting for the same hammer."

Actually, oldtime Alaskan merchants who resist change and want to do business as usual, even to the extent of maintaining high prices when costs go down, are the ones who may be facing real trouble in the near future. This is particularly true in the larger towns, where newcomers are settling in greater numbers and do not have that sense of loyalty other Alaskans show toward merchants in smaller towns.

In sum, the high cost of doing business in Alaska is a real problem but only for the businessman who may not be able to incorporate his costs in his price tags; and it is a problem for the businessman who, when the occasion arises, cannot or will not absorb a part of his costs in order to meet competition or rising consumer resistance.

To some extent, the "high cost" factor within Alaska has influenced the thinking of Outside businessmen who ship and sell goods to Alaska. It has become almost traditional for Outside businessmen to automatically tack shipping costs onto the goods they sell to jobbers and wholesalers in Alaska.

Yet if the same goods were shipped prepaid to Alaska, as they may be to any other part of the U.S., it may be possible for the Alaskan merchant to reduce his selling price accordingly, making it further possible for him to increase his volume, which in turn would mean increased orders for the Outside businessman.

Consider, for instance, this actual analysis made by an Alaskan businessman with cost-accounting training:

A well-known canned goods distributor in Chicago ships his products prepaid all over the U.S. His customers in New York or California pay no more or no less than his customers in Chicago because shipping charges are cost-accounted in advance and become a part of the selling price. In other words, prepaid shipping "spreads" the cost among all the distributor's customers everywhere. But the same distributor, in shipping to Alaska, *adds* the cost of transport to his billing. If he were to prepay shipment to Alaska, however, "spreading" the cost among all his customers, he would have to raise his prices to all by less than one cent per case! But it would enable his Alaskan customers to reduce their prices by at least 15 to 25 per cent, making it possible for them to increase sales volume substantially within Alaska.

THE SHORTAGE OF INVESTMENT CAPITAL

A very real problem for all business in Alaska is the shortage of investment capital. Those who need cash to start or expand a business frequently find it difficult to borrow.

There are two principal reasons for the shortage: (1) lack of interest on the part of Outside investors; (2) a comparatively low rate of savings and deposits in Alaskan banks.

Bank deposits in Alaska total slightly more than $181,000,000, or about $800 per capita. In the over-all U.S., per capita deposits average $1,435. Alaskan bankers have only about half the proportion of deposits that Outside banks have and correspondingly lower funds for making loans.

The net effect of the capital shortage is that Alaskan banks are unwilling or unable to make many *long-term* loans. Most business loans in Alaska are made for short terms—two, three, or five years. Thus a borrower of business capital in Alaska must be certain that the money he borrows will create substantial short-term profits, enabling repayment of the loan. This makes long-range planning difficult and uncertain. (The usual interest rate on bank business loans is eight per cent.)

The shortage of investment capital is a problem that will best be met by Alaska's banks in combination with Outside financing. Most bankers in the 49th State are confident of alleviating the problem in the near future. Robert A. Baker, president of the Matanuska Valley Bank, formerly executive vice president of Alaska's largest bank, the First National of Anchorage, said:

"The bankers throughout the new state face the task of providing financing through their own resources and by attracting loan funds from the Outside. However, we no longer face the question of a declining economy. There are now people, lots of them here and more coming, who wish to make this country their home. Money is staying in the community and supporting many service industries which employ many more people."

Help from the Small Business Administration.

Playing an increasingly important role in Alaska's business world is the Small Business Administration, an independent Federal agency authorized by Congress to aid any American small business through a system of expert consultation, guidance, and loans. The SBA may make loans directly to the small businessman or obtain loans for him from a private lender by participating in the loan with the private lender, in effect guaranteeing the loan. Almost any business grossing less than $1,000,000 a year and employing less than several hundred persons may qualify for SBA assistance.

In Alaska, the SBA recently opened a new office in the Federal Building in Anchorage. Between 1953 and 1956, while operating from its Seattle office, the SBA had arranged only 24 loans for small businessmen in Alaska. But after the Anchorage office had opened in 1956, more than 50 loans totaling $1,500,000 were provided. Some of the loans ranged from as little as $7,200 for aid to a baker who wanted to install modern equipment, to a loan of $10,000 for a one-man stationery business, and a loan of $55,000 for a dentist. By mid-year 1959, the SBA had approved 145 loans for a total of more than $7,100,000, including a loan for as much as $448,000.

The real advantage in Alaska is that the SBA makes it possible to obtain *long-term* loans, up to 20 years, and often will negotiate a loan on "faith" in a man's integrity rather than his tangible assets. Typical was the Alaskan who needed $5,000 to start a one-man lumber mill in an area of increasing homestead activity. The young man felt that many settlers, building their own homes, were potential customers for cut timber. But his only assets were an old shed, a saw, ingenuity, initiative, and energy—no money for purchasing the raw material, timber. Impressed with his good moral character and enthusiasm, the SBA gave him a $5,000 loan. The young businessman was instantly successful, and had to employ four full-time workers.

THE INVENTORY PROBLEM

Many businessmen in Alaska have to carry an inordinately large inventory. This means a larger-than-usual amount of money has to be tied up in stock, and in a stockroom or warehouse.

The usual cause for large inventory is the long distance between the Alaskan businessman and his supplier. Sometimes the problem is one of a business in Anchorage with its main supplier in Chicago; sometimes it is one of a business in Nome with its supplier in Anchorage. In either case, unlike many businessmen in other states, an Alaskan merchant who suddenly finds himself out of stock usually cannot jump in his car, drive to the warehouse and pick up his needs; nor can he telephone the jobber and expect immediate delivery from a warehouse. As a matter of fact, a couple of jobbers in Alaska have increased their volume substantially simply by making it possible for their customers to drive to the warehouse to replenish stocks.

The merchant who sells goods that are subject to whims of fashion or seasonal influences in Alaska must be extremely careful in his selections. If he cannot move his goods, he may go bankrupt in spite of substantial assets in his stockroom. The inventory problem may eventually be resolved in Alaska by more warehouses, a better distribution of warehouses and jobbers, and the growth of specialists in inventory liquidations, such as auctioneers and "surplus" stores.

The need for warehouses in Alaska has been recognized by some enterprising Outsiders, who are attempting to purchase land adjacent to terminals in the hope that the price of such land will soar when needed for a warehouse.

THE TRANSPORTATION PROBLEM

Although air-freight shipping to Alaska is increasing steadily, most businessmen rely on ocean, rail and truck transport for delivery of their goods. Because such deliveries are time-consuming, as well as costly, some businessmen in Alaska can be confronted with a serious problem in returning goods which require repairs or refunds. It is for this reason that many merchants in Alaska, particularly clothiers and appliance dealers, prefer to deal only in quality merchandise, keeping returns at a minimum.

Another aspect of the transportation problem for Alaskan business is damage, or pilferage, or both. While merchants may be covered by insurance for such losses, they are not usually protected against the loss of profits that may ensue as a result of being without goods when needed most.

Fortunately, in recent years, goods shipped by ocean transport, the bulk of which is handled by the Alaska Steamship Co., have been getting through to merchants in Alaska with an extremely reduced "loss" rate. The Alaska Steamship Co. has introduced a system of transport known as "containerized shipping," in which goods are sealed in huge metal containers until they reach their destination in Alaska. Since the Alaska Steamship Co. has invested millions of dollars in research and testing for this system, as well as for new equipment, it is likely that "containerized" shipping may go a long way toward eliminating this problem for most businessmen in Alaska.

LABOR IN ALASKA

From the businessman's point of view, there are two features of Alaskan labor that create problems: (1) a shortage of skilled workers, except in construction crafts; (2) labor that is highly organized and exerts a strong influence in major population centers.

Any businessman who may require skilled workers, apart from construction, may find it necessary to train or pay for the training of the types of skills required. Yet if he should go to the expense of training his own workers, he cannot be certain of their tenure with him. Indeed, he may even risk the prospect of his own trainees eventually competing with him. In one situation, an Anchorage merchant needed a skilled assistant. Unable to find one in all Alaska, after extensive advertising, he trained his own assistant who, within a year, opened a competing business on the same street.

The strength of organized labor in Alaska usually creates a problem for the businessman only when there is a widespread or protracted strike of one of the major construction craft unions. Such strikes have an almost immediate impact on consumer spending and business can fall drastically.

A strike among longshoremen or truckers, however, may compel a businessman to circumvent the problem by air-freight deliveries from his suppliers, in which case the businessman must usually stand prepared to absorb the added cost. Sometimes he must be prepared with cash, too, in order to increase his inventory upon news of an impending strike in transportation.

CHAPTER 12

THE ROLE OF DEFENSE FORCES IN ALASKA

> *"Alaska is the most central place in the world for aircraft . . . I believe that in the future he who holds Alaska will hold the world."* Brigadier General Billy Mitchell, 1935

AN OBSCURE CLOAK-AND-DAGGER EVENT BEGAN EARLY IN World War II when Alaskan and West Coast newspapers carried a routine but prominently placed news report that a cannery was to be erected on one of the Aleutian Islands. The story had been carefully planted by American agents. Its purpose was to cover the frenetic hustle and bustle for the construction of an urgently needed air base to counterattack Japanese forces in Alaska. The Japanese had taken Kiska and Attu in the Aleutians. It was an old story for us—rushing in to fill a breach which had been ignored in the name of economy.

All through the 1930's Congress was warned of our vulnerability in Alaska. Gen. Billy Mitchell, who had a troublesome knack of being too right too soon, urged Congress to appropriate funds for air bases in Alaska. He was ignored. Alaska's Delegate-at-Large in Congress, Anthony J. Dimond, as early as 1934, said the Japanese would attack without a declaration of war and would occupy Alaska immediately. He sought repeatedly but vainly to impress Congress with the need for air bases in Alaska. Even after Hitler had invaded Poland in 1939, Alaska's "defense" consisted almost entirely of 11 officers, 286 enlisted men stationed at Haines, armed to the teeth with .45-cal. pistols and 1903 Springfield rifles, and a small tugboat that could scarcely buck a 15-knot breeze.

It was not until mid-1940 that Congress provided some money

for naval and air bases in Alaska. But before anything substantial could be constructed, the Japanese moved into the Aleutians, as predicted. Finally, when the last of the enemy withdrew under cover of fog in July, 1943, it ended what Alaskans hope and pray was the last enemy occupation of American soil.

We have come a long way since those pitiful days of paper defenses. Today, there is in Alaska a well-organized military bastion of Navy, Army and Air Force, unified under a single command known as ALCOM, the Alaskan Command, established in January, 1947, and greatly expanded since the Korean war.

WHO AND WHERE THEY ARE

Essentially, ALCOM consists of two "heartlands": Anchorage, where ALCOM makes its headquarters; and Fairbanks. Between these are three enormous air bases, and an Army post at Fort Richardson, near Anchorage. The Naval bases are at Kodiak and Adak, and there is an active Air National Guard.

The defense organization is built mainly about the Alaskan Air Command, under which there are two air bases at Fairbanks: Ladd Air Force Base, which adjoins the city of Fairbanks; and Eielson AFB, 26 miles south of Fairbanks on the Alaska Highway. Elmendorf AFB is a few miles from the center of Anchorage. Operating from these bases, which are veritable cities-within-cities, are bombers of the Strategic Air Command, jet interceptors, Nike missile sites, and various support wings for weather reconnaisance, logistics, and research.

A vital instrument in the Air Defense Command is the well-known "Dew Line," a series of complex, costly radar stations strung across the Arctic, connecting with Canada and reaching down into the Aleutians, to serve as "early warning" detectors against an enemy air attack headed for the "lower 48."

ALCOM, as all Alaska knows, is a mighty force indeed. It represents an investment of over three billion dollars! But with Russia almost breathing down Alaska's backbone, can we and will we really defend Alaska? Newcomers frequently ask the question.

The answer is yes, quite definitely. The defense forces are in Alaska not merely to man the "Dew Line," not merely to have bases for striking back at Russia, but also to fight for Alaskan soil if invaded. In an official statement of its mission in Alaska, an ALCOM spokesman said: "We are in Alaska to warn our nation of air attack and to destroy enemy aircraft, to protect military installations, and to *prevent an enemy from gaining a foothold in Alaska."*

Periodically, Alaskans have heard statements, sometimes expressed at Congressional hearings on military appropriations, that the armed forces in Alaska are insufficient or inadequately equipped to defend Alaska. It has been said, for instance, that the armed forces in Alaska should have intermediate range ballistic missiles (IRBMs) in order to destroy the air bases from which Russian planes might take off to bomb Alaska and the other states, and to prevent paratroop invasions of Alaska.

But generally overlooked are these counter-arguments:

The problem is to deal effectively with the over-all Soviet threat, including that portion of the threat based on the Kamchatka Peninsula. Extensive studies show that intercontinental ballistic missiles (ICBMs) based in the interior of the U. S. can do this job better and cheaper than IRBMs based in Alaska. IRBMs in Alaska would be vulnerable and difficult to support logistically. IRBMs in Alaska would not effectively increase the defensive posture of the 49th State.

Although enemy planes might attempt to bomb Alaskan bases and drop paratroopers to "take" Fairbanks or Anchorage, the "heartlands," they would have to contend with Air Force fighter interceptors, constantly on the alert, and with air defense missiles. An enemy paratroop force would have to contend with Army defense forces, trained to fight for Alaska inch by inch. To which would be added, of course, our own capability to reinforce Alaska rapidly.

Finally, in the words of a Defense Department spokesman: "The over-all deterrent and retaliatory capability of the Strategic Air Command to strike the enemy everywhere just as surely defends Alaska as it does any other state of the Union."

But apart from the military strategies involved, Alaskans have always maintained a keen interest in their defense forces—an economic interest.

THE ECONOMIC IMPACT OF DEFENSE IN ALASKA

Many students of Alaska's economy have said that almost everything the state has today it owes to military spending. Were it not for the enormous investments in ALCOM, there would be no cities of Anchorage and Fairbanks as these cities are known today. It is an obvious and accurate observation. Perhaps two-thirds or more of

Alaska's gross volume of business (income) is generated directly or indirectly by the defense forces in Alaska.

Maj. Gen. C. F. Necrason, Commander of the Alaskan Air Command, told me, "For the three services to carry out their missions and responsibilities in Alaska, almost $300,000,000 is required annually for normal operating and maintenance expenses."

Not all of this sum, however, is spent directly in Alaska, although a substantial portion is. Gen. Necrason estimated that at least $41,-000,000 of Air Force expenditures alone go directly into the Alaskan economy.

Col. W. C. Gribble, Jr., Chief District Engineer for the Army's Corps of Engineers in Alaska, produced a massive chart vividly illustrating other expenditures, as for example, an estimated average of $100,000,000 a year since 1952 on Air Force and Army construction contracts carried out by the Corps of Engineers. The spending peak was in 1952, about $160,000,000, and the low point was in 1958, about $60,000,000. It has been shown also that for every $1,000,000 in contracts let by the Corps of Engineers, 100 persons are employed in Alaska.

Added to these figures is the very great sum in salaries paid to military personnel and civilian employees who spend millions locally on food, housing, clothing, services, and recreation. The combined military-civilian payroll of Ladd Air Force Base alone averages some $15,000,000 a year.

Some Alaskan officials don't like to be reminded of these economic facts. They fear that Outsiders might think Alaska could not stand on its own without defense spending. To a great extent, this is true— for the present.

But there is no reason for the economic facts to cause a lessening of faith in Alaska's future. For one thing, nobody is demanding a *cut* in defense spending in Alaska.

Moreover, there are many indications that an important economic shift is taking place. The reliance on military spending is gradually decreasing. While military expenditures may remain at their present or even higher levels, other forms of spending are increasing at a rate that is gradually reducing the ratio of reliance on the military.

Col. Gribble, a man who favors the precise knowledge of charts and figures, told me that if Anchorage was 90 per cent reliant

on military spending five years ago, it was perhaps only half as reliant
on that spending now.

Finally, even if there were little or no expansion of defense facilities and construction in Alaska, the need merely to maintain and
operate the existing three-billion-dollar defense plant in Alaska
should insure a substantial and continuing flow of spending.

This maintenance need also exists for some "hidden" defense services which are not so readily apparent to the casual observer, but
which provide substantial benefits to Alaskans.

Among these "hidden" services are a vast network of communications known as "White Alice," and the Alaska Communication System, which is known to Alaskans simply as "the ACS," but which
has no other counterpart in American military organization except
perhaps the Panama Canal.

ALASKA COMMUNICATION SYSTEM

Many Alaskans place long-distance telephone calls and send telegrams between their cities and the Outside world, without even knowing that "their" telephone and telegraph company is a military organization, which not only has played a historic role in the development
of Alaska, but is indispensable to Alaska's future.

ACS was established by an Act of Congress on May 26, 1900.
The Act provided for a military telegraph system to connect Army
garrisons in Alaska with Washington, D. C. by means of a combination of telegraph land lines and submarine cables. For its time,
it was a daring project, calling upon the men of the Signal Corps to
fulfill a mission of heroic stature. Often to conquer the unknown
vagaries of engineering in frozen wastelands, new skills and ingenious
mechanics had to be devised extemporaneously, sometimes at the cost
of lives. By 1907, the Signal Corps task was completed.

But the Act of 1900 also provided that in addition to its prime
military function, the Alaska Communication System was to be
made available, at the discretion of the commanding officer, for
commercial use whenever conditions were deemed to be "in the public interest."

Fortunately for Alaska, ACS has been made available for commercial use ever since 1907, so much so, in fact, that the ACS is
today to Alaska what AT&T is to the other states.

There are about 15 small (and sometimes colorful) local telephone
companies in Alaska, but all long-distance message communications,

all telegrams, all private teletype lines, go through ACS. When an Alaskan picks up the telephone in Nome to call Anchorage—or New York—he usually has no idea that his call is handled by a unique "corporation" of military and civilian employees.

Thanks to ACS, Alaska has one of the finest and most reliable communications systems in the world. ACS's equipment is so modern that if a caller in Anchorage (or almost any other part of Alaska) wants to reach New York he need only dial 110 and give the number to the operator, who will then "punch" it out on an electronic marvel known as the "key pulse system." Within less than one second after the operator has punched the last digit, the New York telephone will ring! Assuming the Alaskan knows his New York telephone number, from the time he dials 110 to the time his New York number rings, about one minute will have elapsed! There is the same ease and speed of connection between Alaska and almost any other part of the U.S.

However, because ACS lines are sometimes in great demand, especially during business hours, there is usually a delay ranging from five to ten minutes in placing a long-distance call. During holiday seasons, such as Christmas and Easter, delays on calls to the Outside may range up to five hours. Otherwise, any part of the world where there are telephones and telegrams may be reached through ACS.

ACS's rates are based on the same type of fixed schedules and standards employed by commercial telephone and telegraph companies in the other states.

Recently, ACS facilities were augmented by the remarkable communications system, "White Alice," which was installed at a cost of over $100,000,000 under a contract between the Air Force and Western Electric Co., and which will require about $15,000,000 worth of maintenance annually.

The purpose of White Alice is to serve the military with reliable and virtually tamper-proof communications. White Alice is based on a revolutionary principle of microwave propagation known as "tropospheric scatter," in which no telegraph poles or lines are needed to connect the stations. It has been described as 99.4 per cent reliable.

White Alice will loom significantly in Alaska's future. It will help speed the opening of new frontiers by providing reliable communications where previously there had been none. Within months after its recent opening, White Alice "liberated" at least twenty communities from their reliance on highly uncertain voice-radio sets.

Outsiders frequently turn to ACS for information concerning communications in Alaska because ACS knows Alaska's communications problems and setup as no other organization does. ACS even knows where all the "bush" radio stations are located. Consequently, when businessmen, industrial organizations, sportsmen, homesteaders, and prospectors need to know such things as costs of communications and locations of reliable communications in the field, especially for the purpose of deciding where to establish a headquarters site, camp, hunting and fishing lodge, or homestead, they obtain their most reliable information by writing to: Headquarters, Alaska Communication System, 550 Federal Building, Seattle 4, Washington.

THE CORPS OF ENGINEERS

In addition to carrying out Army and Air Force construction in Alaska, the Corps of Engineers has for many years provided a great variety of civilian services involving public welfare, such as the construction of dams for flood control and the improvement of waters and harbors to make rivers navigable. The Corps has even provided safe facilities in harbors used mainly by boating enthusiasts and fishermen. The Corps maintains a full-time staff of nearly 600 in Alaska, about 70 per cent of whom are professional civilian engineers.

One of the most important but least known Corps of Engineers' projects—scheduled for completion in 1962—is the construction of a "portable" nuclear reactor, sometimes called "Army Package Power," at Ft. Greely, about 100 miles southeast of Fairbanks. It has been designed for a capability of 4,000 kw of electricity, to be used in experimental lighting and heat. If the experiment proves successful, "package power" may revolutionize Alaska's industrial potential, making it possible to settle outlying areas rapidly. *This is one of those obscure facts which skeptics often fail to take into account when evaluating Alaska's future, and the potential value of land in outlying areas.*

MISSIONS OF MERCY—AIR RESCUE

In a land where there are more aircraft per capita than any place in the world, where there are more sportsmen in the bush, and where modern pioneering proceeds at a breathtaking pace, there are apt to be numerous emergencies calling for swift action. In this regard, another of the important but "hidden" defense services for the civilian population is frequently performed by the Air Force—rescue and transportation!

On a single day in August, 1959, between 11:10 A.M. and 4:50 P.M., I saw an Air Force squadron log the following orders, and missions accomplished:

(1) Bring in seven-year-old boy from homestead. Was accidentally hit in the head with an axe. Emergency medical treatment required.

(2) Pick up three civilians stranded on 5,000 foot bluff. Their light plane crashed on landing.

(3) Pick up sheep hunter from Los Angeles, California. Was flown into hunting camp in the bush. Pilot was to have returned to pick him up, but "air strip" at camp washed out by heavy rains.

(4) Emergency medical pick-up for man with severe head injuries resulting from a fall; deliver direct to hospital by helicopter.

ARMED FORCES RADIO SERVICE

The Armed Forces Radio network plays an important part in maintaining morale of the servicemen in Alaska. Through its enormous facilities and connections with commercial radio organizations in the U. S., AFRS brings to thousands of servicemen information, news, and entertainment not otherwise available over commercial Alaskan radio. AFRS network, which has 39 stations spotted around Alaska, is often "open" to Alaskans in outlying areas. In and around the major cities, AFRS is "piped" in to the military bases and is usually unavailable to the civilian population.

RESEARCH AT THE TOP OF THE WORLD

How can man work and survive in temperatures best suited for polar bears? What are the best foods to eat in cold climates? What sort of clothing is best to meet the challenge of the elements?

Answers to these questions are important to the armed forces in Alaska. But they are equally important to Alaska's future.

In search of answers is a unique Alaskan Air Command unit, the Aero-Medical Laboratory at Ladd Air Force Base. Its function, of course, is to develop information of military importance. But often its research leads to knowledge which need not be kept secret, and isn't. Any and all information it develops of use to Alaskans is frequently relayed to the public by means of press releases to Alaskan newspapers.

Among the Aero-Medical Laboratory's recent and best-known findings are facts which tend to show that penetrating cold may not always be related to sub-zero temperatures alone. Often you can "feel" equally as cold at -10° F. as at -40° F. when there is just a slight change in wind velocity and humidity.

The Aero-Medical Laboratory has a staff of about 55, among whom are more than 25 civilians possessing advanced degrees in science and highly regarded reputations in their respective specialties. They often go to various field stations in remote areas in order to learn how to live under the most trying conditions known to man. They expose themselves to just about everything from extreme isolation on floating ice islands to dry cold, damp cold, and the effects of profound physical exertion in icy winds. Presently, they are studying the how and why of animal hibernation in cold climate. It is not inconceivable that from the results of Aero-Medical Laboratory research at the top of the world, Alaskans may someday be equipped with the knowledge to live longer, healthier lives in their sub-Arctic land.

When a friend once asked Secretary William Seward what he considered to be the most important of his public services, Seward replied:

"The purchase of Alaska, but it will take the people a generation to find out."

Unfortunately, it took our military forces a little longer than that. But now the Defense Department knows very well what Seward and Billy Mitchell had in mind, and there is not the slightest chance that defense in Alaska will again be fed to wolves crying, "Economize!"

CHAPTER 13

HUNTING AND FISHING:
THE GOLDEN LURE

> *"Alaska is a country where sportsmen don't have to lie—because the truth is strange enough!"* Department of Defense, *Pocket Guide to Alaska*

H OW WOULD YOU LIKE TO SHOOT A MOOSE, A BROWN BEAR, *and your limit of ducks, catch a fighting salmon and six husky cutthroats—all in one day at the same place? I've done it and you can, too. Fantastic? Not in Alaska.* Reports * like these from the experts have been firing the imagination of outdoorsmen the world over.

For vacationers and travelers, hunting and fishing is Alaska's number-one attraction. But it is also the golden lure for an overwhelming number who have made Alaska home. More than 70 per cent of the hundreds I had interviewed in Alaska—men and women—said that their decisions to remain permanently in the new state were influenced by the superb hunting and fishing. For instance, an Air Force colonel, about to retire, told me: "My family and I (five children) have lived in six countries and nearly half the states and we've hunted and fished everywhere. But we've never seen anything like Alaska. We intend to remain here because of the hunting and fishing. My boys will go to the University of Alaska for their education."

In the matter of hunting and fishing, all the superlatives apply to Alaska and without any possible exaggeration. There's good reason. Truly the last great wilderness in the United States, Alaska is blessed

* *Field and Stream*, August, 1959.

with the natural features that make hunting and fishing a sportsman's paradise.

There are more than 33,000 miles of coastline, more than 3,000 islands, of which over 1,100 alone are in the exalted Inland Passage of southeastern Alaska.

There are mountain ranges, rocky slopes, marshes, peninsulas, plateaus, plains, and tundra. There are placid streams and turbulent rivers. Fish, fowl, and furry game of almost every variety abound everywhere. To name a few: Canadian geese, harlequin, pintail and mallard ducks; ptarmigan and grouse; cutthroat trout, rainbow trout, Dolly Vardens, pink salmon, king salmon, silver salmon, halibut; polar bears, grizzly bears, brown bears and black bears; deer, moose, Dall sheep, and wild mountain goats; caribou, fox, and timber wolves. About the only thing that cannot be found in Alaska are lions, tigers, and elephants. Happily, too, there are no snakes of any kind, anywhere!

But Alaska's trophy-size game—like the polar bear—more than make up for the absence of jungle-style big game. As a matter of fact, in its guide for servicemen assigned to Alaska, the Department of Defense advises, "When you start writing home about *your* game trophies, don't expect to be believed."

Ironically, I've heard sportsmen groan that sometimes the hunting and fishing in Alaska was a bit too easy. I'll never forget an incident which occurred shortly after my plane had landed at Gustavus in southeastern Alaska. One of my plane companions, Sgt. Phil Townsend of the Alaska Air National Guard, a slim, youthful, ardent duck hunter, was off the plane within seconds after the landing. Shotgun in hand, he strode gingerly across the field, in the direction of a marsh. He had never been there before, but he seemed to know exactly what he was doing. Within an hour he was back. His face was a picture of dejection. "What's the matter, sergeant," I called out, "no luck? Is the weather too good even for ducks?"

"Heck, no!" he shouted back. "The weather is too darn good and so was my luck." He held up a mess of ducks strung together at the feet. "I've already bagged my limit."

Sometimes, the fishing is also "too good." In some parts of southeastern Alaska, the Dolly Vardens are so plentiful that fishing for them is considered women's or children's sport. Not long ago, as a matter of fact, conservation officials were confronted with a peculiar problem regarding the abundance of Dolly Vardens. It seems that the

Dollies had developed the habit of following salmon during the spawning season, eating the salmon eggs as they went along. This posed a potential threat to the propagation of salmon, which is an important commercial as well as recreational fish in Alaska. Officials, therefore, decided to pay a bounty for every Dolly Varden brought in, dead. As evidence for collecting the bounty (2½ cents), fishermen had to produce Dolly Varden tails. But so many Dolly tails were turned in that the bounty had to be called off. Luckily, it developed that the Dollies were only eating the salmon eggs that could not be hatched anyway.

WHEN, WHERE, AND HOW

As in most states, open-season dates for hunting and fishing are set from year to year. However, for those who may wish to make advance preparations for hunting or fishing in Alaska—whether such preparations concern open-season dates, obtaining licenses, hotel reservations, information about guides, fish and game, transportation, equipment, supplies, or what to wear—there are two excellent sources of information: Alaska Department of Fish and Game, Subport Building, Juneau; and the Division of Tourism and Economic Development, 310 Alaska Office Building, Juneau.

Two additional and frequently useful sources of information are the respective local Chambers of Commerce (see Appendix) and the airlines specializing in Alaskan passenger traffic. Pacific Northern Airlines, 1223 Fourth Avenue, Seattle, Washington, for example, has published a unique 25-page booklet, *Guide Book to Alaska Game Fishing*, compiled by the airline's own employees, nearly all of whom are devoted Alaskan fishing enthusiasts. The booklet, according to the airline, is a condensation of "lifetime know-how on salmon, trout, sheefish, and grayling" fishing and suggests all the best fishing spots, rivers, streams, lakes, together with information on the right kind of tackle.

Also, just about every city, town, and village in Alaska has an air strip out of which expert bush pilots serve as operators of aircraft and as hunting and fishing guides, carrying outdoorsmen into choice game country (see Appendix). Some charge as little as $10 for a round trip to an island literally surrounded by king salmon. At the other extreme, if you want something to talk about the rest of your life, there are guides who will fly you hundreds of miles above the

Arctic Circle and remain with you until you bag a polar bear (guaranteed), at a cost of $1,500 to $2,000, which includes the cost of skinning and fleshing the bear for the taxidermist.

Fishing permits for non-residents may be obtained for ten days at a cost of $5. A year-round license is $10. A non-resident hunting license is $10; a hunting-fishing license, $20. Residents pay $5 for sport fishing licenses; $7 for hunting licenses; and $12 for hunting-fishing licenses.

The state also has its own hunting and fishing magazine, the *Alaskan Sportsman*, a monthly published by the Alaska-Northwest Publishing Co. of Juneau. It is an extremely well written and authoritative publication and frequently contains articles and advertisements of interest to Outsiders, such as accommodations for sportsmen, supply stores in Alaska, camping facilities for rent, and offerings by guides. Incidentally, there are hunting and fishing supply stores everywhere and the owners of these stores are themselves usually among the most ardent and knowledgeable outdoorsmen in the state. Because of the keen competition among them, the cost of outdoor clothing, fishing tackle and hunting supplies is comparatively inexpensive. Many visitors prefer to rent their fishing, camping, and hunting equipment in Alaska. Any local Chamber of Commerce can refer your inquiry to a hunting and fishing supply store for information regarding availability of equipment and prices.

Perhaps the finest and most useful guide to the type of game in Alaska is a beautifully illustrated, 25-cent, 60-page booklet known as *Circular 17, Alaska's Fish and Wildlife*, published by the U.S. Department of the Interior's Fish and Wildlife Service and sold through the Superintendent of Documents, Washington 25, D. C.

One of the authors of *Circular 17* was Clarence J. Rhode, perhaps the most highly regarded authority on Alaskan game. He was recently lost while on an official flight over a rugged mountain range in northern Alaska, and is presumed dead. News of his disappearance touched off the largest air-sea-land rescue missions in Alaska's history. Scores of private pilots and guides, at their own expense, participated in the search, which lasted for weeks. Alaskans consider the late Mr. Rhode's contribution to *Circular 17* a lasting tribute to what every sportsman should know about fish and wildlife in Alaska.

SPORT FISHING IN ALASKA

Alaska offers almost every type of sport fishing imaginable—deep-water marine, coastal, inland lakes, shallow lakes, glacial lakes, inland streams, and coastal streams. Perhaps most popular is fishing for king salmon and silver salmon in southeastern Alaska.

Almost every town in southeastern Alaska sponsors a salmon-fishing contest early in the summer. One of these, the Golden Salmon Derby, sponsored by the Juneau Sportsmen's Club, attracts salmon-fishing enthusiasts by the thousands from every state and from foreign countries. Prizes include new autos and boats and hundreds of items contributed by sporting-equipment manufacturers and dealers within and without Alaska. But the most truly cherished prizes are the salmon, weighing 20, 30, and 40 lbs. A recent first-prize trophy was a king salmon weighing almost 45 pounds. In 1939, a king salmon weighing more than 120 pounds was caught near Petersburg.

However, salmon fishing ranges far into the north. King salmon may be found in the Arctic Ocean. But they appear in greatest numbers in waters adjacent to the Pacific. A king generally takes the hook below the surface and will start battling instantly, often taking the line out 200 feet or more.

Silver salmon, which is most abundant in southeastern Alaska, will take your bait or lure even when it is within sight of your boat. It makes a fast run of 30 feet or more, breaks water and leaps several feet into the air and continues these combative tactics on the surface until played out. Many Alaskans consider the silver salmon a superior game fish because it fights so hard.

The following on fish and game in Alaska is based on information supplied by the U.S. Fish and Wildlife Service, the Alaska Game Commission, and various authoritative wildlife publications of the University of Alaska.

Trout.

Rainbows are found in coastal rivers and in the interior of Alaska, south of the Yukon drainage. They are stocked in some landlocked lakes, particularly in southeastern Alaska. Their average size is smaller than steelheads (although some will argue there is no difference between rainbows and steelheads). Individual rainbows of 27 to 30 inches are common in many areas.

Steelheads average 8 to 10 pounds and may be found in most of the large coastal streams and in many of the smaller ones throughout Alaska.

Rainbows and steelheads will take all types of lures—flies, spinners, or bait. Many Alaskans prefer wet-fly fishing early in the spring and dry-fly casting in the summer.

Dolly Vardens may be fished in almost all coastal streams and lakes, from the British Columbia border to the Aleutians and Bering Strait. Dollies range in length up to 30 inches, although some measuring over four feet have been caught. Many Alaskans won't try for Dollies because they lack fight. Actually, the Dolly has every bit as much fight as the eastern brook trout or the lake trout and few can distinguish the cooked flesh from that of any of the other preferred sport-trout fish in Alaska. Dollies will go for almost any lure, casting or trolling. An outdoorsman who wants to give his wife or children the first thrills of successful fishing usually goes out for Dollies because they are so abundant and easy to catch.

One of the finest game and food fishes in Alaska is the coastal cutthroat trout, which, except for the rainbow, is the only black-spotted trout in Alaska. Adult cutthroats usually enter the streams in the fall, when they are caught in greatest numbers. They have a reputation for being spectacular fighters and will take a variety of lures, including flies, spinners, and salmon eggs. If you encounter a school of cutthroats (usually in salt water) you can take them almost as fast as you can cast a lure and reel in. The favorite salt-water lure is the "pop-gear" type of flasher-spinner combination, trolling. Cutthroats average 3 to 6 pounds, and about 20 inches.

Lake trout, sometimes known as Mackinaw, is one of the lesser-known sport fishes in Alaska. It belongs to the char group, in which are also the Dolly Varden and brook trout. Lake trout is the largest of the char types. Catching 30-pound lake trout is not unusual in Alaska. They are found in the Brooks Range and are abundant in western Alaska. They go mostly for fresh bait or simulated-fish lures.

Northern pike.

Pike, generally a large and favored game fish in other states, is one of the least popular fresh-water fishes in Alaska. According to the Fish and Wildlife Service it is "not even rated as a game fish under Alaska law." Northern pike in Alaska average 80 to 100 pounds and over four feet. They are considered ideal for bait-casting fans and will take spoon, spinner, and plug lures or streamer flies. They are mainly shallow-water lake fish, found in the backwaters, sloughs, and bottomland lakes of the Yukon and Kuskokwim valleys and north to the Arctic Coast.

Grayling.

Ranging up to 23 inches, weighing as much as 4 to 5 pounds, grayling in Alaska are ideal sport for fly fishermen. The grayling is predominantly a surface feeder and will take anything, even gaudy spinning lures. It puts up a tough battle, starting with a quick run downstream, then a cross-current rush, followed by a series of acrobatics and finally a plunge to the bottom. Grayling are found in every major river drainage north of the Gulf of Alaska and throughout the Alaska Peninsula.

Sheefish.

If you've never heard of a sheefish, don't be surprised. It is unique to Alaska. Sometimes it is called the *inconnu* (meaning *unknown*) because it has never been found in any other state. The sheefish has been "loosely described as a cross between a whitefish and a salmon," though in action and appearance it might well be called an Arctic tarpon and is every bit as much a tackle buster as any tarpon. Average weight of a shee is about 20 pounds, and up to four feet; but many have caught 40- and 80-pound shee. They are confined largely to northern rivers. But it takes a great deal of skill and patience to land one. Some prefer to go for shee with a large, bright spoon cast into a deep pool in a northern stream; others prefer spinners, plugs, and flies. Sheefish experts believe that the spoon cast in a deep pool yields the most fruitful results in terms of size.

WHEN FISHING IS BEST

Except for the hardiest anglers, the usual fishing season in Alaska ranges from April through mid-September, when there is good fishing to be found almost anywhere. April through May is considered the best time of the year for giant-size trout and king salmon in southeastern Alaska. Generally, however, the best fishing months are July and August, when the warm and almost nightless days make fishing a supreme and satisfying experience from the Arctic Circle to Ketchikan. During these months you don't always get the largest trout or salmon, but with lakes, streams, and rivers literally boiling with fish at insect-feeding time you are apt to enjoy the most success.

HUNTING IN ALASKA

Many Alaskans can remember when hunting in the north country was a principal source of food. Game was plentiful. Caribou and moose meat was a regular part of the dinner menu. But with the coming of the railroad and highways and defense activities and an increasing population of trophy-minded sportsmen, hunting, according to the oldtimers, is not what it used to be. Nevertheless, Alaska, in the eyes of the experts, is still the last big-game frontier in America, and many a modern homesteader has shot a moose from his bedroom window. In fact, even the gentlest of fishermen is advised not to go into the woods without a sizeable rifle. A housewife, formerly of Brooklyn, now living just a few miles outside Anchorage, told me how she had to learn to shoot a 30-06 because occasionally she'd see some bears snooping around the garbage, although she has since learned they can be scared off easily by banging a few pots together.

It is the rare hunter who cannot bag something during any season anywhere in Alaska. If the wildlife is not as abundant as it used to be in the days of the Klondike, it is still BIG for big game. Recent records in Alaska include an 11'-11" brown bear, an 11' grizzly, and a bull moose with 25-point antlers and 73½-inch spread.

In a recent study on "wildlife in the economy of Alaska," it was found that the average outdoorsman, during a 16-day hunting and fishing trip in Alaska, managed to bag 4 pounds of waterfowl, 14 pounds of small game, and 104 pounds of big game. During the period under study, hunters had taken a total of 126 polar bears; 5,000 moose; 6,000 caribou; 8,000 deer; several hundred mountain goats and Dall sheep; and "well over" 200,000 ducks, geese, grouse and ptarmigan.

Bears.

Alaska's bear population is big and varied. It includes the brown bear, largest meat-eater on land, weighing up to 1,600 pounds, the grizzly, the black bear, and the polar bear.

The brown bear roams vast areas of Alaska, up the mainland coastal mountains to sub-Arctic regions, and the interior mountain ranges. Brown bears are also numerous on Admiralty, Baranof and Chichagof Islands, the Alaska Peninsula, and the Kodiak-Afognak group of islands.

Brown and grizzly bears in Alaska have been classified into nine groups, consisting of 30 species and subspecies, ranging widely in coloration and size. The Toklat grizzly is cream-colored. The Admiralty Island "brown" bear is almost black. The grizzly of Norton Sound is comparatively small, but the Kodiak brown bear is enormous. Brown and grizzly bears are ferocious fighters, especially when wounded or when they believe their cubs are in danger. Mother bears with cubs have been known to go out of their way to attack hunters.

In Juneau, I met a group of citizens who were taking up a collection for a sixteen-year-old boy who had gone into a nearby forest to go fishing. He had a momentary encounter with a brown bear. It was only one swipe of the bear's paw across the boy's face. The collection was for the purpose of sending the boy to a school for the blind.

Black bears range over three-fifths of Alaska and weigh from 200 to 300 pounds in adult size, although hunters have brought them in weighing nearly 500 pounds. Although usually rich black in color, they also are found with cinnamon and blue colorations. As a rule black bears are not hunted for trophies, although the bluish-colored variety, found usually between Lynn Canal and Cape St. Elias, are prized by sportsmen because of the unusual color.

The polar bear is one of Alaska's larger bears. Males weigh from 700 to 1,600 pounds. They cling mostly to the southern border of the ice pack in Arctic waters and a sudden advance of ice sometimes brings them as far south as Bering Strait.

A polar-bear hunt is considered a dangerous venture, which is one reason seasoned pilot-guides are needed, and the cost for a one-week polar-bear hunt may range upwards of $1,000. Usually, the pilot "scouts" the bear from the air and then lands at a safe and convenient distance to track, "corner," and shoot.

Mountain sheep.

The Dall mountain sheep in Alaska is the only wild white sheep in existence. The white coat and long curled ram horns make it one of the handsomest and most prized wildlife trophies in the world. A Dall sheep is not easy to shoot, with gun or camera. It is found only in the rugged, high mountain ranges from Kenai Peninsula to the Arctic coast, and in the isolated high ground of the Brooks Range north of the Arctic Circle. It has an uncanny sense of smell and acute vision. It takes a strong and agile hunter to keep up with a Dall sheep as it scampers along steep, rocky ledges.

Moose.

Moose is one of the most popular "dinner-table" items in Alaska. Hundreds of Alaskans hunt moose to put in a deep-freeze supply of food. One family could live off a moose for a long time. The Kenai moose is the largest animal of its kind in the world, often reaching a weight in excess of 1,400 pounds. A bull moose antler spread not uncommonly will exceed five to six feet and makes an outstanding trophy. Moose are abundant on the Kenai Peninsula and range as far north as the Yukon, Tanana and Kuskokwim Valleys.

Caribou.

At one time, caribou (which look like Santa's famed reindeer) were so abundant throughout Alaska that the population was estimated in the millions and paddle-wheel steamers on the Yukon sometimes had to maintain slow reverse speed while whole herds crossed the river ahead. There no longer are millions of caribou in Alaska, but the animal is still abundant as far as hunting goes. Caribou travel widely and frequently about Alaska, over high plateaus and mountain slopes, preferring chiefly the barren ground in the Brooks and Alaska Ranges. Large herds have been known to migrate hundreds of miles. The caribou is hunted for trophies and meat.

Deer.

According to the U.S. Fish and Wildlife Service, Alaska has only one true deer, the Sitka black-tailed deer. Its natural range is on the islands of southeastern Alaska, with a few on the narrow mainland strip. Characteristic of these deer is their "vertical migration." As the snow melts from higher elevations, many, particularly bucks and yearlings, climb as high as 2,500 feet and remain there until deep snows force them to lower feeding grounds. In late summer or early fall hunting season, the search for black-tail means a climb of 2,000 feet or more; but later in the fall many bucks are taken within a few hundred feet of tidewater, where they feed on kelp and other marine vegetation. More deer are taken each year than any other big game in Alaska. They come in a variety of sizes. Some have spike horns, others five-point antlers, and they are wily as well as swift. Sometimes they will bound through the forest at incredible speeds; sometimes they will practically crawl, seeking fallen logs and depressions in which to remain out of sight.

Birds.

Vast expanses of tundra, muskeg, and river bottoms, dotted with endless potholes, lakelets and sloughs, provide nesting sites for one of the greatest variety of waterfowl and game birds in Alaska. The most outstanding single nesting area is the coastal tundra between the Yukon and Kuskokwin Rivers, where many species of ducks and geese may be found. Alaska plays an important role in maintaining the continental supply of migratory waterfowl. Bird-banding records have shown that Alaska-raised birds find their way to most of the 48 states and Mexico. One great flight path from the north leads through the Cold Bay area at the tip of the Alaska Peninsula, where hundreds of thousands of pintails, black brant, and cackling geese, among others, concentrate before making the long hop to the Pacific states. These birds, together with lesser Canada geese and other species from elsewhere within Alaska, are the waterfowl that provide most of the sport of Pacific-coast hunters.

So far, bird shooting in Alaska has been comparatively incidental to other types of hunting, but to the explorer, prospector, or trapper, grouse and ptarmigan are important sources of food. Ptarmigan and grouse may often be seen in huge flocks. Ptarmigan hunting with a small-bore shotgun is much like quail hunting, and calls for fast, accurate shooting.

Ptarmigan, among the most widely distributed of Alaska's game birds, is found from the Arctic tundra to southeastern Alaska. The blue grouse, sometimes called sooty grouse, dusky grouse, or hooter, is Alaska's largest upland game bird, weighing as much as 3½ pounds. It is distributed throughout southeastern Alaska, from Glacier Bay to British Columbia.

CHAPTER 14

THE 49TH STATE TODAY:
SIGNIFICANCE OF STATEHOOD,
GUIDE TO 23 CITIES AND TOWNS

> *"Alaska, My Alaska*
> *Tho slow thy growth/Through many a year,*
> *Thy motto has been/'Persevere. . . .'"*
> from "Alaska, My Alaska" by Mountin A.
> Snow, Juneau High School, Class of '03

I~~N~~ 1955, ANTICIPATING ULTIMATE VICTORY FOR STATEHOOD, THE Territorial legislature authorized a convention to draft a state constitution for Alaska. Typically, Alaskans sent to the convention about as diverse a representation as you might expect to find in a motley frontier. Among 55 delegates there were lawyers, merchants, fishermen, miners, housewives, truckers, bush pilots, and homesteaders. For technical assistance the convention enlisted experts from the Public Administration Service of Chicago.

Delegates to the constitutional convention had little precedent to go by. It had been nearly half a century since the last state had been admitted to the Union. Besides, there was little in history that could be applied to the unique requirements of a state detached from the mainland, and a state that had to face the complexities of a more modern world.

Nevertheless, after the proposed constitution had been ratified on April 24, 1956, by a vote of more than 2 to 1, experts hailed it as "one of the finest documents of its type ever written," one which adapts "to a remarkable degree the most advanced thinking in political science and public administration . . . as a sound basis for government in Alaska [and] also as a model for use in constitutional revision in other states."

The Alaska Constitution is basically simple. Its essence is a strong central executive in which the Governor is chiefly responsible for the various state departments. Only one other state official, the Secretary of State, is required to stand for election. The theory behind this concept of government is that it prevents the Governor from "passing the buck." There can be no guesswork, no political dalliance, nor evasion of the daggers of criticism. Since almost all officials are subject to the appointment and removal of the Governor, the chief executive must stand or fall on his every act.

The state's basic organization includes a two-house legislature (Senate, four-year term; House of Representatives, two-year term); a single system of courts; strong home rule for the cities and towns; and a system of boroughs, instead of counties. All elected officials are subject to voters' recall, and while the State Legislature may convene a constitutional convention at any time, it must automatically place on the ballot every tenth year the question, "Shall there be a constitutional convention?"

Perhaps the most controversial provision of the constitution is that it has placed the state capital at Juneau which, ironically, by virtue of its inaccessibility and its remoteness from the most dynamic centers of population, may once more afflict Alaska with the debilities of government by "long distance." There is no doubt that the state capital will be the subject of heated debate in Alaska.

THE SIGNIFICANCE OF STATEHOOD

It is not unusual that the state constitution stresses the elimination of "buck passing," a peculiar manifestation of bureaucracy, a disease which had plagued Alaskans eternally under Territorial status. Senator Gruening once characterized Alaska's principal infirmity as "bureaucratic bursitis" and "appropriation anemia," the effects of neglect from stepchild treatment by remote government in Washington.

But stepchild status now is history. It is in this single fact, more than anything else, that the greatest significance of statehood lies. Although to many Americans the Statehood Act was barely more than a ceremonial bit of mumbo-jumbo, with a scrambling for souvenir pens at the White House, to Alaskans statehood means the realization of a dream, a practical dream—of having voting representatives on Capitol Hill, of an opportunity to engage in that *quid pro quo* of political bargaining which yields many tangibles, *e.g.,* roads, rivers and harbor projects, dams, and housing, to name a few.

But there is equally great significance in the fact that statehood has placed Alaska's destiny in its own hands and has nullified a number of laws which were plainly and calculatingly discriminatory. It is no secret that many absentee landlords in industry had exploited (less politely, plundered) Alaska's resources and had done so with impunity. Also, it was easy to exert pressure on Congress to pass laws favorable to some, but not to Alaskans.

The Jones Act of 1920, for example, made it practically impossible for Alaskans to receive or "export" freight in any but American ships departing and arriving from American ports. As a result, Alaskans were unable to take advantage of much lower freight rates that otherwise might have been offered by competitive shipping, as from Vancouver, Canada. The late Senator Richard Neuberger of Oregon, a long-time friend of Alaskan statehood, once cited the case of a budding lumber business that had to quit before it could get started simply because it was compelled, under the Jones Act, to employ American shipping at uneconomical rates. The political rationale behind the Jones Act? It was supposed to be for the national good, enabling America to build its Merchant Marine. That it also conveniently encouraged and protected high American shipping rates was presumably coincidental, as was perhaps the fact that the Congressman after whom the Act was named came from an area of strong West Coast shipping interests.

But with statehood the Jones Act in Alaska is bound to die, and if there is to be again an immolation of Alaska for a "national good" it will probably have to be over the political corpses of two Senators and a Representative with voting power.

As a state, Alaska, of course, will now have to stand or fall on its own abilities, although it is little known that Alaska entered the Union under singular fiscal circumstances—the only state without a debt burden. Moreover, with its tremendous store of natural resources Alaska stands to benefit greatly from developments and discoveries, particularly in commercial production of oil and gas.

Another factor of statehood that must be weighed in Alaska's balance is perhaps less tangible but no less real, certainly no less significant: stability of statehood! It will enable the state to attract and encourage investors, secure in the knowledge that planning is not subject to political veto in Washington.

In the past, whenever a new state had entered the Union its population either doubled, tripled, or quadrupled within five to ten years after statehood, and the character of the new population had always been stable. With greater ease of travel, there is no reason to expect less of Alaska. As the Fairbanks *News-Miner* has said: "A new type of person is coming to Alaska. Before statehood, in Fairbanks, we had a lot of ex's up here—ex-gangsters, ex-husbands, ex-wives, ex-businessmen, people who were flops in many walks of life. They came up here to get away from something. A few years ago you could see only two well-kept lawns around here. Now you see trimmed lawns all over town."

Finally and aptly, in the succinct words of an educator, Dr. Ernest N. Patty, president emeritus of the University of Alaska, "In brief, we think Alaska has been rediscovered, that the old myth of Alaska as a land of ice and snow has been melted and that the state has been set for an era of real and sound advancement."

History is on Alaska's side; so is the same spirit that has moved America past all its frontiers while much older lands in the Old World are still struggling with theirs.

THE CITIES AND TOWNS OF ALASKA

ANCHORAGE, pop. 36,500

On the basis of percentage rate of growth, Anchorage is not only the fastest-growing city in Alaska, but in the entire United States. The population of "greater Anchorage," which includes suburban developments within a ten-mile radius, is approximately 101,000, which includes an estimated 25,000, military personnel stationed primarily at Elmendorf Air Force Base and Fort Richardson, both only a few miles from the center of town, connected by round-the-clock scheduled bus service.

With at least half Alaska's population in "greater Anchorage," the city is the largest population center in Alaska. But it is also the most cosmopolitan and youthful. Its schools, places of entertainment, business establishments, streets and highways, are as modern as those in any other part of the United States. Although the adjacent military establishments are large, there is virtually no social conflict between the military and civilian residents. In fact, the military frequently appear in the streets in their civilian dress and are happily "integrated" into all phases of Anchorage life.

The city is the financial and commercial hub of Alaska. It was estimated that in 1959, business in the greater Anchorage area registered an all-time high of $172,000,000 gross, more than one-third of the total gross income for all Alaska. The largest share of the dollar-volume of business went to the retail industry, which hit an estimated $80,000,000 gross.

Property rentals 1960-61 in prime downtown areas are about 40 to 60 cents per square foot; property purchases in the same areas ranged from $1200 to $1750 per square foot.

Much of the oil and gas industry expenditures for exploration and development is felt in the greater Anchorage area, since the hub of oil and gas activities is on nearby Kenai Peninsula. It is expected that oil and gas expenditures will increase substantially within the coming generation.

Newcomers usually feel right at home in Anchorage, not only because it is a well-developed modern metropolis, but also because the overwhelming number of people in and around Anchorage are relative newcomers themselves. The pervading atmosphere is one of informality, optimism, confidence, and cheerful friendliness. While these characteristics are perhaps true for most of Alaska, with the exception of a few of the more settled southeastern areas, they are seen and felt more in Anchorage.

The city has two daily afternoon newspapers: Anchorage *Times*, about 19,000 circulation (daily except Sunday); Anchorage *News*, about 12,000 circulation (daily except Sunday). There are two television stations, KENI-TV (affiliated with ABC and NBC) and KTVA-TV (CBS affiliated). There are three radio stations: KBYR (independent); KENI (CBS, ABC, and Mutual); and KFQD (CBS).

There are two large modern motion picture theatres and the exceptionally modern high school auditorium is frequently the scene of dramatic productions and concerts produced either by active local groups or visiting professionals.

Centrally located, there is a very modern and tastefully furnished library, which houses a small museum of Alaskan historical exhibits, 37,000 books, a substantial reference collection, and receives nearly 200 magazines and 29 different newspapers from all over the United States. The library is an active center for students as well as the adult population and is open 11 hours daily, 26 days of the month.

Numerous social, civic, fraternal and medical-benefit groups are active in Anchorage. Among the general population there is a higher-than-average college level.

The city is also the most accessible, by air and road, to all other parts of Alaska, and the world. With increasing scheduled jet flights stopping to refuel, discharge, and receive passengers, Anchorage is well on its way toward becoming the Bagdad of the North. One of the few cities in Alaska with an active planning commission, Anchorage should expand rapidly and in an orderly fashion with respect to streets, highways, sewage, airports, utilities, and possibily shipping.

BARROW, pop. 1,200

Located on the extreme northern tip of Alaska, the town of Barrow is the largest Eskimo settlement in the world, and the farthest-north town on the American continent. This is the Alaska of fictional fame, where Eskimos live principally by and for hunting and fishing.

It is a popular summer stop-over for tourists, Alaskans as well as Outsiders, although it is accessible only by air, dog-sled or boat. Between June 1 and September 15, Wien-Alaska Airlines makes daily flights to Barrow, where it maintains the "Top O' the World" hotel, with unpretentious but colorful accommodations.

There are often in Barrow interesting groups of scientists, engineers, and skilled technicians assigned to research or maintenance projects nearby. Between May, June, and July there are 80 days of all-day sunshine.

Most of the Eskimos live in modern, frame-type dwellings, although a few may still be seen in their ancient igloos. The village itself centers about a trading post, a few small restaurants, and a cluster of Quonset-type dwellings. The atmosphere is distinctively frontier, and so are the prices. Food costs are perhaps highest in Alaska. During the July thaw boots are needed to negotiate the gravel-packed muddied streets. About a dozen miles from the village is a famed monument, marking the spot where the celebrated humorist Will Rogers died in a crash with his pilot, Wiley Post.

When the Eskimos catch their first big whale, usually July, there is considerable feasting and celebration. The festivities include many competitions between natives, tantamount to the Eskimos' "Olympics."

BETHEL, pop. 1,100

Although situated in the extremely isolated southwestern portion of Alaska, at the northern tip of the Kuskokwim Bay, Bethel is an active little town and well organized. One of its ambitions is to install street lights.

Bethel became a legal entity in the fall of 1957. It has an apartment house and its residents, mainly employed by Federal agencies such as the U. S. Public Health Service and the Bureau of Indian Affairs, are proud home owners. It enjoys a fairly wide trading area. A recent publication prepared under the supervision of the local school superintendent states that there are many "opportunities in Bethel for the man who wants to start a business." The presence of an active boat and motorboat repair shop testifies to fishing and boating as major recreational and commercial activities.

It has a large, airy and well-constructed school house, with an average enrollment of 270 pupils and 14 teachers, including an accredited high school.

The town also boasts the largest field hospital in Alaska for natives, rebuilt in 1954 at a cost in excess of $4,000,000 serving about 12,000 natives "widely scattered" among 70 villages. Settled originally by Moravians, and still a bustling Moravian missionary center, Bethel has no public drinking places, but it has two small motion picture houses, a small hotel, a couple of restaurants, and a library. Fishing in the Kuskokwim River for pike, salmon, sheefish, and smelt is highly rated, as is fishing for trout in nearby lakes. Ample game is also found within a 15-mile radius of the village, including moose, wolves, beaver, muskrat, ducks, geese, and ptarmigan.

CORDOVA, pop. 2,000

Located in south central Alaska, almost on the Gulf of Alaska, Cordova was once the center of a thriving copper-mining industry. A 195-mile railroad built inland from Cordova to the Kennecott copper mines, an incredible feat immortalized in Rex Beach's *The Iron Trail,* once filled Cordovans with great hopes of becoming a rail and ocean terminus. But when the copper bubble burst, the town returned to its customary means of earning a livelihood, fishing. Thus, while the population has been officially estimated at 2,500, it may be at times considerably less during a poor fishing season or "between" seasons.

The town has salmon, crab, and clam canneries and a small but excellent boat harbor. According to a report in the Fairbanks *News-Miner,* "Petroleum exploration south of Cordova in the Ice Bay region has brought hope that an oil field might be developed. Oil is known to exist in the area, and a small refinery operated at Katalla, near Cordova, until it burned down in the 1930's."

Another hopeful outlook for Cordova is the possibility that it may become the site of a pulp mill because the town is surrounded by dense forests. There are also reports that other mining activities may be launched (coal) to take the place of the once-thriving copper industry. According to the U.S. Bureau of Mines, there are in areas near Cordova an estimated 3,000,000,000 tons of bituminous and anthracite coals.

The town is accessible only by air or water but it has three hotels and its seafood restaurants are considered among the finest in the North.

DILLINGHAM, pop. 900

In southwestern Alaska, on the Nushagak River, near Bristol Bay, Dillingham lies in a flat wooded area on "the largest red salmon fishing grounds in the world." Its Chamber of Commerce virtually guarantees "an animal for every hunter"—moose, bear, and caribou.

Most of the population earn their livelihood chiefly from fishing and trapping, but because of its growing reputation as a "sportsman's paradise," tourist traffic is contributing to the Dillingham economy.

Proximity to the warming effects of the Japanese current gives

Dillingham a more moderate climate than many midwestern and northern states.

There are five different churches, two motion picture houses, a dance hall, two bars, and a pool hall. In the summer, two commercial canneries are active and the population is swelled by cannery workers as well as commercial fishermen. There is also a public school and two parochial grade schools, run by the Seventh Day Adventists, and the Holy Rosary Mission, and the town maintains a 50-bed hospital.

Areas nearby are known to be mineralized and offer opportunities for prospectors. One commercial mercury mine has been established and its production has been described as "extremely high mercury content."

FAIRBANKS, pop. 12,500

As Alaska's second largest city, and the farthest-north large town in America, Fairbanks is experiencing rapid growth. The greater Fairbanks area, *not* including two military installations nearby (Ladd Air Force Base and Eielson Air Force Base), totals about 38,500 population, representing a 400 per cent increase in the past 20 years. However, the town itself relies to a great extent on military personnel and construction projects for income.

Like Anchorage, it is a spirited youthful town, although it still retains a fair measure of the Old Klondike atmosphere, which many are not too anxious to alter because it has become a tourist attraction. Even Alaskans like to go north to Fairbanks, to see its large gold placer mining operation in action and to pan a little gold for themselves in nearby rivers and streams. They especially like to be in Fairbanks around July 28, "Discovery Day," when the entire town turns out in colorful costumes (including bearded men) to commemorate the day a Klondiker named Felix Pedro made the gold discovery that touched off the wildest gold rush in Alaska. On "Discovery Day," and for days thereafter, the entire town reverts to the Klondike era. People pan for gold on the streets bordering the Chena River, which flows through Fairbanks, merchants dress as in days of old, the bars are filled with "hussies" in frontier costume, and "uncooperative" (beardless) males are locked up in the hoosegow.

The main part of town is well paved and expanding, but it represents an intriguing mixture of the new (modern apartments) with the old (small log cabins), which inspired the setting and story for

Edna Ferber's *Ice Palace*. With the University of Alaska nearby, Fairbanks also has a campus atmosphere at times.

In addition to many churches, modern apartment houses, and modern office buildings, there are several hotels and motels, two motion picture theatres, a hospital, several modern medical clinics, an excellent daily afternoon newspaper (*News-Miner,* 10,000 circulation), *Jessen's Weekly,* perhaps the most famous and most colorful newspaper in Alaska (circulation 5,200), two television stations (KFAR-TV, KTVF) and two radio stations (KFAR, KFRB).

Fairbanksians also have a fairly active cultural schedule, which includes concert and dramatic presentations by local and "imported" groups. The town seems to be a haven for artists. Not only is there a fine arts guild, but many residents—oldtimers and newcomers alike—pursue active art hobbies. Most people are also very sports-minded and participate in a wide variety of activities, which include curling, archery, and parachute jumping. The local Chamber of Commerce also describes Fairbanks as the "center of the last and greatest hunting and fishing territory in the Western Hemsphere," a fact which seems to be supported by the great number of hunting and camping supply stores in town and by the steady traffic of sportsmen to Fairbanks during the various hunting and fishing seasons.

Like Anchorage, Fairbanks has become an important stop-over for increasing jet Pole flights and the town looks forward to this activity as a growing source of revenue. Local business leaders are also striving earnestly and intensively to make Fairbanks the number-one tourist center in Alaska, and many have already made substantial investments with this in mind. Fairbanks will perhaps continue to benefit greatly from the fact that it is usually the first major stop for travellers coming off the Alaska Highway.

It has several excellent paved highways leading out of town and connecting with the main network of roads through the Richardson Highway south, and also into the Denali Highway which carries a steady flew of Alaskans and Outsiders to Alaska's most famous attraction, McKinley National Park.

Employment, however, is largely seasonal and depends mostly on the construction industries.

Housing has generally been fairly "tight" and may remain so for several years while intense urban renewal projects are underway. During the summer months, nine trailer courts with modern facilities, including sewer and water connections, help take up the slack, and trailer space rentals are moderate, ranging from $30 to $40 per month, plus utilities. There is often an active market in used trailers for sale and rent.

With business growing almost daily, prime property in downtown Fairbanks costs about as much to rent or purchase as it does in Anchorage, ranging upwards from about 40 cents per square foot for rentals to $1,200 per square foot, purchased. Assessed valuation of property in the greater Fairbanks area has increased from $23,000,-000 in 1947 to well over $100,000,000.

HAINES, pop. 800

When World War II broke out, the town of Haines in southeastern Alaska, near Skagway and the Lynn Canal, happened to be the only place in Alaska with an Army garrison. Today, it is the only southeastern town which connects directly with the Alaska Highway via Haines Junction to the north. Its neighboring settlement is Port Chilkoot, which has a hotel, and the two areas are often considered as "one" town.

The local industries are fishing and lumbering. There is a 625-mile pipeline which runs from Haines to Fairbanks.

The area around Haines is known to be highly mineralized but largely unexploited. It is a pleasant place in the summer, when temperatures frequently climb to a comfortable 85 and annual precipitation—about 50 inches—is quite low for that part of Alaska.

There are two hotels in town, one quite modern, and its restaurants are also noted for seafood. The area is also known for its strawberries, three of which may fill a coffee cup. During late June or early July there is a Strawberry Festival, at which there are a variety of festivities, including strawberry-eating contests and dances by Indians.

HOMER, pop. 1,100

About 120 air miles southwest of Anchorage, at the tip of the Kenai Peninsula, Homer is a rapidly growing community in choice hunting country (said to have the biggest moose in Alaska) and is serviced by daily flights from Anchorage. It can also be reached via the Sterling Highway from Anchorage, a factor which is contributing to its growth.

The area surrounding Homer is picturesque and dotted with farms. It has a friendly, youthful population nearly all of whom share an intense optimism for the town's future, many confidently expecting the population to mushroom to at least five times its present size within the next decade. Some of this optimism is generated by the fact that heavy oil and gas expenditures on the Kenai Peninsula will benefit the town, which already has several modern motels and a supermarket. Optimism is stimulated also by an expected increase in tourist trade and the possibility of developing a cannery based on shrimp known to abound in nearby waters.

A thriving mail order business was recently established in Homer, based on the unique wild berries which grow in the area. A mimeographed weekly newspaper adds to the town's informal, genial atmosphere. Adjacent to beaches are enormous coal beds, from which residents pick up free coal for fuel; others purchase it from venders at about $5 a ton. A local hotel has about 25 rooms and also offers "dormitory beds" at rates ranging from $2 to $3.50 per person.

The local hunting and fishing supply store, "Sporter Arms," is considered an "information center for hunting, fishing, boating and hiking." Excellent and moderately priced small-airplane service can take sportsmen from Homer to a wide variety of hunting and fishing spots, including islands and inlets. With expanding population and increasing tourism southbound from Anchorage, Homer promises to become a town with many opportunities for service-type businesses.

JUNEAU, pop. 9,500

The controversial capital of Alaska, Juneau is typical of that part of the Panhandle which clings to the western border of Canada. It rests at the foot of steep mountains, almost as if it were cradled between the toes of a giant, with no place to grow but up. The center of town consists of less than half a square mile of streets, almost all running uphill. It is a popular tourist stop-over in the summer, when Canadian steamship lines bring vessels crowded with passengers from Vancouver.

Most of the residents are real oldtimers in Alaska, and many consider those with less than 20 years in Alaska as "newcomers." The town itself is colorful and the scenery is incomparable. Many businesses make an effort to eschew the new and the modern in order to retain the old flavor of Alaska which apparently appeals to tourists.

The Baranof is perhaps the most famous hotel in Alaska and a Juneau landmark, where the old and the new blend inoffensively.

Among the notable points of interest are a fascinating museum-library in the Federal Building, which contains the most complete collection of Eskimo and Indian crafts, artifacts, rare books, and minerals in Alaska, and the Red Dog saloon, which has retained its Klondike flavor, complete with sawdust on the floor, swinging doors, and honky-tonk piano. Equally intriguing is the famous Mendenhall Glacier, 13 miles from town.

The largest single payroll in town is the state and Federal government. After that it is fishing and forestry, although a local airline with 80 employees is "big business." The people give the impression of being more sedate and conservative than the rest of Alaska. It is not hard to come by many who still think statehood was a mistake. The one thing most Juneau residents now seem to fear is that Anchorage will take the capital away from them—an extremely justifiable fear. There are about 60 miles of roads within and without Juneau, but most of these lead to nowhere. Cut off by mountains, it may be a generation or more before Juneau finds a highway link to interior Alaska, its most dynamic center. The future for Juneau appears to be in the development of tourism, for which it is apparently ideal as a scenic attraction and sportsman's paradise. When the Salmon Derby is on in Juneau, the entire town virtually comes to a standstill.

There are two hospitals, 20 churches, excellent schools, two radio stations (KINY, KJNO) and one television station (KINY-TV); a daily newspaper, the Alaska *Empire* (circulation 4,100) which also appears Sundays, and a semi-weekly newspaper, the *Independent* (circulation 3,100).

About a dozen or so miles over a bridge leading out of Juneau is a suburban town, Douglas, of exceptional beauty and largely a growing residential area for people who work in Juneau. Douglas has been labelled by many visitors as the "ideal home community" in Alaska.

There are three outstanding hunting and fishing lodges—the Taku, the Tongass, and the Thayer Lake—which are readily accessible to sportsmen via brief, inexpensive air hops.

KENAI, pop. 400

Although still a small town, Kenai, situated on the Sterling Highway southwest of Anchorage on the Cook Inlet, is in the heart of the booming oil and gas country and its future has been predicted as nothing less than "spectacular." One report estimates that "in the not-too-distant future" the population of Kenai will zoom to 50,000!

It is principally a fishing town with a salmon cannery, but its residents enjoy many of the comforts and "culture" available to Anchorage, including television. Kenai is one of the earliest Russian settlements, founded in 1791. It has an old Russian church, and Indian burial ground, an airport, a motel, restaurants, and taxi service. Many businessmen in Alaska, as well as a large bank, are maintaining a watchful vigilance over Kenai's prospects for business opportunities as oil and gas activities increase on the peninsula.

KETCHIKAN, pop. 10,500

Like its sister towns in the Panhandle, Ketchikan, the southernmost city in Alaska, clings to a mountainside and has steep streets. It is the third largest city in Alaska, and its future has been brightened by the recent establishment of a $55,000,000 pulp mill, providing steady employment for hundreds. Other principal industries are fishing, lumbering, and some mining, although discovery of radioactive ore on nearby Prince of Wales Island, west of the city, may play a significant role in its mining future.

Ketchikan is the first port of call for cruise ships from Canada; like Juneau, it has an annual Salmon Derby which is popular within and without Alaska, attracting fishermen by the thousands from all over the United States.

Its climate is among the mildest in the Panhandle and it has been described as "the city where it rains but never snows."

Saxman Park, about two miles from town, is the site of many famous old totem poles, and a popular feature for many travellers is a visit to one of several neighboring Indian villages which are accessible by short charter airplane rides or charter boats. For outdoorsmen there are several resorts, relatively low-priced, where cabins, boats, hot spring baths, and fishing are featured.

The city itself is located on an island with a name which residents themselves don't care to pronounce, Revillagigedo. Some of the streets are picturesque, propped up by timber trestles, like small railroad bridges, because they cling to the steep slope of a mountain.

Although barely out of its frontier fishing age, Ketchikan was named one of the 11 winners for the All-American cities title in 1958, an honor awarded to dynamic, forward-looking cities in a nationwide U.S. competition. The city has enjoyed excellent management and has made numerous improvements in recent years, particularly in school construction and public utilities. In 1958, it dedicated the largest and finest small boat harbor in Alaska, built at a cost of nearly $2,500,000.

Ketchikan, boasting four canneries in town and several others in the surrounding areas, is also known as the "Salmon Capital of the World," and it has a number of cold-storage processing plants for halibut, cod, and herring as well as salmon.

An anticipated passenger-vehicle ferry, linking Ketchikan with nearby Prince Rupert in Canada, may boost tremendously Ketchikan's future as a center for tourism, particularly in view of the fact that its cost-of-living factor is extremely low, relative to the rest of Alaska, and its recreational value is quite high.

There are two radio stations (KTKN, KABI), a weekly newspaper, the *Alaska Chronicle,* and a daily newspaper, the *News* (circulation 3,100), a large, modern high school, a community college, nearly two dozen churches, and one of the best housing situations in Alaska since, as one report said, "the community was over-built during the pulp mill construction boom."

According to the Chamber of Commerce, "Special tax incentives are available for new industries locating in the area and a trained work force in these fields of endeavor is available at Ketchikan."

KODIAK, pop. 5,000

The city of Kodiak is located on Kodiak Island, part of a lush green group of islands which measure about 50 by 200 miles in area, and is about 75 miles southwest of the Kenai Peninsula. The city lies at the foot of a 1,400-foot hill which the islanders, naturally, call a "mountain," Pillar Mountain, although some parts of the island are rugged in terrain, with peaks exceeding 5,000 feet.

The city was first settled by the Russians around 1792, and has long been noted for one of the world's greatest hunting trophies, the Kodiak brown bear, the largest carnivore in the world. In addition to about 700 natives, the population, an admixture of Russians and Scandinavians, is augmented by a nearby Naval station and Coast Guard Air detachment. Total military personnel and their dependents are estimated at about 3,000.

There are very few roads on the island. Most people get around by boat or airplane. About half the population relies on the Naval and Coast Guard installations for a livelihood, the remainder on fishing. Salmon has been the mainstay, but king crab is coming up fast, and there is also a clam cannery in the city. There are six cattle ranches in the island group, but a small dairy near Kodiak supplies fresh milk to a pasteurizing and bottling plant in town.

There is a Catholic-operated, 23-bed hospital, a weekly newspaper (*The Mirror,* circulation 1,500), radio and television outlets supplied by Naval units and the Armed Forces Radio Service, and a very modern (completed in 1955) combination grade and high school located on a hillside which commands a magnificent view of St. Paul's Harbor and surrounding mountains. The school has an enrollment of about 800 pupils and a teaching staff in excess of 40. There are also several churches in the city, including a Christian Science center.

KOTZEBUE, pop. 1,000

About 50 miles north of the Arctic Circle, above Seward Peninsula. Kotzebue is almost entirely a native village, native-run, with no liquor, no sidewalks, a trading post, and two small hotels, largely to accommodate tourists brought in by Wien-Alaska Airlines. It is headquarters for polar bear and wolf hunters around March and April. Between mid-May and mid-June, visitors like to watch the massive ice break-up from their hotel windows and then go shee-fishing, which is said to be excellent after the ice moves out. Also, after the ice break-up the natives go for beluga whales, and visitors can arrange to join a whale hunt. Between June and July there are a number of native festivities, including the famous blanket-tossing games, dancing, demonstrations of kayak riding, craftsmanship in jade, ivory and fur, and rides for visitors in "oomiaks," huge, sturdy boats made from tough walrus hides.

The Wien Arctic Hotel serves sourdough pancakes, pickled beluga whale, reindeer stew, and luscious wild blue berries. After June 3, the sun, for 36 days, never sinks below the horizon.

The area around Kotzebue is said to be rich in jade, lead, silver, and copper, but like much of the Arctic slope remains virtually unexplored and unexploited.

McGRATH, pop. 300

Several hundred miles northwest of Anchorage, just west of the rugged Alaska Range (about 200 miles due west of McKinley National Park), McGrath is perhaps one of the most isolated settlements in Alaska, consisting of a few small stores and an airfield. It is in the heart of a great valley, where many rivers converge. The population of 300 is strictly "estimated." Most of those who live in or around McGrath are employed by the government, the stores, the bush pilots, and the airlines that land there mainly to deliver supplies for natives in the trading area and for employees of various Federal units, such as an aviation station, health center, and Bureau of Land Management fire-fighting field headquarters.

NOME, pop. 2,600

Nome, in the southwest corner of the Seward Peninsula facing Norton Sound and the Bering Sea, was the locale of a fabulous gold rush in '98, when gold was panned on the beaches and more than 20,000 people poured in to seek their fortunes, living in an enormous tent city which Rex Beach was to make famous in *The Spoilers.* Today, panning for gold around Nome is still a part-time hobby or business for residents and visitors alike.

Nome is the business center for northwestern Alaska and has a hospital, school, bank, several hotels, including one that is modern, trading posts, and curio stores selling the handicrafts of the famous master ivory carvers from King Island. There is also a tri-weekly newspaper, *The Nome Nugget,* and a local television station, KNOM-TV.

If the price of gold should be increased, Nome may well again become an active gold-panning and mining area. In the depression of the 1930's, because the price of gold had risen, Nome, unlike the rest of Alaska, was a fairly prosperous town.

For the past 25 years, the harbor has been maintained by the U. S. Army Corps of Engineers, who provide a dredge, tugboat, and two scows to make it possible for supply ships to unload offshore. In 1934, a wind-swept fire, starting at the edge of the town, raced through the wooden-planked streets (still boardwalks), burning to the ground almost every structure in sight. The courageous residents rebuilt the town.

The Corps of Engineers' harbormaster for the past 26 years has been a colorful, tall, steely-haired Scotsman, Bill Brown, who has won renown for his unceasing and heroic labors, in the face of many violent Bering Sea storms, to keep the harbor open.

PALMER, pop. 6,000

Palmer is the "capital" of the lush agricultural area known as Matanuska Valley, about 50 miles northeast of Anchorage off the Glenn Highway. Although the population of the town itself is only about 900, it is a modern, active center for the entire area. Nearby is the only hydroelectric power project worthy of the name and vivid evidence that hydroelectric power in Alaska is feasible.

The town has its own school system, including a high school of extremely modern design, and there is another modern high school at Wassila, a few miles from town. Very recently, the streets were paved and a modern dial telephone system was installed. There are many active fraternal and social clubs in the area, as well as modern stores, banks, a motion picture theatre, 10 churches, and a new 25-bed hospital.

Every August, the proud farmers of the valley hold an agricultural fair at Palmer. It has become a popular "state fair," attracting visitors from all over Alaska. Also, in May, there is a day of festivities to mark the founding of the unique Matanuska Valley Colony.

A monthly magazine (the *Alaskan Record*) and a weekly news-paper (*The Frontiersman*) are published in Palmer, and the area can tune to the two television stations in Anchorage.

PETERSBURG, pop. 1,800

A colorful bit of "old Scandinavia," the town of Petersburg is located on Mitkof Island in the Panhandle. It is surrounded by the majestic Tongass National Forest. Although incorporated as far back as 1910, the town has not grown with any notable speed. However, as a choice hunting and fishing center its harbor is often an anchoring center for sportsmen who arrive from the big cities in yachts. A world's record king salmon (125½ pounds) was taken by a commercial fisherman in water nearby.

The economy of the town is based almost entirely on fishing, salmon, and shrimp canneries. There is a small hotel and a weekly newspaper (the *Press*) and restaurants feature Scandinavian cooking. Around mid-May there are several days of old-country (Norwegian) festivities.

SELDOVIA, pop. 650

Population in the town of Seldovia has fluctuated between 400 and 650 in recent years on account of erratic employment at the town's salmon cannery, chief source of income for Seldovians. The town is located in a scenic area on the southern tip of Kenai Peninsula, facing Homer across Kachemak Bay. Unlike Homer, however, Seldovia has no road connection. Recent developments in carp, shrimp, and halibut processing may continue to support the bulk of the population.

SEWARD, pop. 3,500

Midway down the eastern coast of Kenai Peninsula, the city of Seward, third largest in central Alaska, is known as "City of Contrasts." Many of its streets are unpaved and a frontier atmosphere prevails everywhere, yet there are modern stores and schools, a fine hospital, electric power to homes 25 miles out of town, a film society, a theatrical and concert group, hotels and motels.

As one of the most active posts in Alaska and as the southern terminus for the Alaska Railroad, its principal industries are shipping, railroading, trucking, and lumbering. Most of the supplies for interior Alaska are shipped through its port. During peak seasons, more than 300 cargo handlers are employed on the docks. Another major source of employment (about 120 people) is the Seward Sanatorium, a tuberculosis hospital. The city is expected to expand and benefit greatly from the growing oil and gas activities on the Kenai Peninsula, particularly if pipelines and storage facilities (including refineries) are established when production reaches commercial proportions.

There is a radio station (KIBH) but no television reception from Anchorage because mountains are in the way. But the town has been planning a cable installation to make TV reception possible.

A major event in Seward is an annual silver salmon derby held over two weekends in August, in which prizes totaling more than $10,000 are offered, attracting contestants from Scandinavia and every state in the union. Another annual feature, one that has gained international fame, is a grueling race (inaugurated in 1915) from downtown Seward, up and over the peak of 3,022-foot Mt. Marathan. Contestants from all the states and several foreign lands show up for the event for which the record (51 minutes 40.7 seconds) was set by an Alaskan in 1957.

Gardening is very popular among residents who grow many root crops, including potatoes, cabbage, broccoli, lettuce, peas, radishes, onions, squash, and strawberries. A few have experimented, not too successfully, with fruit trees, although one man has managed to get a yield from a large crab apple tree. Small greenhouses are seen everywhere, and raising tomatoes in pots or cans inside glass porches is popular too.

In 1953, the city suffered a disastrous fire during which the newspaper plant burned down. But an enterprising group of women began publishing a weekly, which they "half-derisively" called the *Petticoat Gazette,* and it has proven popular within Seward. Some 125 subscriptions also go to readers Outside.

SITKA, pop. 4,000

Located on Baranof Island in the Panhandle, Sitka was the original Russian capital of Alaska, founded in 1799. It retains much of its Old World influence and color. Featured attractions are an old Russian church, St. Michael's Cathedral (where many Old World religious treasures are on display) and an old blockhouse where warring Indians were fought off.

A recently opened pulp mill, representing an investment of more than $50,000,000, is expected to contribute significantly to Sitka's economic future and to provide stable employment for almost 1,000 people. Other principal sources of employment and income are a fishing industry, the immense Mt. Edgecumbe school and hospital, a large home for old folks (Pioneer Home), and the Sheldon Jackson High School and Junior College.

The area is noted for its deer hunting, as well as other Alaskan game, such as bear and mountain goat. Lakes and streams around Sitka abound in trout; and in the bays and inlets, king salmon fishing is a major attraction for sportsmen who arrive from all over Alaska by chartered boats and planes.

The city itself, except for highlights and nuances of Russian architecture, appears small and very much like a New England coastal village. There is a daily newspaper (the *Sentinel*), and two radio stations (KFIW, KSEW). Modern medical and hospital facilities are available to all residents, and the town maintains high educational standards and an excellent school system.

During October 16-18, the town goes all out to celebrate Alaska Days, commemorating the transfer of Alaska from Russia to the United States. Since Sitka was the site of the transfer, the festivities resemble traditional July 4th celebrations, which include historical pageants and costume parades.

SKAGWAY, pop. 800

Skagway is a beautiful little town located at the head of the Lynn Canal in the northeast corner of the Panhandle, just above Haines. It has one of the most colorful and historic backgrounds related to the gold rush of '98, when it was one of the major gateways to Dawson City on the storied Klondike River. It is the town where the legendary "Soap" Smith and his gang ruled the Klondikers with violence and terror.

Its buildings and stores still retain the false "gingerbread" fronts made famous in fact and fable. The town itself is virtually surrounded by towering peaks, ranging to 7,000 feet, and is connected to Canada via the unique narrow-gauge railway of the White Pass & Yukon Railroad. The town's economy is based principally on transportation, serving as headquarters for the railway and steamship lines. It has a small but modern motion picture theatre and a weekly newspaper (the *Lynn Canal Weekly*).

The town supports a fully accredited high school and several small hotels. It has a fairly good future as a tourist stop-over, and one of its annual features, the re-enactment of the "Shooting of Dan McGrew," plus kangaroo courts, and costume balls, is becoming widely known to travelers.

SOLDOTNA, pop. 700

There are many maps of Alaska that still do not show or list Soldotna as a town. Located off the Sterling Highway on the Kenai Peninsula, just north of the town of Kenai, Soldotna typifies the speed with which an otherwise unpopulated area can be developed in Alaska. A few years ago, an area of nearly 100 square miles around Soldotna would probably not have held two dozen people. Today, its population is growing rapidly. There are quite a few who now support themselves as part-time homestead farmers, in addition to working for nearby salmon canneries or in one of about thirty service businesses, among which is a motion picture theatre.

An extremely youthful town, Soldotna is planning to build a school but meanwhile sends about 100 of its children to school by bus to nearby Kenai. The town expects rapid growth as a result of oil and gas activities on the Peninsula.

VALDEZ, pop. 750

Located in south central Alaska at the end of an exquisite 30-mile fjord in Prince William Sound due east of Anchorage, Valdez is the northernmost ice-free port on the American continent and connects with interior Alaska via the Richardson Highway. The Highway actually originated as a trail out of Valdez, at the turn of the century, when it was used by Klondikers headed north for the gold fields of Fairbanks. Since then it has played an important role in Alaskan transportation, and trucking is one of its main supporting industries, which include canneries. Valdez might have been the Anchorage of Alaska had not a last-minute decision been made to route the Alaska Railroad through Anchorage instead of Valdez.

However, there is considerable optimism that future recommendations of the Alaska International Rail and Highway Commission may lead to substantial transportation developments for Valdez, perhaps sufficient to restore its hopes of becoming a sprawling metropolis like Anchorage. At present, as one of the most picturesque towns in Alaska, Valdez is content to thrive on its very apt description as the "Switzerland of America."

There are motels, hotels, banks, a modern hospital, a motion picture theatre, and excellent fishing streams. A tourist attraction is the beautiful and intriguing Worthington Glacier, a few miles outside of town, accessible by a side road, and travelers delight in having their photographs taken atop a chunk of ice known to be millions of years old. Another road leads through an abandoned mining town and the main highway goes through the Keystone Canyon, which is beautifully decorated with waterfalls cascading down the sides of mountains.

APPENDIX A

SCHOOLS IN ALASKA

Listed below are the cities, towns and settlements in which there are grade schools, high schools, and colleges in Alaska. School systems incorporating a four-year high school are preceded by an asterisk (*) and those with a limited high school program are preceded by a double asterisk (**).

DISTRICT

*Anchorage
Angoon
*Cordova
**Craig
*Fairbanks
*Haines
Hoonah
Hydaburg
*Juneau
Kake

*Ketchikan
King Cove
Klawock
*Kodiak
**Neenana
*Nome
North Pole
*Palmer
Pelican
*Petersburg

**Seldovia
*Seward
*Sitka
*Skagway
Unalaska
*Valdez
*Wrangell
Yakutat

STATE OPERATED

Afoknak
Akutan
Aleknagik
Alitak
Allakaket
Ambler
Anchor Point
Aniak
Annette Island
Anvik
Belkofski
Bettles Field
*Bethel
Candle
**Cantwell
Chenega
Chignik
Chignik Lagoon
Chugiak
Clark's Point
Circle

Cooper Landing
Crooked Creek
*Dillingham
Dot Lake
Edna Bay
Egegik
Ekuk
Ekwok
Fortuna Ledge
**Fort Yukon
Gakona
Galena
Girdwood
**Glenallen
Gustavus
Healy
Hollis
*Homer
Hughes
Huslia
Karluk

Kasaan
*Kenai
Kenny Lake
King Salmon
Kobuk
Kokhanok
Koyukuk
Lakewood
Larsen Bay
Levelock
Manley Hot Springs
McGrath
Mentasta
**Metlakatla
Moose Pass
**Naknek
Neets Bay
Newhalen
Nikolai
Nikolski
**Ninilchik

252

Nondalton
Northway
Nyac
Old Harbor
Ouzinkie
Pauloff Harbor
Pedro Bay
Perryville
Pilot Point
Port Graham
Port Heiden
Rampart

Red Devil
Ruby
Russian Mission
Sand Point
Slikok Valley
South Naknek
Sterling
Suntrana
Talkeetna
Tanana
Tatitlek
Teller

Tenakee
Thorne Bay
**Tok Junction
**Tustumena
Two Rivers
Tyonek
Unga
Venta
*Wasilla
Willow
Woody Island
Yakutat F.A.A.

ALASKA ON-BASE SCHOOLS

*Adak
*Eielson
Elmendorf
*Ft. Greely

Ft. Richardson
Kodiak
Ladd
*Whittier

APPENDIX B

HOSPITALS IN ALASKA

Listed below are the general hospitals in Alaska, shown according to location and sponsorship. Figures in parenthesis indicate the number of beds. The abbreviations ANHS, and USPHS, and USF&WLS represent the Alaska Native Health Service, United States Public Health Service, and the United States Fish and Wildlife Service, respectively.

Anchorage: Providence Hospital (74), Catholic; Anchorage Medical Center (133), ANHS, USPHS; Elmendorf Air Force Base Hospital (Number of beds not available), Air Force.

Barrow: Barrow Government Hospital (14), ANHS, USPHS.

Bethel: Bethel Government Hospital (56), ANHS, USPHS.

Big Delta: Fort Greely Dispensary (Number of beds not available), U.S. Army.

Cordova: Cordova Community Hospital (22), Baptist.

Dillingham: Kanakanak Government Hospital (57), ANHS, USPHS.

Eielson: Eielson Air Force Base Dispensary (Number of beds not available), Air Force.

Fairbanks: St. Joseph's Hospital (70), Catholic; Ladd Air Force Base Hospital (Number of beds not available), Air Force.

Fort Yukon: Hudson Stuck Memorial Hospital (13), Episcopal.

Glenallen: Faith Hospital (3), C.A.M. Inc. Mission.

Homer: Homer Hospital Health Center (3), Public Utility District.

Juneau: St. Ann's Hospital (79), Catholic.

Ketchikan: Ketchikan General Hospital (74), Catholic.

Kodiak: Griffin Memorial Hospital (19), Catholic; Naval Air Station Dispensary (Number of beds not available), U.S. Navy.

Kotzebue: Kotzebue Government Hospital (38), ANHS, USPHS.

Mt. Edgecumbe: Mt. Edgecumbe Medical Center (100), ANHS, USPHS.

Nome: Maynard MacDougall Memorial Hospital (27), Methodist.

Palmer: Valley Presbyterian Hospital (25), Valley Hospital Association.

Petersburg: Petersburg General Hospital (21), Community.

St. George Island: St. George Island Hospital (6), USF&WLS.

St. Paul Island: St. Paul Island Hospital (8), USF&WLS.

Seldovia: Seldovia Community Hospital (6), Community.

Seward: Seward General Hospital (30), Community.

Sitka: Sitka Community Hospital (23), Community.

Skagway: White-Pass Yukon Hospital (8), White Pass & Yukon Railroad.

Tanana: Tanana Government Hospital (30), ANHS, USPHS.

Wrangell: Bishop Rowe General Hospital (13), Community.

There are also two nursing homes in Alaska, Woodhaven Rest Home (15 beds) at 309 E. Fireweed, Spenard; and the Alaska Pioneers Home (65 beds) at Sitka. Special hospital beds for tuberculars are maintained at the Mt. Edgecumbe Medical Center, the Anchorage Medical Center, and at the Wesleyan Hospital for Chronic Disease in Seward.

As of Nov., 1959, a community hospital in Valdez was reported closed. The hospital in Fort Yukon was also closed.

APPENDIX C

CHAMBERS OF COMMERCE IN ALASKA

Listed below are the various Chambers of Commerce and the addresses at which mail inquiries are received.

Alaska Chamber of Commerce
Box 1079, Ketchikan

Anchorage Chamber of Commerce
304 G. Street, Anchorage

Arctic Circle Chamber of Commerce
Kotzebue

Bethel Chamber of Commerce
Bethel

Cordova Chamber of Commerce
Cordova

Dillingham Chamber of Commerce
Dillingham

Fairbanks Chamber of Commerce
Northward Building, Fairbanks

Haines Business Council
Haines

Homer Chamber of Commerce
Box 93, Homer

Juneau Chamber of Commerce
155 So. Seward St., Juneau

Kenai Chamber of Commerce
Kenai

Ketchikan Chamber of Commerce
Box 2651, Ketchikan

Kodiak Chamber of Commerce
Kodiak

Matanuska Chamber of Commerce
Box 1242, Palmer

North Pole Chamber of Commerce
North Pole

Petersburg Chamber of Commerce
Box 583, Petersburg

Seward Chamber of Commerce
Box 963, Seward

Sitka Chamber of Commerce
Box 435, Sitka

Skagway Chamber of Commerce
Skagway

Valdez Chamber of Commerce
Valdez

Wrangell Chamber of Commerce
Wrangell

APPENDIX D

PRESS AND BROADCASTING IN ALASKA

Listed below are the principal news publications and broadcasting facilities, according to location.

Anchorage: Daily News; Times (both daily, except Sunday); Radio stations: KBYR, KFQD, KENI; Telvision stations: KENI-TV, KTVA.

Cordova: Times (daily); Radio station: KLAM.

Fairbanks: News Miner (daily except Sunday); *Jessen's Weekly;* Radio stations: KFRB, KFAR; Television stations: KFAR-TV, KTVF. Three other weekly publications also circulate in Fairbanks: *The Polar Star,* published by the students of the University of Alaska; the *Eielson Friendly Times,* Eielson Air Force Base; and the *Midnight Sun,* published at Ladd Air Force Base. The Air Force publications are free.

Juneau: Alaska Empire (daily and Sunday); the *Independent* (semi-weekly); Radio stations: KINY, KJNO; Television station: KINY-TV.

Ketchikan: the *News* (daily except Sunday); *Alaska Chronicle* (weekly); Radio stations: KTKN, KABI.

Kodiak: The Kodiak Mirror (weekly).

Nome: Nome Nugget (Mon.-Weds.-Fri., tri-weekly); Television station: KNOM-TV.

Palmer: Frontiersman (weekly).

Petersburg: Press (weekly).

Sitka: Sentinel (daily, except Sat. & Sun.); Radio station: KSEW.

Seward: Radio station: KIBH.

Skagway: Lynn Canal Weekly.

Wrangell: Sentinel (weekly).

The Armed Forces Radio Service operates non-commercial news and recreational radio programs 24 hours a day, seven days a week throughout Alaska. Similar Naval radio stations are operated at Kodiak.

APPENDIX E

ALASKA AIRCRAFT OPERATORS AVAILABLE FOR HIRE
FOR HUNTING AND FISHING TRIPS

The law no longer requires the use of a registered guide for hunting and fishing trips into various parts of Alaska. However, most aircraft operators either serve as expert hunting and fishing guides or provide such guides, as well as special flights and charter aircraft into virtually all parts of Alaska.

The information below has been adapted from a special list of certificated pilot owners (as of August, 1958) made available by the Federal Aviation Agency of the Department of Commerce in Anchorage, Alaska. Their specialties are indicated by a code.

Most of these operators have 2-, 3- and 4-place airplanes. Some have twin-engine amphibians. Larger aircraft are usually available from scheduled carriers.

Code

PL, private lodge; *Gu*, registered guide; *Fl*, floats; *Sk*, skies; *W*, wheels; *B*, bear; *M*, moose; *C*, caribou; *G*, mountain goats; *S*, mountain sheep; *F*, fishing; *H*, all kinds of hunting.

Name	Location	P.O. Box or Street Address	Code
Barton Air Service	Anchorage	1600 E. 5th St.	
L.A.B. Flying Service	Anchorage	2003 Sunrise Drive	W, Fl, Sk, B, F, M, C, G, S
Baumann Skylines	Anchorage	2316 E. 5th St.	
Branha, E. G	Anchorage	Box 759	H, F
Dunne's Flying Service	Anchorage	333 E. Concrete Ave.	Fl, Sk, F, M, C
Gay Airways	Anchorage	2600 E. 5th Ave.	W, Fl, Gu, PL, F, H
Lee's Flying Service	Anchorage	1528 Kinnikinnick St.	Fl, H, F, Gu
Lenhart, Victor	Anchorage	Box 646	
Rasmussen, Jack	Anchorage	1600 E. 5th Ave.	
Spernak Airways	Anchorage	Box 2255	W, F
Stoddard Aero Service	Anchorage	2550 E. 5th Ave.	W, Fl, Gu, H, F
Sutton, Richard L.	Anchorage	1600 Medfra St.	
Witham Air Service	Anchorage	Box 3712, East-chester Br.	
Frankes, Fred	Anchorage	112 E. 7th Avenue	

Name	Location	P.O. Box or Street Address	Code
Sea Airmotive, Inc.	Anchorage	Box 828	H
Alcan Airways	Anchorage	Box 2173	
Clark, H. C.	Aniak		W, Fl
Helmericks, Harmon	Barrow		W, S, B, M, C, S, F
Arctic Alaska Air Service	Barrow		
Bethel Charter Service	Bethel	Box 362	W, Fl
Samuelson, John R.	Bethel		W, Fl
Falls, James J.	Bettles		W, Fl
Wilson, Jack E.	Chitina		Fl, Gu, H, F
Jones, Marvin	College	Box 23	Fl, W, Gu
Bear Paw Flying Service	Cooper Landing		W, Fl, B, F, M, G, S
Maves Airways	Dillingham	Box 12	W
Wood, Wilfred	Egegik		W
Black, Horace E.	Fairbanks	Box 504	
Fairbanks Air Service	Fairbanks	Box 1027	
Fricks Flying Service	Fairbanks	Box 1222	
Alaska Bush Airways	Fairbanks	Box 1127	W
Arctic Air Service	Fairbanks	Box 2021	W
Arctic Air Taxi	Fairbanks	1101 6th Ave.	W
Pitts Polar Flight Service	Fairbanks	Box 886	
Rud, Clyde N.	Fairbanks	Rm. 114 International	
Marc's Air Service	Fairbanks	Box 514	W, H
Raven Charter Service	Fairbanks	813 Austin St.	W
Fleet Airways Co.	Galena		W, H, F
Fox Air Service	Haines	Box 95	W, Fl
Ace Flying Service	Haines	Box 91	W, Fl
Inlet Airways	Homer	Box 50	Fl, Gu, F, M, B, C, G, S
Klingbeil, John W., Jr.	Homer	Box 18	Fl, F, B, G, M
Lawrence Aircraft Service	Homer	Box 8A	S, M, B
Homer Air Service	Homer	Box 207	S, M, B
Roadhouse Flying Service	Iliamna		Fl, W, S
Hudson, Oren B.	Iliamna		W, Sk
Goodwin, Dean H.	Juneau	Box 1262	Fl
Gibson, James S.	Kenai	Box 187	W

Name	Location	P.O. Box or Street Address	Code
Jacobs, Robert E.	Kenai	Box 106	Fl, Sk, W, Gu, F, M, G, S
Johnson, Donald L.	Kenai	Box 152	Fl, W, Sk, F, M, B, S
Webber Air Service	Ketchikan	Box 2436	Fl, F
Simpson Aircraft Rental	Ketchikan	Box 2146	Fl, H, F
Hollenbeak Flying Service	Ketchikan	Box 2015	Fl, H, F
Alaska Aero Marine	King Salmon		H, F
Alaska Aero-marine	King Salmon	Box 15	W, H, F
Seiler, Edwin W.	King Salmon		W, Fl, H, F
Harve, James W.	Kodiak	Box 1125	Fl
Kodiak Airways, Inc.	Kodiak	Box A-1	Fl
Almasy, Theordor J.	McGrath		W, Fl, B, F, S, M
Smith, Daniel	McGrath		W, Fl
Tibbetts Flying Service	Naknek	Box 110	Fl, F, H
Floyd Miller Enterprises	Northway		
Green's Flying Service	Palmer	Star Route	W
Matanuska Air Trading Service	Palmer	Box 825	
Houston, C. R.	Palmer	Mile 147 Glenn Highway	W, Fl, B, M, C, G, S, F
Sutter, Charles W.	Palmer	Mile 156 Glenn Highway	Fl, Gu, H, F
Polar Flying Service	Pt. Barrow		W, S, B
Boyette, John	Seldovia	Box 95	Fl, M, G, B, F, Gu
Jay Carroll-Guide & Outfitter	Seward		H, F
McDonald Airways	Seward	Box 655	W
Vanderpool Flying Service	Sleetmute		W, H
Branham, Dennis	Spenard	Box 4-1351	H, F
Hurst, James L.	Spenard	Star Route A, Box 588	
McDonald, Terrence W.	Spenard	2300 McKinley Ave.	
Novak, Stephen N., Jr.	Spenard	2409 McRae Road	

Name	Location	P.O. Box or Street Address	Code
Polar Helicopters, Inc.	Spenard	Box 4502	
Vaughn's Air Service	Spenard		
Sheldon, Donald E.	Talkeetna		W, S, Fl, Gu, F, M, C, S, B
Frank's Air Service	Tanana	Box 58	Fl, M, C, B, S, F
Peninsula Airways	Ugashik		W
Kennedy Air Service	Valdez		
Hansen, Paul B.	Pacific Palisades, California	1269 Chautauqua Boulevard	Fl

SCHEDULED AIR CARRIERS

Name	Location
Alaska Airlines	Anchorage
Alaska Coastal Airlines	Juneau
Cordova Airlines	Anchorage
Ellis Airlines	Ketchikan
Munz Airlines	Nome
Northern Consolidated Airlines	Anchorage
Pacific Northern Airlines	Anchorage
Reeve Aleutian Airlines	Anchorage
Western Alaska Airlines	Dillingham
Wien Airlines	Fairbanks

For additional information regarding certificated aircraft operators in Alaska: Fifth Region, Federal Aviation Agency, Federal Building, Anchorage.

APPENDIX F

AVERAGE HOURLY WAGES PAID TO WORKERS IN 16 OCCUPATIONS, IN ANCHORAGE AND FAIRBANKS

The information below has been adapted from tabulations made available by the Army-Air Force Wage Board in Washington, D. C. It is based on actual hourly wages paid to various groups of workers in 43 firms between Anchorage and Fairbanks. However, since averages tend to wash out the highs and the lows, the last column has been adapted from the data to show the range between the lowest and the highest hourly wage paid.

Occupation	Average Hourly wage	Range of Hourly Wages	
		Low	High
Laborer, skilled	$ 3.24	$ 3.00	4.09
Fork lift operator	3.08	2.60	4.09
Truck driver (heavy)	3.76	3.40	4.19
Helper (trades)	3.01	2.40	4.19
Carpenter	4.36	3.80	4.59
Electrician	4.20	3.60	5.10
Pipefitter	4.47	3.60	5.10
Sheet metal worker	4.38	3.40	5.09
Machinist	3.67	3.00	4.09
Aircraft mechanic	3.63	3.30	3.79
Mechanic, maintenance	3.98	3.10	4.99
Automotive mechanic	3.68	3.30	3.89
Electrical lineman	4.88	4.60	5.10
Heavy equipment operator	4.07	3.70	4.49
Plumber	4.89	3.80	5.10
Welder	4.01	3.40	4.59

Generally, fully qualified skilled craftsmen and those in recognized unions usually receive the highest hourly wage. Sometimes the *highest* is a *minimum* wage which is further augmented by premium payments. Consequently it would not be unusual, for example, to find truck drivers being paid $5 or more per hour. Sometimes, if there is a shortage in certain skills, an employer will pay the highest wage for an employe who may not otherwise be fully qualified for the skill. On one occasion, the author met a man who had been drawing pay as a roofing foreman, although he had been in the trade for only about 18 months.

SOURCES OF INFORMATION, ANNOTATED

Listed below are various sources of information regarding Alaska, according to categories devised by the author. Most of these sources were utilized, personally or through research, by the author and were found extremely valuable in obtaining general data and answers to specific questions regarding every conceivable phase of life in Alaska.

No one source is entirely exclusive. For instance, while a Chamber of Commerce (see Appendix C) is always a useful source on many questions, especially in Alaska—whether these questions concern business or obtaining the name and address of a local fishing and hunting guide—other sources of information may and should be utilized, if only to be certain that the information received is reliable. For this reason, the list below is also annotated by the author in order to call attention to the possibilities of utilizing more than one specific source of information and to call attention to otherwise obscure facts.

General

Chambers of Commerce in various Alaskan cities and towns. (See Appendix C)

Alaska Resource Development Board, 309 Alaska Office Building, Juneau, Alaska. This is a state agency and a particularly reliable and efficient source for information regarding business and economics as well as the natural resources of Alaska.

The United States Government Printing Office, Superintendent of Documents, Washington 25, D. C. This is an exceptionally reliable source for the kind of information that may be found in *any* official report, brochure, booklet, or book that may have been written either for public information, or for official internal use in one or more government agencies. Learning how to make use of USGPO facilities may yield some of the most obscure yet surprisingly useful and reliable information. The technique is fairly simple. Two basic steps: (1) A request addressed to the Superintendent of Documents, asking for a *List of Publications* regarding Alaska in general, or regarding a *specific* subject in Alaska. These lists are free. Lists describe publications available, contents, and prices and you order in accordance with instructions. Usually, there is a nominal charge for various publications that are available for public distribution. (2) The USGPO publishes a *Monthly Catalog of United States Government Publications.* Each catalog contains an index. Checking the index under "Alaska" will disclose the existence of official information, even if it has *not* been made available for public distribution. But the catalog will tell you where such a publication can be obtained, sometimes free. Also, a cumulative index for the year is published in the December issue of the *Monthly Catalog.* These catalogs are usually available at public or college and university libraries. When unable to locate a library possessing the catalog, a letter addressed to the USGPO, asking for the name and address of the nearest library, will bring the required information since there are, scattered about the country, a number of "depository libraries" which receive all publications of the USGPO. It is also possible to purchase individual issues of the *Monthly Catalog* at 25 cents per copy, or to obtain a yearly subscription for $3.

United States Bureau of Census, Department of Commerce, Washington 25, D. C., for general information regarding population and economic reports.

Fairbanks News-Miner, 514 Second Avenue, Fairbanks, Alaska, publishes in December of each year a *Progress Edition,* an outstanding and comprehensive report, in several sections, covering all phases of life in Alaska, including surveys, data, and feature material which should prove of great interest to anyone, whether or not living in Alaska. The *Progress Edition* may be purchased directly from the *News-Miner.*

Alaskan Command, APO 942, Seattle, Washington, is a source of general information regarding defense activities in Alaska. These activities, of course, include employment of civilian personnel, construction projects underway or planned; it is also the most reliable source of information regarding life in general on the various military and naval bases in Alaska.

Airlines. (See Appendix E) The various major airlines which fly to and from Alaska, and the scheduled aircraft carriers of Alaska, frequently publish a variety of pamphlets and brochures on subjects of general interest and distribute these to the public upon request.

Employment

Alaska Employment Security Commission, Box 2661, Juneau, Alaska, is an official state agency for information regarding jobs in Alaska, the availability of labor in businesses and wages paid. *No one* should pay any fee to any company or individual, either for information about jobs or the promise of a job in Alaska, without first consulting this agency. In this regard, there have been many fakers and their numbers will probably grow as interest in Alaska increases over the years.

United States Department of Labor, Washington 25, D. C., has various units, such as the Bureau of Labor Statistics, and the United States Employment Service, where general information regarding labor developments, problems, and employment may be obtained from one or more of the appropriate offices. The United States Employment Service is a Federal-state organization which has a unique "clearing" system, wherein you can learn about the availability of a specific type of job in Alaska merely by visiting a local U. S. Employment Office.

Associated General Contractors, Alaska Chapter, Anchorage, Alaska, is a source of information regarding construction projects in Alaska. Since construction is a major source of employment for a great variety of jobs, knowledge of specific construction projects underway or planned may prove useful.

Alaska Construction News, 518 I Street, Anchorage, Alaska: for the same reasons outlined in the previous paragraph, this bi-monthly publication may prove useful. Periodically, it publishes a list of contractors who are members of the Alaska Chapter of the Associated General Contractors. Single copies are 35 cents. Yearly subscriptions, $2.

Alaska Communication System, 550 Federal Office Building, Seattle 4, Washington, is the best source of information for possible employment in the vast communications network of Alaska. In this regard, it should be remembered that part of the network are the "White Alice" and "Dewline" systems which are maintained by private contractors, who do the hiring. The names of these contractors may be obtained from the ACS office in Seattle. In any event, there is almost always a need for operators, trouble shooters, engineers, and electronics technicians as well as a variety of skilled craftsmen for maintenance.

In the professional and career areas, there are also the following sources:

ACCOUNTANCY: Board of Accounts, Juneau.

CHIROPRACTIC: Board of Chiropractic Examiners, Box 1192, Juneau.

COSMETOLOGY: Board of Hairdressing and Beauty Culture, Juneau.

DENTISTRY: Board of Dental Examiners, Juneau.

ENGINEERING OR ARCHITECTURE: Board of Engineers' and Architects' Examiners, Box 1511, Juneau.

LAW: Board of Law Examiners, Juneau.

MEDICAL AND PUBLIC HEALTH: Medical Officer-in-Charge, Alaska Native Health Service, Department of Health, Education and Welfare, Anchorage; State Department of Health, Juneau; Board of Medical Examiners, Juneau.

OPTOMETRY: Board of Optometry, Box 468, Ketchikan.

PHARMACY: Board of Pharmacy, Box 800, Anchorage.

TEACHING: University of Alaska, College, Alaska Methodist University, Anchorage, Commissioner of Education, Juneau; Bureau of Indian Affairs, Juneau.

WEATHER: U.S. Weather Bureau, Department of Commerce, Washington 25, D. C.

Civil Service Employment information for Alaska is obtainable from: Alaska Branch, Eleventh Civil Service District, Seattle, Washington.

Housing

Alaska State Housing Authority, Box 179, Anchorage, Alaska, is the best and most reliable source of information on all questions pertaining to the availability of housing, costs of construction, loans, and housing problems in general. If the Authority cannot answer a question from its own resources, it will almost certainly be able to refer an inquirer to the next best available source, perhaps a bank or a specific Chamber of Commerce.

Business

Chambers of Commerce (see Appendix C) in Alaska are most cooperative in providing information regarding business problems. In this regard, too, the author calls particular attention to the various reports and publications mentioned in the Bibliography, namely publications prepared by J. Walter Thompson and Co., Benton and Bowles, *Sales Management Magazine*, and the National Industrial Conference Board.

University of Alaska, Division of Business Administration, recently completed a special study of wholesaling and retailing in Alaska, for the Small Business Administration. Copies of the full report are available from the University at $2.00 each.

The Small Business Administration, Federal Building, Anchorage, is particularly useful for information regarding problems of running and financing a small business in Alaska.

U. S. Department of Commerce, Washington 25, D. C., through its many domestic and foreign offices has a great variety of experts in many different departments where special studies regarding Alaska have been made and probably will continue to be made for the benefit of those who may contemplate doing business in or with Alaska.

Public Lands
For Homesites, Homesteading, Business and Recreation

U.S. Department of the Interior, Bureau of Land Management, Washington 25, D. C., is the best and most reliable source of information regarding public lands in general in Alaska, including questions pertaining to oil and gas leasing, prospecting on the public domain and lands in the national forests. Specific questions regarding public lands in Alaska are best answered by the various BLM land offices in the state. These are: Area Office, Box 1481, Juneau; Operations Office, Box 480, Anchorage; Operations Office, Bink Building, Fairbanks.

It should also be noted that the Bureau of Land Management recently completed for public distribution a 28-minute color, sound motion picture showing the public land and resource development programs of the BLM. It is a 16-mm film which was made in Alaska and, according to the BLM, it depicts BLM's role in past and future Alaska development, covering "oil and gas leasing through agricultural homesteading and townsite planning." The film is available, free of charge, on a loan basis, to any interested group. Information on obtaining the film may be had from the BLM's Washington office.

The University of Alaska, Agricultural Extension Service, College, Alaska, cooperating with the U. S. Department of Agriculture, makes available a great variety of publications regarding agriculture in Alaska. It is also the best single source of information pertaining to any type of "farm" problem, from lists showing the names and addresses of other agricultural sources of information to buying a farm in Alaska or homesteading as a livelihood. The Extension Service also has field offices in Alaska, as follows: ANCHORAGE: Room 58, Federal Building, Box 2086; FAIRBANKS: Room 3, Federal Building, Box 1913; HOMER: Husky Building, Box 70; JUNEAU: Room 208, Municipal Building, Box 1109; KETCHIKAN: 622 Mission Street; NOME: Box 657; PALMER: American Legion Building, Box 1736.

Religion

The Alaska Council of Churches, 711 Ninth Avenue, Anchorage, Alaska, Reverend Fred McGinnis.

Health

Department of Health, Alaska Office Building, Juneau, Alaska.
Arctic Health Research Center, Anchorage, Alaska.

Cities and Towns

League of Alaskan Cities, Box 1764, Palmer, Alaska, publishes a yearly *Alaska City Officials Directory* which is sold for $1. It contains a great deal of reliable information pertaining to various cities and towns in Alaska, such as names of officials, property evaluation reports, tax rates, utilities, reports on city finances and resources, bonded indebtedness, definitions of classes of cities, and even shows when the various city councils meet.

Travel: to, from, and within Alaska

Division of Tourist and Economic Development, Alaska Office Building, Juneau, Alaska.

The Alaska Railroad, Anchorage, Alaska.

The Bureau of Public Roads, Department of Commerce, Washington 25, D. C.

Two excellent and reliable guides for highway travelers and tourists in general are: *The Milepost,* Box 457, Cathedral City, California; and Lou Jacobin's *Guide to Alaska and the Yukon,* Box 586, Cathedral City, California.

The author is compelled to note that many persons traveling the Alaska Highway to and from Alaska have reported distressing experiences. It is a trip of great scenic excitement and color but, in many respects, an adventure as well. Anyone planning to travel the Alaska Highway would do well to heed the advice of experts and plan accordingly. An important and useful publication on the Alaska Highway is *Travel in Alaska,* published by the U.S. Bureau of Public Roads and available from the Superintendent of Documents, Washington 25, D. C., for 5 cents. This publication also lists other sources of information regarding the Alaska Highway.

Since traveling the Alaska Highway means going through a large portion of Canada, useful information may be obtained from Canadian Government Travel Bureau, Ottawa, Canada.

Private Flying: to, from, and within Alaska

The best single source of information is the Federal Aviation Agency, Fifth Region, Box 440, Anchorage, Alaska.

This office has prepared an extremely useful and entertaining report an excellent 6-page mimeographed report entitled *Central Information* prepared for widespread public distribution, but it has become so popular with pilots within Alaska that it may soon be published in quantity.

However, for those increasing numbers of pilots who want to fly their own airplanes to Alaska, this office has made available, free of charge, an excellent 6-page mimeographed report entitled, *Central Information on Flying to and in Alaska,* providing the necessary information as to desirable routes, flight plans, and radio frequencies.

This office also recommends that interested private pilots obtain from the Superintendent of Documents in Washington, D. C., a pocket-sized booklet called *Terrain Flying,* which sells for 30 cents and contains a special chapter on Alaska.

Further recommended, and sold by the Superintendent of Documents, is *The Alaska Flight Information Manual,* also 30 cents.

Climate and Weather

The Weather Bureau, U.S. Department of Commerce, Washington 25, D. C., is, of course, the most authoritative source of information regarding climate in general or weather in particular for any area, city, or settlement in Alaska.

Hunting and Fishing

Alaska Game Commission, Juneau, Alaska.
United States Fish and Wildlife Service, Juneau, Alaska.
Not to be overlooked is the fact that the various Chambers of Commerce in Alaska are excellent sources of information regarding hunting and fishing within their respective areas.

Maps and Charts

Often, the best, most authoritative and least expensive maps and charts are available through two Federal agencies: The Map Information Office, U.S. Geological Survey, and the Coast and Geodetic Survey, both units of the Department of the Interior, with main offices in the Interior Building, Washington 25, D. C.

The U. S. Geological Survey is constantly preparing new maps and revising old ones. Now that Alaska will be choosing its land from the public domain, under the Statehood Act, surveying work will be greatly accelerated.

Maps published by the Geological Survey are useful for many purposes in Alaska. A topographical map, for example, is so incredibly complex, detailed and costly to produce that only the Government could afford the undertaking and the professional skills required. Yet some of these maps, which are indispensable to sportsmen, prospectors and homesteaders, sell for as little as 25 cents. The Map Information Office in Washington has available, free of charge, a variety of publications which are designed to help people select Government maps.

SELECTED BIBLIOGRAPHY, ANNOTATED

The publications and reports listed below have been compiled and selected by the author from the following sources: Library of Congress, Washington, D. C.; The New York Public Library at 42nd Street and Fifth Avenue, New York City; The Lousac Library, Anchorage, Alaska; The Greater Anchorage Chamber of Commerce, Anchorage, Alaska; The Fairbanks Chamber of Commerce, Fairbanks, Alaska; Alaska Resources Development Board, Juneau, Alaska; Extension Service Information Office, College, Alaska; Information Service Office, Alaskan Command, Elmendorf AFB, Alaska; Information Service Office, Air Force,

Ladd AFB, Fairbanks, Alaska; Public Information Office, U. S. Department of Commerce, Washington D. C.; the Public Information Office, Bureau of Land Management, Department of the Interior, Washington, D. C., and Benton & Bowles, Inc., New York City.

The bibliography has been organized according to various classifications of subject interest and is annotated to highlight certain information or to clarify the availability and sources of publications.

General and Historical

Albee, Mrs. Ruth: *Alaska Challenge,* Dodd, 1940.

Barbeau, Charles M.: *Pathfinders in the North.*

Caldwell, Joseph B.: *Introducing Alaska,* Putnam, 1947.

Carrighar, Sally: *Moonlight at Midday,* Knopf, 1958.

Coe, Douglas: *Road to Alaska, Story of the Alaska Highway,* Messner, 1943.

Crisler, Lois: *Arctic Wild,* Harper, 1958.

Day, Beth: *Glacier Pilot,* Holt, 1957.

Duffresne, Frank: *Alaska's Animals, Fishes,* Binfords, 1955.

Greely, Maj. Gen. A. W.: *Handbook of Alaska, Its Resources, Products, and Attractions,* Scribner's, 1909.

Gruening, Ernest, H.: *The State of Alaska,* Random House, 1954. This is perhaps the most definitive and authoritative history and interpretation of many phases of Alaska's past and current problems, including the struggle for statehood. The author is a former Governor of Alaska, currently a United States Senator from Alaska, whose reputation and long experience in Alaska are highly regarded.

Herron, Edward A.: *Alaska, Land of Tomorrow,* Whittlesey House, 1947.

Hilscher, Herbert, H.: *Alaska Now,* Little-Brown, 1950.

Hulley, C. C.: *Alaska, 1941-53,* Binfords, 1953.

Illingworth, Frank: *Highway to the North,* Philosophical Library, 1955.

Small, Marie: *Four Fares to Juneau,* Whittlesey House, 1947.

U. S. Geological Survey: *Landscapes of Alaska,* University of California Press, 1958.

U. S. War Department: *What Has Alaska to Offer Post-War Pioneers,* Educational Manual EM 20, Roundtable Series, Prepared for the U.S. Armed Forces by the American Historical Association USAFI, Madison, Wisconsin, 1944.

Whishaw, Lorna: *As Far as You'll Take Me,* Dodd, 1959. Interesting account by a girl who hitch-hiked to Alaska via the Alaska Highway.

Winslow, Kathryn, *Big Pan-Out,* W. W. Norton & Co.

Periodicals

National Geographic: "North Star Cruises Alaska's Wild West," p. 57, July, 1952.

———: "When Giant Bears Go Fishing," p. 195, August, 1954.

: "Alaska, The Big Land," p. 776, June, 1956.

———: "Alaska's Warmer Side," p. 737, June, 1956.

———: "Alaska Proudly Joins the Union," p. 42, July, 1959.

Holiday: "Untamed Alaska," p. 100, July, 1953.

———: "Favorite American Tours," p. 24, July, 1956.

———: "Alaska," p. 26, August, 1959. A very comprehensive report that should prove of great interest to tourists and travelers.

Yachting: "In the Waters of Alaska," p. 69, January; p. 51, February; p. 54, March, 1953.

Reader's Digest: "Why Live in Alaska," p. 159, September, 1956.

Nature Magazine: "Gateway to Alaska," p. 456, November, 1958.

Travel: "Railroading Across Alaska," p. 31, June, 1954.

Colliers: "Alaska Range," p. 68, February 19, 1949.

Independent Woman: "Alaska Diary," p. 127, April, 1955.

Cosmopolitan: "Wilderness Vacation in Comfort," p. 88, July, 1956.

Industries and Resources

Water Resources Development in Alaska, U.S. Army Corps of Engineers, January, 1959.

Alaska Oil Report, (published weekly) September 5, 1959, Box 442, College, Alaska.

Oil Lease Speculation, subject of a press release issued by the Department of the Interior, April 1, 1958, based on remarks of the Secretary of the Interior.

Alaska's Mineral Resources, an article on "Our Public Lands," January, 1959, published by the Bureau of Land Management, Washington, D. C.

Alaska, Frontier for Industry, published by the Economic Research Department, First National Bank, Seattle, Washington.

Alaska, U.S.A., Business Record, published by the National Industrial Conference Board, of New York City, February, 1959.

Nuclear Power Experiment, subject of a press release report issued June 15, 1959, by the U. S. Army Engineer, Alaska District, Box 7002, Anchorage, dealing with an experimental nuclear power installation at Ft. Greely, Alaska.

Federal Records Relating to Oil and Gas Rights, subject of a press release issued August 2, 1957, by the Bureau of Land Management, Washington, D. C., based on a speech by Earl J. Thomas.

Business

Retail and Wholesale Trade, subjects of 3 bulletins published by the Bureau of Census, Department of Commerce, Washington, D. C., Bulletins: R-2-7, S-2-10, W-1-51.

Economic and Business Situation in Alaska, With Special Reference to Wholesale and Retail Trade in Fairbanks and Anchorage, a special and unique study by Prof. Vernon R. Kiely of the University of Alaska, Business Administration Division, underwritten by a special grant from the Small Business Administration. The study is available from the

University of Alaska at $2.00 per copy. Free summaries of the study are available from the Small Business Administration, Washington 25, D. C. The summary is called, "Expanding Distribution and Warehousing in Alaska," Management Research Summary, No. 5, January, 1961.

County Business Patterns, First Quarter, 1956, a joint publication of the U. S. Department of Commerce and the U.S. Department of Health, Education and Welfare, covering Alaska as well as Hawaii, Puerto Rico, and the Virgin Islands.

The Alaskan Market, published by the J. Walter Thompson Co., New York City, 1958. A concise description of Alaska as a market, intended as an introductory survey, compiled October, 1958.

Our 49th State, An Adventure in Marketing, a report on the present and future of the Alaskan market; information gathered in Alaska during September-October, 1958, published by Benton & Bowles, Inc., New York City.

How to Rate Alaska as a Market, article in *Sales Management Magazine,* August 1, 1958, p. 50.

Financing Large Industrial Projects in Alaska, problems, and possibilities, subject of a prepared address delivered by Arthur L. Wadsworth, vice president, Dillon, Read & Co., Inc., New York City, before the Pacific Northwest Trade Association meeting, Fairbanks, Alaska, August 28, 1959. An excellent, detailed, and entertaining account of the problems encountered in financing a large pulp mill in which Japanese interests are involved, plus a concise and penetrating analysis of Alaska's business and financing problems.

Employment, Labor, and Wages

Monthly Labor Review, various issues, especially those of November, 1953; and December, 1953; in which there are comprehensive and authoritative reports on Alaska's labor laws and its administration, wages, and working conditions, plus a symposium and specific bibliography; published by the U. S. Department of Labor, Washington, D. C.

Income in Alaska, published by the U.S. Department of Commerce, Office of Business Statistics, available from the Superintendent of Documents, Washington 25, D.C., 35 cents.

Status of Labor in Alaska, Bulletin No. 1191, United States Department of Labor, Bureau of Labor Statistics, December, 1955.

The Labor Market and Employment Security, various issues, especially those of: October, 1956; March-April, 1957; November, 1958; December, 1958; and January, 1959. This is a publication of the United States Department of Labor. While generally not well-known to the public at large, this publication is an excellent and authoritative source regarding job prospects, the labor market, economics, major industries and employment characteristics, trends and outlook in the field of employment and labor.

Outlook for Construction in Alaska, an excellent article written by the Commissioner of Labor Statistics, Ewan Clague, January, 1959, U. S. Department of Labor, Washington, D. C.

Civilian Employment in Alaska, Information Pamphlet, prepared and issued by the Alaskan Air Command, Elmendorf AFB, Anchorage, Alaska, July 1, 1958.

Engineering Opportunities in Alaska, prepared and issued by the U. S. Army Corps of Engineers, District Office, Anchorage, Alaska.

Job Facts, Job Information, separate brochures published February, 1959, and 1958, respectively, by the Alaska Employment Security Commission, Juneau, Alaska.

Public Lands

How to Get Land from Uncle Sam, Harry Kursh, W. W. Norton & Co., New York City, contains a special chapter on getting land in Alaska as well as a discussion of the public domain in general throughout the United States.

Small Tracts, Information Bulletin No. 1, Bureau of Land Management, 1958.

Information Relative to the Use and Disposal of Public Lands, and Resources in Alaska, Information Bulletin No. 2, Bureau of Land Management.

Land Occupancy, Ownership and Use of Homesteads in the Kenai Peninsula, Bulletin No. 21, November, 1956, Alaska Agricultural Experiment Station, University of Alaska; 31 pp. with map of the Peninsula, photos, and considerable data.

Background for an Alaskan Land Policy, by Kay Hitchcock, research assistant, Alaska Agricultural Experiment Station, University of Alaska, originally prepared as a term paper for a course in economic history at the University of Alaska, May, 1959, 27 pp., mimeographed. While it does not represent necessarily the views of the University or the Alaska Agricultural Experiment Station, it is an excellent discussion of problems regarding the public domain and resources, and contains an annotated bibliography that should prove of interest for historians, economists, teachers, and students.

State of Alaska, Chapter 169, reprint of the law establishing a Division of Lands in Alaska and relating to the disposals of lands and resources, approved May 2, 1959.

Homesteading, Past and Present, booklet, Bureau of Land Management.

What Lies Ahead for Alaska's Homesteaders, James W. Matthews, an article in the *Extension Service Review,* June, 1959. Mr. Matthews is the Fairbanks District Agent, Alaska.

Alaska Withdrawal Atlas, $5.25, publication sold by the U.S. Government Printing Office, showing Federal land withdrawals and reservations in Alaska, and location of the boundaries of lands reserved or withdrawn as of June, 1958, contains 60 plates, 22"x20".

Education and Teaching

Report of the Alaska White House Conference on Education, Alaska section, Commissioner of Education, Juneau.

Teach in Alaska, the 49th State, 8 pp., mimeographed brochure issued by the Commissioner of Education, Juneau. A concise explanation of the Alaska school system and teacher employment.

Alaska Public Schools, 3 pp., mimeographed, Department of Education, Box 1841, Juneau.

Alaska Story, Journal of the National Education Association, October, 1955.

Federal Schools for Native Children in Alaska, School Life, May, 1958, publication of the U. S. Office of Education, Washington, D. C.

Health and Medical

Alaska's Health, a Survey Report, The Graduate School of Public Health, University of Pittsburgh, under contract for the U. S. Government, published 1954, a comprehensive and authoritative study containing extensive statistical data, charts, maps and discussion of demographic factors, health conditions, health agencies, health facilities and personnel health problems in Alaska, plus an important bibliography on health and medicine in Alaska.

Publications List, an extensive bibliography of general and specific health reports and research papers, issued by the Arctic Health Research Center, Anchorage, Alaska.

Public Health in Alaska, American Journal of Public Health, June, 1952.

Alaska's Health, bi-monthly publication of the Alaska Department of Health.

Economics and Cost of Living

Basic Economic Data, compiled as of June 1, 1958, for the Alaska Territorial Employment Service, Alaska Employment Security Commission, Juneau, containing information relative to the labor market areas of Anchorage, Fairbanks, Juneau, Ketchikan, and Petersburg.

"Alaska Development," *Commercial and Financial Chronicle,* p. 197, July 17, 1958; also special report in the issue of January 8, 1959, p. 109.

"Purpose and Source of Seasonal Migration to Alaska," *Economic Geography,* Clark University, Worcester 10, Mass.

"Unlocking Alaska's Wealth," *The Economist,* September 6, 1958.

"Alaska, from Frontier to 49th State," *Business Horizons,* School of Business, Indiana University, Bloomington, Indiana, 1958-59.

Housing

Annual Report, 1958-59, Alaska State Housing Authority, Anchorage, Alaska.

"Building a 49th State," *Architectural Forum,* p. 112, December, 1958.

Hunting and Fishing

Field and Stream Magazine, following issues: May, 1953; January, March, April, August, September, 1954; February, May, December, 1955; July, November, December, 1957; June, December, 1958.

Outdoor Life Magazine, following issues: February, June, 1953; February, September, October, 1954; January, February, 1955; March, April, July, 1956; June, November, 1957; January, 1958.

Alaska's Fish and Wildlife, Circular 17, U.S. Fish and Wildlife Service, Washington, D. C., 1953, sold by the Superintendent of Documents, 25 cents, an excellent and beautifully illustrated guide.

Agriculture

Agriculture in Alaska, Information for Prospective Settlers, 1958, Bulletin 22, Revised, Agricultural Extension Service, University of Alaska.

Questions and Answers Regarding Farming in the Matanuska Valley, Alaska Rural Rehabilitation Corp. Palmer, Alaska, revised, October, 1958, 10 cents.

Yearbook of Agriculture, Alaska chapter published as a separate reprint, Bulletin No. 2923, Extension Service, University of Alaska.

Farm Management Research Progress Report, C. F. Marsh, economist, Alaska Agricultural Experiment Station, University of Alaska, July, 1959.

The Relation of Agribusiness to the Management of Alaskan Farms, C. F. Marsh, 11 pp., mimeographed report, AAES, University of Alaska.

Publication List for the Alaskan Farmer, Homesteader, Homemaker, a 24-p. catalog containing list of varied publications available free of charge from the Agricultural Extension Service and the Agricultural Experiment Station, University of Alaska.

Population

Bureau of Census, Department of Commerce, "Current Population Reports," February 16, 27, 1959; October 27, November 13, 1958.

The Population of Alaska, Statistical Bulletin, October, 1958, Metropolitan Life Insurance Co., New York City.

Aviation and Air Travel

Selected Aviation Safety Discussions, Don M. Gretzer, Chief, General Safety Division, Federal Aviation Agency, Region Five, Anchorage, Alaska, an excellent, informative and entertaining 139-p. mimeographed booklet on safety for civilian pilots in Alaska, written by one of the best-known veterans in flying safety who has had more than 15 years of flying experience in Alaska alone.

Flying Magazine, issues of: April, 1957; June, October, 1958.

Popular Mechanics, December, 1957, p. 96, "Report from a Roving Editor."

"Aviation Week," *Commercial Aviation Problems,* August 11, 1958, p. 29.

Defense

"Top of the World Guardian," *Air Force Magazine,* August, 1958.

"Alaska's Partner in Progress," *Army Information Digest,* September, 1959.

"Rampart to the North," *Army Information Digest,* January, 1959.

Helpful Hints for Personnel Ordered to U. S. Army, Alaska Headquarters, Department of the Army, June, 1958; also available from the Government Printing Office, Washington, D. C., 10 cents.

Impact of Military Spending on the Economy of Alaska, subject of a prepared and illustrated address by Maj.-Gen. C. F. Necrason, Commander, Alaskan Air Command, September 5, 1959, before a luncheon meeting of the Pacific Northwest Trade Association, Fairbanks, Alaska, an extremely well-organized report containing significant information on military spending in Alaska and its possible effects on the economy of Alaska.

Politics, Government, and Public Affairs

"Colonialism in Alaska," *Current History,* December, 1955.

"How the 49th State Will Change the U. S.," *U. S. News & World Report,* July 11, 1958.

"Alaska's Herald Constitution," *Journal of the American Bar Association,* December, 1958, p. 1147.

Alaska, Information from Non-Self Governing Territories, United Nations General Assembly, May 5, 1959 (1959, a/4088/add.14).

Documents Pertaining to the Acceptance of Alaska into the Union, Communication from the U. S. Government to the United Nations (1959 a/4115), June 11, 1959, 43 pp.

Alaska Omnibus Bill, U. S. Senate Committee on Interior and Insular Affairs, Report, May 28, 1959, to accompany S. 1541, 86th Congress, 1st Session, Senate Report No. 331, 60 pp.

Weather

Climates of the States, Alaska, Climatography of the United States, No. 60-49, published by the Weather Bureau, Department of Commerce, for sale by the U. S. Government Printing Office, 15 cents.

Miscellaneous Government Publications

Mid-Century Alaska, 1957, 170 pp., $1, Catalog No. I 35.10/2:al 1s/16/957.

Mineral Industry of Alaska, reprint from Minerals Yearbook, 1957, vol. 3, 27 pp., il. 15 cents, Catalog No. I 28.37/a2:al ls/957.

Pocket Guide to Alaska, 1956, 69 pp., il. 30 cents, Catalog No. D2.8:al 1/956.

Travel in Alaska and the Alaska Highway, 1958, 8 pp., il., 5 cents, Catalog No. C37.2:al ls

Federal Jobs Overseas and in Alaska, 1958, 10 pp., il., 10 cents, Catalog No. CS 1.48:29/13.

Guide to Popular Flores of United States and Alaska, annotated, selected list of nontechnical works for the identification of flowers, ferns, 1954, 56 pp., il., 25 cents, Catalog No. al.60:23.

Legal Status of Women in Alaska, 1958, 14 pp., 10 cents, Catalog No. L133.3:157-51.

INDEX

INDEX

277

0|2461

DATE DUE

OCT 17 1996	

GAYLORD   PRINTED IN U.S.A.

← Pocket Inside

STATISTICAL SUMMARY OF ALASKA'S CLIMATE

District	Station	Temperature — Length of record (Yr.)	January average (°F.)	July average (°F.)	Maximum (°F.)	Minimum (°F.)	Killing frost average dates — Length of record (Yr.)	Last in Spring	First in Fall	Growing season (Days)	Precip. Length of record (Yr.)	January (In.)	February (In.)	March (In.)	April (In.)	May (In.)	June (In.)	July (In.)	August (In.)	September (In.)	October (In.)	November (In.)	December (In.)	Annual (In.)
Southeastern	Annex Creek	21	22.7	54.9	84	−12	20	May 6	Sept. 30	147	22	9.04	7.85	6.20	5.65	5.14	4.33	6.21	10.22	13.42	16.61	13.41	9.36	107.44
	Bell Island	9	29.0	58.2	90	−4		May 8	Oct. 28	173	9	10.63	8.51	7.12	6.64	5.33	5.49	5.71	7.19	11.26	15.29	15.11	11.78	110.06
	Haines	15	22.9	57.6	90	−15	14	May 20	Sept. 19	122	15	5.42	5.14	4.76	3.34	2.01	1.58	1.80	2.27	4.98	10.24	7.74	7.15	56.43
	Juneau	40	27.5	56.6	89	−15	23	Apr. 28	Oct. 17	172	40	7.18	5.63	5.41	5.46	5.22	3.95	5.03	7.33	10.15	11.18	9.10	7.61	83.25
	Kassan										13	9.21	7.59	6.32	6.22	5.65	3.76	3.68	4.44	6.30	10.17	10.39	10.27	84.00
	Ketchikan	28	32.6	57.5	96	−8	23	May 5	Oct. 17	165	28	13.71	11.63	12.20	10.79	8.31	6.55	8.24	11.51	12.14	20.13	19.74	15.94	150.89
	Petersburg	8	28.5	55.2	81	−5	6	May 18	Sept. 24	129	9	8.50	9.85	7.29	6.39	5.79	4.49	5.31	6.94	11.97	15.32	12.79	11.81	106.45
	Seclusion Harbor	6	30.3	55.8	92	−2	6	May 6	Oct. 9	156	6	11.89	9.08	8.20	6.68	5.49	4.14	4.70	6.67	8.52	17.45	15.40	12.33	110.55
	Sitka	40	32.4	54.9	87	−5	23	May 10	Oct. 16	159	40	7.84	6.78	5.97	5.58	4.15	3.36	4.29	7.02	10.33	12.64	10.07	9.10	87.13
	Skagway	32	21.1	57.7	92	−19	21	May 27	Sept. 15	111	30	2.05	1.40	1.30	1.46	.89	.92	1.45	1.91	3.52	5.02	4.14	2.79	26.85
	Tree Point	9	34.1	54.4	86	−3	8	May 22	Sept. 23	124	9	10.85	7.23	6.97	6.47	5.46	5.66	5.72	5.41	8.38	12.69	13.45	11.38	99.67
	View Cove	7	35.1	56.0	88	5	6	Apr. 25	Nov. 3	192	7	17.74	12.17	12.36	10.97	9.50	6.65	6.20	7.23	12.58	18.37	22.57	19.18	155.52
	Wrangell	23	29.0	58.2	92	−6	19	Apr. 26	Oct. 12	169	22	7.71	7.25	5.43	4.89	4.38	3.55	4.49	5.31	8.35	11.21	11.79	8.59	82.95
Pacific coast	Cordova	26	27.2	54.8	87	−19	22	May 8	Oct. 4	149	27	9.49	10.70	8.49	8.69	9.09	6.03	8.51	13.24	19.96	22.94	15.51	12.78	145.43
	Kodiak	36	29.8	54.3	85	−12	23	May 5	Oct. 12	160	40	4.66	4.73	3.83	3.93	6.03	4.91	3.60	5.00	5.43	7.55	5.72	6.09	61.48
	Seward	26	22.4	55.3	82	−20	18	May 18	Sept. 27	132	26	4.46	4.91	3.34	4.25	3.39	2.42	2.83	5.92	9.60	11.06	14.85	6.70	73.73
	Valdez	27	19.1	53.3	83	−24	20	May 23	Sept. 16	116	25	4.55	4.92	4.22	2.90	2.81	2.15	3.53	6.18	9.05	8.38	5.99	5.70	60.38
	Whale Island	14	28.8	53.1	83	−9	14	June 3	Sept. 17	106	15	3.87	4.62	2.84	3.52	6.88	4.22	3.16	3.46	3.66	7.43	5.75	4.62	54.03
	Yukutat	17	29.3	52.8	82	5	12	May 9	Oct. 8	152	18	10.77	9.67	8.75	7.84	7.80	4.17	8.18	10.17	14.65	17.73	16.92	12.48	129.13